Tourism Agility in Times of Crisis and Uncertainty 2

Tourism and Mobility Systems Set

coordinated by
Philippe Violier

Volume 12

Tourism Agility in Times of Crisis and Uncertainty 2

Between Marketing-Communication and Sustainability

Edited by
Sylvie Christofle

ISTE

WILEY

First published 2025 in Great Britain and the United States by ISTE Ltd and John Wiley & Sons, Inc.

ISTE Ltd
27-37 St George's Road
London SW19 4EU
UK

www.iste.co.uk

John Wiley & Sons, Inc.
111 River Street
Hoboken, NJ 07030
USA

www.wiley.com

Library of Congress Control Number: 2025933205

British Library Cataloguing-in-Publication Data
A CIP record for this book is available from the British Library
ISBN 978-1-78630-995-2

Contents

Foreword

Thinking on Tourist Destinations as Complex Systems in Times of Uncertainty

Covid-19, climate change and the increasing social, political and ecological tensions of today's world have enriched both academic and political debates on tourism (Cheer et al. 2019; Prayag 2020; Gössling and Higham 2021). These tensions represent new challenges for tourist destinations, while also intensifying others that were already latent (Prideaux et al. 2020).

From November 8 to 10 2022, the 11th edition of the international multidisciplinary symposium AsTRES (Association for Tourism, Research and Higher Education) was held in Nice. The aim of this event, *Tourism Agility in Times of Crises: Replications, Accelerations, Reinventions…?* – which led to the publication of this book – was to identify the elements that characterize the "agile" dimension of tourism through a multidisciplinary approach. As suggested in the call for papers, agility or even flexibility should enable tourism and tourist destinations to cope with crises and periods of uncertainty.

Agility can be understood as the capacity of complex spaces, such as tourist destinations, to anticipate and capitalize on ongoing changes. Based on this definition, concepts related to complexity were employed throughout the symposium to analyze how destinations, as places, can adapt, evolve and

---

Foreword written by Salvador Anton CLAVÉ.

reduce their vulnerability in the face of crises. The various speakers explored how the iterative, incremental and adaptive structure of agility could be particularly valuable in developing economically, socially and environmentally successful strategies.

In this context, this preliminary contribution to the works presented in this volume seeks to broadly reflect on the need to consider complexity and agility in shaping new alternative pathways to articulate what can be termed "tourism transitions" across various levels or scales.

The evolution of destinations and the creation of trajectories

Research on the evolution, transformation and change in tourist destinations has demonstrated that they are in constant flux (Saarinen 2004) and can respond to critical events due to their dynamism and forward-looking vision. Destinations find the necessary resources to overcome their vulnerability and adapt to new scenarios in diverse ways (Brouder et al. 2017). It is also well established that the transformation of tourist destinations extends far beyond models based solely on tourism performance indicators (Sanz Ibáñez and Anton Clavé 2014). Destinations can be differentiated by the evolving quality of their tourism offerings as they adapt to changes (Equipe MIT 2002), as well as by the transformation of their core activities (Prideaux 2004).

Research on the transformation of tourist destinations has also shown that, during times of crisis, they shape their sustainability through innovation and learning (Hudson 2010), which act as mechanisms for building capacity to overcome vulnerability and increase adaptability (Cheer and Lew 2017; Saarinen and Gill 2018). Historical analyses have illuminated these processes (Walton 1983), as have the application of models like the tourism area lifecycle (Butler 1980, 2014), the study of restructuring dynamics (Agarwal 2002) and investigations into the trajectories of tourist destinations (Coëffe and Stock 2021). In all cases, adaptation strategies lead to varied outcomes, ranging from the redevelopment and reconfiguration of tourism dynamics (Anton Clavé 2012) to the metamorphosis of places (Clivaz et al. 2014), or even the abandonment of tourism activities altogether (Baum 1998).

To grasp the diversity of these situations and the outcomes of these change processes, it is necessary to employ complex, nonlinear and non-deterministic conceptual and analytical models. This analysis can be approached through the lens of evolutionary economic geography (EEG) (Boschma and Lambooy 1999). Key concepts within EEG, such as path dependence (Bramwell and Cox 2009; Ma and Hassink 2013), path creation (Gill and Williams 2014), path plasticity (Halkier and Therkelsen 2013) and path shaping (Bramwell 2011), are useful for understanding how tourist destinations transform into complex places governed by varied processes interacting across different scales (Benner 2023).

We can identify three fundamental pillars that simultaneously influence and distinguish the evolutionary performance of tourist destinations and determine their agility: the role of actors, context and dependency (Sanz Ibáñez and Anton Clavé 2022). From this perspective, the dynamics of destinations cannot be viewed as a simple linear trajectory from less developed to more consolidated states. Instead, this evolution results from multiple forces that produce a diversity of situations, each with different timelines and cycles.

Within this conceptual framework, the intervention of actors can deliberately and consciously shift evolutionary paths away from their inertia (Baekkelund 2021). The context either creates or limits the possibilities for economic actions and interactions (Li and Bathelt 2011). Lastly, past events and decisions, even the most random or involuntary, have long-term consequences (Martin and Sunley 2006).

As a result, each destination, shaped by its own geographical, socioeconomic and cultural conditions, the negotiating power among its various subgroups of actors, its technological penetration, leadership and the governance regime that has emerged, formulates specific responses to the challenges posed by current global change forces and local transitions (Cheer et al. 2021). A clear example of this is the diversity of policies implemented in response to climate change in French winter sports resorts, where organizational transformation and actors' responsiveness were critical in understanding the trajectory of these spaces (Rech et al. 2019).

Uncertainty and the adaptation processes of destinations

Recent disruptive trends in tourism production and consumption, such as low-cost travel, the rise of peer-to-peer platforms (like Airbnb, for example), Web 2.0, the climate emergency and social networks, have forced destinations to adapt more quickly and confront urgent social, environmental and economic challenges (Fayos-Solà and Cooper 2019). Other more or less long shocks, whether ecological (e.g. Hurricane Katrina), health-related (e.g. Covid-19), economic (e.g. global financial crises) or political (e.g. wars and regional political instability), have also impacted tourist destinations to varying degrees. Depending on their capacity to adapt, these destinations have initiated processes of reorganization, shifted to a different state, or renewed themselves (Brouder 2020).

Thus, while the pandemic was seen by many as an opportunity to critically reassess the prior trajectory of tourism growth, and even used to develop alternative research and action scenarios (Bianchi 2020), there have been diverse responses and dynamics at the destination level, driven by local characteristics and the power interactions among decision-makers. For instance, some destinations have started implementing actions that, at least conceptually, emphasize degrowth (Langer and Schumude 2024), while others have focused their development on social and environmental well-being, promoted sustainable consumption among both residents and visitors, or advanced corporate social responsibility programs aligned with the United Nations Sustainable Development Goals (European Parliament 2021). Nevertheless, apart from some political actions, there have been notable market inertia following the Covid period, with the pandemic merely acting as a temporary pause in many destinations' growth dynamics and ability to attract visitors (Mansilla and Hughes 2021).

It is also well documented that tourism is a growing source of conflict within the communities where it develops. This may be due to nuisances (noise, waste, privatization of spaces, incivility and crime), structural transformations in the form of tourism development (such as the opening of hotels, the proliferation of legal and illegal tourist apartments, disruption of commercial activities, transformation of buildings, rising rent prices and gentrification) or the commodification of culture and the environment, which often leads to folklorization: the loss of identity, dilution of cultural identity and the overexploitation of heritage (Novy and Colomb 2019).

The above points clearly illustrate the link between uncertainty and tourism, particularly the relationship between uncertainty and the evolution of destinations (Ghaderi et al. 2015). These changes are shaped by the actions and interactions (whether agile or not) of actors and their ability to adapt or create new trajectories in response to structural disruptions or situational shocks, in addition to local challenges (Lew 2014). In this context, the concept of resilience, which originates from disaster studies and challenges the sustainability-based approach to analyzing the transformation of socioeconomic systems (Vale and Campanella 2005; Mehmood 2016), is especially relevant for analyzing destinations as complex socioeconomic and environmental systems in today's era of uncertainties.

In this regard, analytical models such as the *adaptive cycle* by Gunderson and Holling (2002) allow the application of the resilience concept to destinations. In this framework, where destinations are both evolving/reactive territories and systems of actors undergoing change processes catalyzed by tourism (Butler and Dodds 2022), uncertainty plays a crucial role, whether linked to new social dynamics or triggered by major shocks. The *adaptive cycle* comprises four phases: exploitation, conservation, release and reorganization. Without delving into detail, it is evident that this model emphasizes a complex approach to the evolving dynamics of destinations, underlining the pivotal role of agility. As McLeod (2020) demonstrated in the case of the Bahamas, the relationship between governance and resilience, as well as the importance of agent networks, are key to understanding the process of destination evolution.

From this perspective, the agility of human action (actors, leadership, political intervention and collaborative dynamics) largely determines destinations' ability to respond to short-term trigger events and shape new development paths toward more resilient (innovative and sustainable) long-term goals (Gill and Williams 2014). This is essential for defining objectives such as social innovation, sustainability and inclusive and cohesive growth in tourist destinations, which are inherently complex (McDonald 2009).

The complexity of destinations and the challenge of resilience

In a context of uncertainties where nearly all actors, despite differing approaches (Hall 2019), share similar principles concerning sustainability, there is a consensus on the need to renew tourism on a different foundation, in which resilience would play a significant role (Transforming Tourism Initiative 2017; European Travel Commission 2020). The challenge lies in rethinking and acting on the evolutionary trajectories of the tourism phenomenon in a new way (Knafou 2023). These trajectories are linked, on the one hand, to the ability of destinations to adapt to new conditions of attractiveness, and, on the other hand, to the management of factors correlated with the transformation of the primary productive activity and the broader context of global change (Gibson 2021).

In this framework, establishing destination policies focused on promoting sustainability and the digitization of tourism to revive growth post-crisis is insufficient (European Commission 2022). It must be acknowledged that the challenges faced by destinations are inherently connected to global factors, associated with productive, social and environmental dynamics on a global scale. These factors are ultimately fundamental for resilience (Cheer et al. 2021): the climate emergency, the energy transition shifting market preferences driven by environmental awareness, over- or under-tourism, or even the "infusion" of tourism and leisure into developed societies.

Given that a destination is a multifunctional, multi-component and multi-activity system (Gretzel and Scarpino Johns 2018), managing it poses a significant challenge. To address this, there is a need for complex conceptual, analytical and governance models with a systemic perspective that facilitate the development of its social, physical, environmental and financial capital (Fabry and Zeghni 2019).

Complexity is, in fact, a key term in defining destinations. Here, complexity is understood as the nature and behavior of a system whose components interact non-linearly, without a predetermined plan, spontaneously leading to the emergence of new processes based on the available information. This results in behaviors that are difficult to predict (Colchester 2016). Complexity pertains to open systems, which implies that a destination must be understood within its environment, considering the multiple and varied relationships and interactions that shape it (Baggio and Sainaghi 2011), and that enable its adaptive capacity (Hartman 2018).

The analysis of tourist destinations as complex systems has proven valuable for studying interdependent and multifaceted concepts related to resilience, such as sustainability, vulnerability and equity, among others

(Huang and Bahja 2022). These analyses have also contributed to improving classic models of the lifecycle of tourist areas by accounting for turbulence, change and unpredictability (Russell and Faulkner 2004). Additionally, it is important to recall that the complexity approach is one of the three theoretical pillars on which evolutionary economic geography is built, alongside path dependence and generalized Darwinism (Martin and Sunley 2015).

From a resilience perspective, the complexity of destinations can thus be understood as their ability to produce change in order to enhance their capacity for adjustment, and gain flexibility to overcome vulnerability and increase adaptability (Hall et al. 2018). In this context, the actions of actors, particularly their agility, refer to the specific actions taken in particular places and times, driven by the envisioning of one or more different futures. These futures are made possible by combining knowledge, networks and other resources in new and sometimes unexpected ways (Grillitsch and Sotarauta 2020). Relatedly, and in agreement with Scutarri and Corradini (2018), it is important to emphasize that resilience should be understood as a property of a complex system. This is useful for defining future trajectories at the scale of each destination, as well as for renewing its alternatives and competitive advantages (Gretzel and Scarpino Johns 2018).

Agility as a guiding principle for the governance of complex destinations towards resilience

Understanding complexity helps to define the actions of stakeholders who participate in the governance dynamics of destinations, leading them toward new scenarios when external forces, with short- or long-term consequences, impact their trajectory (Gössling et al. 2021).

The major challenge for a destination, then, is to establish governance tools in a context of constant change and learning (Fabry and Zeghni 2019), and this by facilitating the change (transformation) rather than merely the reaction (recovery). In this context, resilience, as an inherent characteristic of complex systems, must be a fundamental component of destination governance (Anton Clavé and Matus 2023) and transformation processes of destinations for two reasons. First, studies on resilience demonstrate that while a system‘s ability to react is important, its ability to evolve toward a more sustainable state is even more so. Second, the hegemonic battle between different groups over the definition of resilience criteria (Paidakaki and Moullaert 2017) complicates a "politics of resilience" in which it is essential to disentangle the implicit responses to questions such as "resilience for whom and against what?" (Vale 2014, p. 191).

In the field of tourism studies, the concept of resilience has primarily focused on the capacity to recover following catastrophic events or gradual long-term changes (Hall et al. 2018); however, interest in the evolving resilience of complex destinations extends to their capacity to evolve toward equitable conditions of social and spatial justice, more ecological mobility, mitigation of climate emergency, commitment to low-carbon emission, and social and gender equality. As Zacher et al. (2022) argue, the resilience of destinations thus encompasses the willingness and competence to anticipate crises, implement efficient strategies in case of a crisis, and, in the long-term, grow and adapt for the benefit of all stakeholders, especially the community in which tourism develops.

As such, adaptability is an ongoing process that, from an evolutionary perspective, must consistently involve all stakeholders in the dynamics of a destination. This includes societal change throughout a persistent learning, more and more focused on resilient processes of reflection, preparation, action, governance and execution (Fabry and Zeghini 2019). This largely relies on collaborative efforts among tourism actors and it can be assumed that implementing this can be more difficult for certain destinations than others, depending, among other factors, on the robustness of their structures and the dynamics of their governance (Bono Gispert and Anton Clavé 2020).

With increased leisure time, reduced long-distance mobility, limited purchasing power, a digital lifestyle, more developed environmental awareness, an increasing concentration of economics power and global ecosystemic emergency, to cite some important factors of global change, we can assert that destinations can reduce vulnerability and enhance resilience without compromising on social justice and environmental integrity (Njoroge 2022).

However, the role of agility in meeting the challenge of reinforcing resilience (in the sense of increasing the ability of local destinations to anticipate, prepare for, respond to and recover from disruption while reducing vulnerability) is limited in part due to two shortcomings. First, the lack of coherence amongst most action plans developed by destinations following the recovery policies implemented after the Covid-19 crisis, primarily focused on digitalization and sustainability than on long-term resilience objectives (European Parliament 2021). Second, the lack of measures and tools to help decision-makers in tourism to evaluate the success of the actions and decision undertaken in terms of resilience.

In any case, to conclude, it is necessary to further reflect on the role of tourism in our future society from the perspective of governance for tourist destinations as complex systems (Amore et al. 2018). In this regard, the two volumes that compile the contributions from the symposium *Tourism Agility in Times of Crises: Replications, Accelerations, Reinventions...?* are of great value. The first volume concerns the uncertainties linked to the dynamics of tourist destinations and tourism in the context of an increasingly digital and technological society that requires agility. The second volume focuses on adaptability, marketing and sustainability, with contributions on territorial attractiveness, digital marketing and sustainability as a key issue for tourism agility.

Acknowledgments

This publication is part of the ADAPTOUR research project (contract number PID2020-112525RB-I00) created by MCIN/AEI/10.13039/50110 0011033.

References

Agarwal, S. (2002). Restructuring seaside tourism: The resort lifecyle. *Annals of Tourism Research*, 29(1), 25–55.

Amore, A., Prayag, G., Hall, C.M. (2018). Conceptualizing destination resilience from a multilevel perspective. *Tourism Review International*, 22(3/4), 235–250.

Anton Clavé, S. (2012). Rethinking mass tourism, space and place. In *Routledge Handbook of Tourism Geographies: New Perspectives on Space, Place and Tourism*, Wilson, J. (ed.). Routledge, London.

Anton Clavé, S. and Matus, S. (2023). Governance: Tourism. In *Encyclopedia of Tourism*, Jafari, J. and Xiao, H. (eds). Springer, Cham. doi: 10.1007/978-3-319-01669-6_747-1.

Bækkelund, N.G. (2021). Change agency and reproductive agency in the course of industrial path evolution. *Regional Studies*, 55(4), 757–768.

Baggio, R. and Sainaghi, R. (2011). Complex and chaotic tourism systems: Towards a quantitative approach. *International Journal of Contemporary Hospitality Management*, 23(6), 840–861.

Baum, T. (1998). Taking the exit route: Extending the tourism area life cycle model. *Current Issues in Tourism*, 1(2), 167–175.

Benner, M. (2023). Revisiting path-as-process: Agency in a discontinuity-development model. *European Planning Studies*, 31(6), 1119–1138.

Bianchi, R. (2020). Covid-19 and the radical transformation of tourism. *ATLAS Tourism and Leisure Review*, 2, 1–8.

Bono Gispert, O. and Anton Clavé, S. (2020). Dimensions and models of tourism governance in a tourism system: The experience of Catalonia. *Journal of Destination Marketing & Management*, 17, 100465.

Boschma, R. and Lambooy, J. (1999). Evolutionary economics and economic geography. *Journal of Evolutionary Economics*, 9, 411–429.

Bramwell, B. (2011). Governance, the state and sustainable tourism: A political economy approach. *Journal of Sustainable Tourism*, 19(4/5), 459–477.

Bramwell, B. and Cox, V. (2009). Stage and path dependence approaches to the evolution of a national park tourism partnership. *Journal of Sustainable Tourism*, 17(2), 191–206.

Brouder, P. (2020). Reset redux: Possible evolutionary pathways towards the transformation of tourism in a COVID-19 world. *Tourism Geographies*, 22(3), 484–490.

Brouder, P., Anton Clavé, S., Gill, A., Ioannides, D. (2017). Why is tourism not an evolutionary science? Understanding the past, present, and future of tourism destination evolution. In *Tourism Destination Evolution*, Brouder, P., Anton Clavé, S., Gill, A., Ioannides, D. (eds). Routledge, London.

Butler, R.W. (1980). The concept of a tourist area life cycle of evolution: Implications for management of resources. *The Canadian Geographer*, 24(1), 5–12.

Butler, R.W. (2014). Coastal tourist resorts: History, development and models. *ACE: Architecture, City and Environment (Arquitectura, Ciudad y Entorno)*, 9(25), 203–228.

Butler, R.W. and Doods, R. (2022). Overcoming overtourism: A review of failure. *Tourism Review*, 77, 35–53.

Cheer, J.M. and Lew, A.A. (eds) (2017). *Tourism, Resilience and Sustainability: Adapting to Social, Political and Economic Change*. Routledge, London.

Cheer, J.M., Milano, C., Novelli, M. (2019). Tourism and community resilience in the Anthropocene: Accentuating temporal overtourism. *Journal of Sustainable Tourism*, 27(4), 554–572.

Cheer, J.M., Lapointe, D., Mostafanezhad, M., Jamal, T. (2021). Global tourism in crisis: Conceptual frameworks for research and practice. *Journal of Tourism Futures*, 7(3), 278–294.

Clivaz, C., Crevoisier, O., Kebir, L., Nahrath, S., Stock, M. (2014). The circulation of wealth: Resort development and touristic capital of place. Working Paper, Maison d'analyse des processus sociaux. Université de Neuchâtel, Neuchâtel.

Coeffe, V. and Stock. M. (2021). Tourism as urban phenomenon and the crux of "urban tourism". In *Progress in French Tourism Geographies*, Stock, M. (ed.). Springer, New York.

Colchester, J. (2016). *Systems + Complexity. An Accessible Introduction to the New Area of Complex Systems*. Create Space Independent Publishing Platform, Scotts Valley, CA.

Equipe MIT (2002). *Tourismes 1. Lieux communs*. Belin, Paris.

European Commission (2022). *Transition Pathway for Tourism*. Publications Office of the European Union, Luxembourg.

European Parliament (2021). EU Strategy for Sustainable Tourism. European Parliament Resolution of March 2021 on Establishing an EU Strategy for Sustainable Tourism (2020/2038(INI)). Publications Office of the European Union, Luxembourg.

European Travel Commission (2020). European tourism manifesto. Priorities [Online]. Available at: https://etc-corporate.org/tourism-manifesto/ [Accessed 27 April 2023].

Fabry, N. and Zeghni, S. (2019). Resilience, tourist destinations and governance: An analytical framework. In *Tourismes et adaptations*, Cholat, F., Gwiazdzinski, L., Tritz, C., Tuppen, J. (eds). Elya Editions, Paris.

Fayos-Solà, E. and Cooper, C. (2019). Introduction: Innovation and the future of tourism. In *The Future of Tourism*, Fayos-Solà, E. and Cooper, C. (eds). Springer, Cham.

Ghaderi, Z., Som, A.P.M., Henderson, J.C. (2015). When disaster strikes: The Thai floods of 2011 and tourism industry response and resilience. *Asia Pacific Journal of Tourism Research*, 20(4), 399–415.

Gibson, C. (2021). Theorising tourism in crisis: Writing and relating in place. *Tourist Studies*, 21(1), 84–95.

Gill, A.M. and Williams, P.W. (2014). Mindful deviation in creating a governance path towards sustainability in resort destinations. *Tourism Geographies*, 16(4), 546–562.

Gössling, S. and Higham, J. (2021). The low-carbon imperative: Destination management under urgent climate change. *Journal of Travel Research*, 60(6), 1167–1179.

Gössling, S., Scott, D., Hall, C.M. (2021). Pandemics, tourism and global change: A rapid assessment of COVID-19. *Journal of Sustainable Tourism*, 29(1), 1–20.

Gretzel, U. and Scarpino Johns, M. (2018). Destination resilience and smart tourism destinations. *Tourism Review International*, 22(3), 263–276.

Grillitsch, M. and Sotarauta, M. (2020). Trinity of change agency, regional development paths and opportunity spaces. *Progress in Human Geography*, 44(4), 704–723.

Gunderson, L.H. and Holling, C.S. (2002). *Panarchy: Understanding Transformations in Systems of Humans and Nature*. Island Press, Washington, D.C.

Halkier, H. and Therkelsen, A. (2013). Exploring tourism destination path plasticity: The case of coastal tourism in North Jutland, Denmark. *Zeitschrift fur Wirtschaftsgeographie*, 57(1/2), 39–51.

Hall, C.M. (2019). Constructing sustainable tourism development: The 2030 agenda and the managerial ecology of sustainable tourism. *Journal of Sustainable Tourism*, 27(7), 1044–1060.

Hall, C.M., Prayag, G., Amore, A. (2018). *Tourism and Resilience: Individual, Organisational and Destination Perspectives*. Channel View Publications, Bristol.

Hartman, S. (2018). Resilient tourism destinations? Governance implications of bringing theories of resilience and adaptive capacity to tourism practice. In *Destination Resilience: Challenges and Opportunities for Destination Management and Governance*, Innerhofer, E., Fontanari, M., Pechlaner, H. (eds). Routledge, London.

Huang, A. and Bahja, F. (2022). Complex systems. In *Encyclopedia of Tourism Management and Marketing*, Buhalis, D. (ed.). Edward Elgar Publishing, London.

Hudson, R. (2010). Resilient regions in an uncertain world: Wishful thinking or practical reality? *Cambridge Journal of Regions, Economy and Society*, 3(1), 11–25.

Knafou, R. (2023). *Réinventer (vraiment) le tourisme. En finir avec les hypocrisies du tourisme durable*. Faubourg, Paris.

Langer, M. and Schmude, J. (2024). COVID-19 as a paradigm shift? Insights from the de-growth debate in tourism. *European Journal of Tourism Research*, 36, 3607.

Lew, A.A. (2014). Scale, change and resilience in community tourism planning. *Tourism Geographies*, 16(1), 14–22.

Li, P.F. and Bathelt, H. (2011). A relational-evolutionary perspective of cluster dynamics. *SPACES*, 9 [Online]. Available at: www.spaces-online.com [Accessed 22 April 2021].

Ma, M. and Hassink, R. (2013). An evolutionary perspective on tourism area development. *Annals of Tourism Research*, 41, 89–109.

Mansilla, J. and Hughes, N. (2021). En dos años no nos vamos a acordar de la pandemia. Análisis del discurso sobre el decrecimiento turístico en Barcelona. *Barataria, Revista Castellano-Manchega de Ciencias Sociales*, 30, 30–52.

Martin, R. and Sunley, P. (2006). Path dependence and regional economic evolution. *Journal of Economic Geography*, 6, 395–437.

Martin, R. and Sunley, P. (2015). Towards a developmental turn in evolutionary economic geography? *Regional Studies*, 49(5), 712–732.

McDonald, J.R. (2009). Complexity science: An alternative world view for understanding sustainable tourism development. *Journal of Sustainable Tourism*, 17(4), 455–471.

McLeod, M. (2020). Tourism governance, panarchy and resilience in The Bahamas. In *Tourism Development, Governance and Sustainability in The Bahamas*, Rolle, S., Minnis, J., Bethell-Bennett, I. (eds). Routledge, London.

Mehmood, A. (2016). Of resilient places: Planning for urban resilience. *European Planning Studies*, 24(2), 407–419.

Njoroge, J.M. (2022). Sustainable adaptation. In *Encyclopedia of Tourism Management and Marketing*, Buhalis, D. (ed.). Edward Elgar Publishing, London.

Novy, J. and Colomb, C. (2019). Urban tourism as a source of contention and social mobilisations: A critical review. *Journal Tourism Planning and Development*, 16, 358–375.

Paidakaki, A. and Moulaert, F. (2017). Does the post-disaster resilient city really exist? A critical analysis of the heterogeneous transformative capacities of housing reconstruction 'resilience cells'. *International Journal of Disaster Resilience in the Built Environment*, 8(3), 275–291.

Prayag, G. (2020). Time for reset? COVID-19 and tourism resilience. *Tourism Review International*, 24(2/3), 179–184.

Prideaux, B. (2004). The resort development spectrum: The case of the Gold Coast, Australia. *Tourism Geographies*, 6(1), 26–58.

Prideaux, B., Thompson, M., Pabel, A. (2020). Lessons from COVID-19 can prepare global tourism for the economic transformation needed to combat climate change. *Tourism Geographies*, 22(3), 667–678.

Rech, Y., Paget, E., Dimanche, F. (2019). Uncertain tourism: Evolution of a French winter sports resort and network dynamics. *Journal of Destination Marketing & Management*, 12, 95–104.

Russell, R. and Faulkner, B. (2004). Entrepreneurship, chaos and the tourism area life cycle. *Annals of Tourism Research*, 31(3), 556–579.

Saarinen, J. (2004). Destinations in change: The transformation process of tourist destinations. *Tourist Studies*, 4(2), 161–179.

Saarinen, J. and Gill, A. (2018). *Resilient Destinations and Tourism: Governance Strategies in the Transition towards Sustainability in Tourism*. Routledge, London.

Sanz Ibáñez, C. and Anton Clavé, S. (2014). The evolution of destinations: Towards an evolutionary and relational economic geography approach. *Tourism Geographies*, 16(4), 563–579.

Sanz Ibáñez, C. and Anton Clavé, S. (2022). Destination evolution. In *Encyclopedia of Tourism Management and Marketing*, Buhalis, D. (ed.). Edward Elgar Publishing, London.

Scuttari, A. and Corradini, P. (2018). Multidisciplinary approaches to resilience in tourism destination studies. In *Destination Resilience: Challenges and Opportunities for Destination Management and Governance*, Innerhofer, E., Fontanari, M., Pechlaner, H. (eds). Routledge, London.

Transforming Tourism Initiative (2017). *Berlin Declaration on Transforming Tourism* [Online]. Available at: http://www.transforming-tourism.org/berlin-declaration-on-transforming-tourism.html [Accessed 22 April 2021].

Vale, L.J. (2014). The politics of resilient cities: Whose resilience and whose city? *Building Research & Information*, 42(2), 191–201.

Vale, L.J. and Campanella, T.J. (2005). *The Resilient City: How Modern Cities Recover from Disaster*. Oxford University Press, Oxford.

Walton, J.K. (1983). *The English Seaside Resort: A Social History 1750–1914*. Leicester University Press, Leicester.

Zacher, D., Philipp, J., Pechlaner, H. (2022). Destination resilience. In *Encyclopedia of Tourism Management and Marketing*, Buhalis, D. (ed.). Edward Elgar Publishing, London.

Acknowledgments

This book would not have been possible without the involvement of organizations and individuals whom I would like to thank.

First, the collective project of the AsTRES symposium and later this book could not have come into fruition without the invaluable support of the members of the Tourism Research Group. This multidisciplinary research group, consisting of scholars from various fields (information and communication science, economics, geography, management and sociology-STAPS) and multiple laboratories of Université Côte d'Azur (ESPACE, GRM, SIC.Lab, GREDEG, LAMHESS and URMIS), has been supported since its inception, within the framework of the tourism project that I coordinate, by the Maison des Sciences de l'Homme et de la Société du Sud-Est, Nice, and specifically by Axis 4: Territories: Construction, Uses, Powers. I would especially like to warmly thank Franck Debos, Bernard Massiera, David Huron, Otto Regalado-Pezúa, Jacques Spindler and Jean-Charles Briquet-Laugier for their unwavering support and wise counsel.

Simultaneously, the Institut du Tourisme Côte d'Azur-ITCA, a federative research institute in tourism, has been a key contributor to this book, and I would like to express my gratitude to Jean-Christophe Gay, scientific director of the institute, and Vincent Tricard, operational director, a driving force and steadfast pillar of university tourism in the Côte d'Azur.

Finally, I wish to thank Jean-Hugues Matelly and Christine Fernandez for their patience and support, both material and immaterial, in the completion of this book.

Introduction to the Authors of the Two Volumes

Henri Alexis

Henri Alexis is Professor Emeritus in Information and Communication Sciences. He is a member of the SIC.Lab Méditerranée at the Université Côte d'Azur in France. His research works are fully aligned with the communication of organizations and territories, particularly questioning them in their innovative, technological and ethical dimensions. His latest research primarily sheds light on interculturality and heritage-making from a largely international perspective.

henri.alexis@univ-cotedazur.fr

Alexis Annes

Alexis Annes is a professor–researcher in sociology at the École d'Ingénieurs de Purpan in Toulouse, France, and a member of the UMR CNRS 5193 LISST rural dynamics. His research works describe and analyze current changes affecting rural societies and agricultural population. He has focused in particular on questions of gender and agriculture for the past decade. His research has been the subject of numerous articles published in national and international journals.

alexis.annes@purpan.fr

Claudine Batazzi

Claudine Batazzi is a university professor in information and communication sciences at the Université Côte d'Azur in France. She is deputy director of the SIC.Lab Méditerranée research lab. Her research work focuses on digital mediation in territories, heritage-making as a tool for the enhancement of territories, sustainable tourism as an economic model, etc. Her latest work is titled *Les symboles au cœur des organisations : des managers en quête de sens*, ISTE Éditions, collection "Gouvernance et sacré", 2022.

claudine.batazzi@univ-cotedazur.fr

Jacinthe Bessière

Jacinthe Bessière is a lecturer authorized to direct research in sociology at the Université de Toulouse, Jean-Jaurès (France) and is a member of the CERTOP UMR CNRS 5044. She teaches at the ISTHIA (Institut supérieur du Tourisme, de l'Hôtellerie et de l'Alimentation), where she is responsible for studies and oversees the Master's Program in Tourism and Development. Her research activities, supported by several research programs, lie at the intersection of tourism sociology and development sociology. Through the study of food heritage, she aims to understand the processes and mechanisms of development in rural spaces. The proposed works seek to understand the process of heritage-making, analyzed as a social construct at the interface of tourism and food issues. Her research, primarily focused on the French Southwest, has resulted in several books and articles being published in national and international journals.

jacinthe.bessiere-hilaire@univ-tlse2.fr

Denis Bories

Denis Bories, PhD in Management Sciences, is a lecturer in Marketing at the Institut supérieur du tourisme, de l'hôtellerie et de l'alimentation (ISTHIA), Université de Toulouse, Jean-Jaurès in France. His research focuses on adopting new technologies and the trust placed in them in the tourism, hospitality and food sectors. He teaches digital marketing to the students of ISTHIA.

denis.bories@univ-tlse2.fr

Sylvie Christofle

Sylvie Christofle is a lecturer, authorized to direct research in Geography at the Université Côte d'Azur in France, affiliated with the UMR ESPACE. She is Deputy Scientific Director of the ITCA (Institut du Tourisme Côte d'Azur, Federative Institute of Tourism Research) and is responsible for the Master 2 International Management Hospitality (IAE Nice). Her research focuses on event tourism, with a specific focus on MICE (Meeting Incentive Convention Event), territorial marketing and communication of destinations via digital social media, as well as smart tourist destinations.

sylvie.christofle@univ-cotedazur.fr

Sylvie Clarimont

Sylvie Clarimont is Professor of Geography and Planning at the Université de Pau et des Pays de l'Adour in France, affiliated with UMR 6031 TREE (energy and environmental transitions). Her research focuses notably on the interrelation between tourism, leisure and the environment.

sylvie.clarimont@univ-pau.fr

Salvador Anton Clavé

Salvador Anton Clavé is Full Professor of Regional Geographical Analysis at the Universitat Rovira i Virgili (URV) in Catalonia, Spain. He has been Visiting Senior Research Scholar at the International Institute of Tourism Studies at the George Washington University. His research focuses on analyzing the evolution of tourist destinations, tourist attractions and theme parks, visitor spatial behavior and data analysis for planning and decision-making in the tourism industry. His research also focuses on the research traditions in the geography of tourism.

salvador.anton@urv.cat

Fabrice Decoupigny

Fabrice Decoupigny is Lecturer of Geography at the Université Côte d'Azur in France. An urban planner and developer by training, his research focuses on the modeling of mobility and development processes as well as on urban growth dynamics of urban metropolitan systems.

fabrice.decoupigny@univ-cotedazur.fr

Sascha Diwersy

Sascha Diwersy is a lecturer at the Université Montpellier 3 in France specializing in computational linguistic semantics and affiliated with the Praxiling laboratory. His skills and expertise focus on corpus linguistics, natural language processing, lexical semantics, discourse studies, lexicography, corpus compilation, linguistic text partitioning, contrastive linguistics and variational linguistics.

sascha.diwersy@univ-montp3.fr

Nathalie Fabry

Nathalie Fabry is a university professor in Information and Communication Sciences at the Université Gustave-Eiffel in France, specializing in Tourism and Territorial Economic Intelligence. Her research, conducted within the Dicen-IdF laboratory, focuses on the strategic management of tourist destinations with an adaptive resilience and smart city approach, as well as on the impact of climate change on the future of tourism.

nathalie.fabry@univ-eiffel.fr

Marie-Ève Férérol

Marie-Ève Férérol holds a PhD in Geography (Université Clermont Auvergne, France). Her thesis focused on the small towns of the south of Massif Central and the west of the Spanish Meseta. Qualified as a lecturer in Geography-planning, she pursues her research on the sustainability and attractiveness of places. One of her specializations is thermalism and spa towns.

mefererol@gmail.com

Carine Fournier

Carine Fournier is Lecturer of Geography at the Aix-Marseille Université in France, affiliated with the ESPACE laboratory (UMR 7300). Her works focus on tourism in the Mediterranean coastal area.

carine.fournier@univ-amu.fr

Sandrine Fournier

Sandrine Fournier is a lecturer at the Université de Picardie Jules Verne in France, affiliated with the CRIISEA (Centre de recherche sur l'industrie, les institutions et les systèmes économiques d'Amiens) laboratory. Her research focuses on human resources in public and private organizations. Her two research axes are secondary school teachers (involvement, performance, satisfaction and stress) and tourism (loyalty, meaning given to work and recruitment).

sandrine.fournier@u-picardie.fr

Isabelle Frochot

Isabelle Frochot is a senior lecturer authorized to direct research at the Université de Bourgogne France, UFR STAPS and is affiliated with the CREGO research unit. Her specialization covers the client experience in tourist consumption, and more specifically mechanisms of disconnection during holidays, the perception of overtourism by local populations and sustainable tourist behavior.

isabelle.frochot@u-bourgogne.fr

Jean-Christophe Gay

Jean-Christophe Gay, holder of an agrégation in geography, is a university professor at the Université Côte d'Azur in France. He is part of the URMIS laboratory and is Scientific Director of the Institut du Tourisme Côte d'Azur. His research focuses on the geo-history of tourism, overseas territories and spatial discontinuities.

jean-christophe.gay@univ-cotedazur.fr

Émeline Hatt

Émeline Hatt is a lecturer at Aix-Marseille Université in France and member of the Interdisciplinary Laboratory in Environment and Urban Planning (LIEU). Rooted in the field of tourism development, her research focuses on public policies, planning and development projects in the mountains and along the coastline.

emeline.hatt@univ-amu.fr

Vincent Herbert

Vincent Herbert is a geographer, professor at the Université du Littoral Côte d'Opale (ULCO) in France, and member of the TVES laboratory (territories, cities, environment, society, recognized research unit 4477). He is the director of the Institut de Recherche et d'Enseignement en Tourisme (scientific interest group InREnT) and has directed the Master's program in Tourism since 2010. His research subjects, founded on a systemic analysis of coastal territories, are focused on studying the interactions of societies and the effects of their activities on their surroundings. For the period 2023–2025, he is on secondment to the Université de Polynésie Française and Deputy Director of the SECOPOL laboratory (health and services of the Polynesian ecosystems, mixed research unit 241).

dir.inrent@univ-littoral.fr

Jean-Denis Hue

Jean-Denis Hue is a doctoral student at the Université du Littoral Côte d'Opale (ULCO) in France, member of the TVES laboratory (territories, cities, environment, society, recognized research unit 4477). He dedicates his doctoral thesis to ecotourism on the Opal Coast in relation to the network of actors with a mesological approach for the actors of the social and solidarity economy. He is also a member of the SAP association (Société Anonyme et Populaire), whose activities are devoted to projects in the social and solidarity economy.

saponyme@gmail.com

David Huron

David Huron is Professor of Management Sciences and Management at the Université Côte d'Azur (IAE Nice) in France. Holder of an accreditation to supervise research, he has supervised around 10 doctoral theses, several of which are in the field of tourism. His research is primarily focused on public management and marketing.

david.huron@univ-cotedazur.fr

Boualem Kadri

Boualem Kadri is Professor of Tourism Studies at the School of Management Sciences of the Université du Québec à Montréal in Canada. His areas of research are the epistemology of tourism studies, the critical analysis of the concept of tourism studies and the process of touristification of cities.

kadri.boualem@uqam.ca

Patrizia Laudati

Patrizia Laudati is a professor at the Université Côte d'Azur in France and a researcher at the SIC.Lab Méditerranée laboratory. With a Doctorate in Information and Communication Sciences, as well as being an architect and specialist in urban projects, she is a visiting professor at DIDA, the architecture department at the University of Florence (Italy), and at the

MediaLaB at the University of Pisa. Her work focuses in particular on the reception and mediation of architectural and urban spaces using a transdisciplinary SHS/SPI and semiopragmatic approach.

patrizia.laudati@univ-cotedazur.fr

Véronique Magri

Véronique Magri, holder of an agrégation in Modern Letters, is a professor of French language and stylistics at the University of Côte d'Azur in France and a member of BCL (Bases, Corpus, Language), CNRS. Her research combines stylistic and computational analysis of literary texts from the 19th century to the present. She is the author of several books and articles, particularly on the poetics of travel narratives and the issue of otherness.

veronique.magri@univ-cotedazur.fr

Jean-Bernard Marsat

Jean-Bernard Marsat is a researcher at INRAE within the UMR Territoires in Clermont-Ferrand, France, holding a doctorate in Management Sciences and Environmental Sciences from AgroParisTech Abies. His work focuses on the relationships between economic activities, especially tourism, territorial development and the management of natural and cultural heritage through strategic analysis and governance studies.

jmarsat@club-internet.fr

Cyril Martin-Colonna

Cyril Martin-Colonna is Lecturer in Tourism and Urban Studies at the Université du Québec à Montréal and the Université du Québec Trois-Rivières in Canada. Currently in the process of validating his doctoral thesis, his research areas include urbicide, the commercialization of cities and regions for tourism, the role of new technologies in tourism resilience and tourism geopolitics.

martin.cyril@uqam.ca

Véronique Mondou

Véronique Mondou is a geographer and lecturer at ESTHUA, Faculty of Tourism, Culture, and Hospitality at the Université d'Angers in France and is affiliated with the mixed research unit CNRS 6590 ESO-Angers. Her research focuses on the relationships between tourism and transport. She specifically addresses issues of accessibility and tourism development, as well as the transformation of modes of transport into tourism products.

veronique.mondou@univ-angers.fr

Paul-Emmanuel Pichon

Paul-Emmanuel Pichon has been Lecturer of Marketing at the Université de Toulouse, Jean-Jaurès in France since 2007. He is a member of CERTOP (Research Center on Work Organizations and Policies, UMR CNRS 5044). In 2016, he co-authored the book *Marketing du tourisme et de l'accueil* (6th edition, Pearson). His research topics focus on strategies of risk perception and reduction by consumers (including food consumers, wine consumers, as well as tourists and travelers), the role of nostalgia and trust in consumer reassurance strategies. His research also addresses influencer marketing as well as e-communication policies (social media, videos, etc.).

paul-emmanuel.pichon@univ-tlse2.fr

Étienne Polge

Étienne Polge is a research fellow at INRAE at the UMR Territories in Clermont-Ferrand in France and holds a Doctorate in Economic Sciences from the Université Paris-Saclay. His research focuses on changes in practices driven by territorial collectives, including those that ensure the management of natural heritage sites within tourist reach.

etienne.polge@inrae.fr

Noémie Ravas

Noémie Ravas was a Master's student in Applied Social Sciences in Food Studies at ISTHIA (Institut supérieur du Tourisme, de l'Hôtellerie et de l'Alimentation), Université de Toulouse, Jean-Jaurès in France. She is particularly interested in the direct relationship between tourism and food heritage when participating in the Touralim research program, which was coordinated by Jacinthe Bessière and Alexis Annes.

noemieravas@hotmail.fr

Otto Regalado-Pezúa

Otto Regalado-Pezúa is Full Professor and Director of the Academic Department of Marketing at ESAN Graduate School of Business (Lima, Peru). He holds a Doctorate in Management Sciences from the IAE Nice from the Université Côte d'Azur in France. He is also a visiting researcher at the GRM Research Laboratory at IAE Nice. His research focuses on sustainable tourism management, sustainable marketing strategy and digital transformation applied to business management.

oregalado@esan.edu.pe

Shiwei Shen

Shiwei Shen is an associate professor at Ningbo University, China, where he founded the Sino-European Institute of Tourism and Culture in 2011 and the joint institute between Ningbo University and the Ningbo-Université d'Angers in 2017. His research focuses on the evolution of tourist destinations and on tourism practices. A large part of his work has focused on enhancing the understanding and performance of multiple stakeholders in tourist destinations.

shiwei_shen@163.com

Juan Carlos Sosa Varela

Juan Carlos Sosa Varela is Dean of the Department of Business, Tourism, and Entrepreneurship at the Ana G. Méndez University in San Juan, Puerto Rico and Professor of International Business and Marketing. His research focuses on marketing strategy, brand management, corporate responsibility, digital transformation and intercultural management. He was a visiting professor at European, Latin American and Indian business schools, and holds a Doctorate in Economic and Social Sciences.

jsosa4@uagm.edu

Marios Sotiriadis

Marios Sotiriadis is an International Professor and Expert at the Ningbo University, China. He obtained his PhD at the Université Nice-Sophia-Antipolis, Nice in France. He authored nine books, seven textbooks and five study guides. His research and writing focus on tourism marketing, tourism business marketing and consumer behavior.

sotermarios@outlook.com

Jacques Spindler

Jacques Spindler is a professor emeritus in Management. He was Director of the IAE Nice (Université Côte d'Azur, France). He specializes in public administration and policies, and, as such, his research has focused on the evolution of tourism organizations (theories and practices).

jacques.spindler@univ-cotedazur.fr

Leonardo Toro

Leonardo Toro holds an MBA and a Master's in Marketing from ESAN in Peru and ESIC in Spain. He specializes in business innovation at EAFIT, consulting in business marketing, strategic planning and innovation in Columbia and Peru. He is also a part-timer lecturer in the fields of marketing, business and entrepreneurship, with notable projects in the internationalization of Latin America and higher education.

mtoro@esan.edu.pe

Laurent Vanni

Laurent Vanni is a research engineer at the CNRS, affiliated with the BCL (Bases, Corpus, Language laboratory) of the Université Côte d'Azur in France. His research focuses on the statistical analysis of textual data and on deep learning applied to humanities and social sciences (HSS). He designs and develops the Hyperbase Web[1] research platform as well as a suite of tools dedicated to textual corpus analysis.

laurent.vanni@univ-cotedazur.fr

Philippe Violier

Philippe Violier is a geographer and professor emeritus at ESTHUA, Faculty of Tourism, Cultural, and Hospitality at the Université d'Angers in France and affiliated with the mixed research unit CNRS 6590 ESO-Angers. He was a member of the MIT team (mobility, itineraries, territories) from 1996 to 2011. His research focuses on relationships between stakeholder strategies and tourist destinations at different scales.

philippe.violier@univ-angers.fr

Sylvain Zeghni

Sylvain Zeghni holds a Doctorate in Economics and is qualified to lead research. He is a lecturer at the Université Gustave-Eiffel in France and conducts his research within the City, Mobility, Transport Laboratory (LVMT). His research primarily addresses the governance of cities, the environmental diplomacy of cities, smart cities, the resilience of territories and tourism policies. He directs the first year of the Master's program in Tourism as well as the "Destination Management" track within the same Master's program at the Université Gustave-Eiffel.

sylvain.zeghni@univ-eiffel.fr

1 See: https://hyperbase.unice.fr.

Introduction

The objective of this book is to identify elements that make it possible to characterize the "agility" dimension of tourism.

Two meanings exist to define the original term. The first refers to lightness and flexibility in body movements. The second relates to intellectual liveliness. Tourism refers to these two definitions (Paris 2015). The term "agile" appeared in the English-speaking economic world in 1991, introduced by James Martin, who, based on a vision of continuous evolution of computer techniques, proposed a method of rapid application development. The iterative, incremental and adaptive structure of this method is based on current agile approaches, particularly useful in periods of crises and uncertainties.

In fact, the Covid pandemic was not the first downturn that tourism has gone through. However, with at least a billion fewer international arrivals[1], the UN Tourism deemed 2020 as the "worst year in tourism history"[2]. Other crises have hit this sector head-on, leading to a decrease (or even a halt) in activity for extended periods (the major recession of the last decades of the 19th century in Europe, the 1929 crash, world wars, etc.). The magnitude of

---

Introduction written by Sylvie CHRISTOFLE, based on a collective text including contributions by Franck DEBOS, David HURON, Jean-Christophe GAY, Bernard MASSIERA, Otto REGALADO-PEZÚA and Jacques SPINDLER.

1 Against 1.5 billion international arrivals in 2019, UNWTO. See: https://www.unwto.org/international-tourism-growth-continues-to-outpace-the-economy.

2 2020: Worst Year in Tourism History with 1 Billion Fewer International Arrivals, UNWTO, 28 January 2021. See: https://www.unwto.org.

these crises, sometimes unpredictable (Dubuc 2020), has often led to the proclamation that post-crisis tourism would no longer be the same as before. The hope placed in transformed tourism nevertheless seems symptomatic of the distrust of elites toward tourism. This lack of trust, relayed by many media, seems to come from a contemporary "tourismphobia", criticizing and even conspiring against "mass" tourism, somewhat delegitimizing popular tastes and practices. However, it highlights the importance of approaching communication channels differently, which are now multifaceted. Certainly far from perfect, tourism is subject to certain denigration in favor of an ideal or idealized tourism. The latter would comprise tourists who travel little, use eco-friendly modes of transport, engage in "sports tourism" or "cultural tourism" with ethical and responsible behavior, all of which seems to mask an unabashed "social racism" (Bourdieu 1979), disregarding the fact that tourism is now one of the components of happiness in our societies, even though, on a global scale, it still only affects a minority of the population.

Notwithstanding, the time of crises and uncertainties that we are going through occurs in a period of climate change, for which tourism, and particularly the modes of transport that it involves, is partly responsible (Lenzen et al. 2018; ADEME 2021; Delaplace 2021). The carbon footprint of global tourism is indeed considerable. In order to make tourism more environmentally respectful, it would be appropriate to examine its role with respect to the conservation of natural and cultural heritage.

Establishing agile, creative and integrative tourism can help avoid a concentration of travelers in hotspots while involving locals. At the same time, it is feasible to involve visitors in varied experiences that reflect the identity of the territory, within a logic of co-creation between residents and tourists. The latter thus become co-producers, as they mobilize the information intended for them and assign added value to it (Esnault et al. 2006).

It is then interesting to question the territory and the new ways of approaching space and time, heritage and individual and collective identities, as well as the cultural implementation of sustainable development based on a pedagogy of belonging and engagement; these approaches could demonstrate their aptitude to fruitfully resolve tensions between identity and otherness, and between globality and locality, two pairs of forces that are characteristic of globalization (Sauvé 2007).

Furthermore, smart tourism can, through the creation of quality digital content, help reduce visit overcrowding (such as the acceleration of digital heritage in China, the online streaming of live performances like the Metropolitan Opera, or even events like the Milan and London fashion weeks). With digitalization potentially catalyzing various processes of agility, will tourism have a paradigm shift and evolve from a standardized approach to a system prioritizing innovation and "customization"? The integration of digital technology creates a new dynamic, as well as a structural and cultural change (Blanc 2016). This evolution leads to a genuine restructuring of the relationship of forces between the individual and the actors in their environment, in favor of the former (Debos and Boillot 2014).

Faced with difficulties and contingency, measures have been taken and will continue to be taken in order to prevent companies from sinking and disappearing. The state and local authorities, notably in developed countries, have assisted the actors in the world of tourism, particularly by granting economic aid during major crises (Fialaire 2018; Christofle 2023). At the same time, companies adopt original measures and strategies, demonstrating agility in the face of a deeply unbalanced environment and tourists whose behavior is also changing (temporarily or permanently?).

Agility could then constitute the common denominator of these actors grouped in tourist destinations, which is the site of their activity. Agility also requires thinking differently – with a genuine synergy – about the modalities and intentions of communication between tourism professionals, those responsible for the territories, citizens and visitors. This is all the more important as public authorities seek to "make the temporary permanent" by adopting agile structures (Kerleo 2020) in order to make "local tourism" dynamic (Pellegrin-Romeggio 2020). This trendy expression seems like an oxymoron, since tourism by definition involves movement, but corresponds well to the emerging moral question: is it good or bad to move? Is it possible to defend the leisure and tourism economy, and thus "useless" transportation? We may question the strategy of "greenwashing" that hides behind the promotion of "local tourism"/staycation, or remote work, which could be valuable to certain tourist, coastal and winter sports resorts. The pandemic crisis only highlighted a phenomenon that started decades ago. This phenomenon corresponds to the metropolization of tourist sites and to the development of the residential or local economy (Davezies 2008). The ski resorts Crans-Montana and Zermatt in Switzerland are good examples.

Their ski lifts have been closed, and they have (agilely?) changed their target by wishing to welcome remote workers, "digital nomads", sometimes seen as "unidentified tourist objects" (Gourlay et al. 2024). Will this strategy endure? Will we witness an increasingly marked decline in tourism in favor of complex mobilities combining work and leisure, described as "heliotropism and residential hedonism" by Veltz (2017)?

What are destinations' trajectories, adaptability and resilience in the face of challenges posed by current accelerated transformations, behavioral changes due to climate change concerns and the shift toward a low-carbon economy? In this dynamic, each tourist place develops its evolutionary process. As a result, it is essential to understand the ability of destinations to anticipate, prepare for, respond to and recover from any critical moment thanks to a continuous and complex process involving all stakeholders in a dynamic that includes societal change.

Hit hard by the crisis, numerous tourist destinations are thus facing "the challenge of having to strategically distinguish themselves [...] to attract opportunities" (Thomas et al. 2020). With the massive expansion of digitization, new questions arise, for example, what business model(s) (Falk and Hagsten 2022), what communication, and what impacts on territories?

At the same time, the use of social media and communication based on social networks (Facebook, Instagram, etc.) are rising at all scales (Kemps 2023). It is then a question of grasping the strategies implemented by various public and private stakeholders, and the representation that netizens, professionals, tourists and inhabitants have of them (Christofle et al. 2019).

This context of crisis and uncertainty leads to the question of the agility of tourist organizations as well as of private and public organizations. Indeed, the mutations resulting from the search of the "right distance" forces actors in the tourism industry to reinvent their managerial practices, in particular, marketing. As highlighted by Briant et al. (2020), "the natural gestures of tourist hospitality are banned in favor of all sorts of digital and mobile applications, sometimes featuring avatars that serve as guides". The introduction of artificial intelligence and data (Guetchouli et al. 2020) can facilitate an even greater agility in proposing products better adapted to consumer needs, especially responsible tourism (Mandal and Dubey 2020).

The connection, the local and the participatory aspects seem to be the foundations of a new tourism positioning. Some recent books thus highlight theories associating marketing and agility (Kalaignanam et al. 2021). Homburg et al. (2020) identified agile marketing as a key dimension of marketing excellence and conceptualized it as a strategic means for a company to execute growth activities through simplified structures and processes, as well as rapid decision-making and learning through trial-and-error. On the basis of this definition, concepts linked to adaptability, speed and iteration can be mobilized to understand agile marketing. Furthermore, the marketing dimension is now strongly territorialized for both companies as for collectives, from territorial brands designating cities and regions (#ilovenice; #cotedazurfrance; #onatousbesoindesud, etc.) to citizen ambassadors capable of making the destination "shine" and enhancing its attractiveness in terms of both its image and quality of life. Such an approach is a valuable contribution to the development of tourism communication, which can no longer be reduced to the classic triptych concerning a destination's image – lived, desired and perceived.

This context calls for new forms of communication and new meditation practices. Questions related to sustainable development and eco-citizenship (Roesch 2003) thus appear at the heart of issues related to sociability and cultural mediation.

At the same time, there exists a fundamental research point around the digitalization of uses and the study of social–digital devices (Pélissier et al. 2015). It also takes into account more specifically the major impact of information and communication technology, the resulting opportunities and risks, particularly in terms of the communication device. The development of the Internet, singularly due to social networks, coincides with a need for reviving interactivity, which is strongly present in individuals. Clients and tourists are increasingly expressing themselves by commenting, recommending, denouncing and "playing" with brands, all while listening to each other and increasingly trusting one other. Concurrently, the shared innovation between the designer and the user is increasingly shifting toward the end user (Musso et al. 2007). The aim is thus to better understand and anticipate the impact of digital technology on the evolution of tourist behavior as well as the stakeholders of this sector. Through increased digitization, the communication of stakeholders in the tourism industry must not only be more agile, but also more responsible, particularly in an educational and awareness-raising approach to preserving the heritage of the tourist destination considered.

In conjunction, public action on a tourist destination (state and local authorities) can manifest in two ways (Thoenig 2014). The first type of intervention works with materially identifiable practices: controls, constructions, maintenance of infrastructures, allocation of subsidies, etc. The second type of intervention is less tangible via regulations, communication, discourse, etc., able to limit or even eliminate situations such as "overtourism" or "undertourism", or by generating positive externalities, for example, airport access and securing certain tourist spaces. For that reason, we can understand the reasons that are leading public administrations involved in tourism to support this sector today (Spindler 2019). This move, which favors a memorable experiential value for tourists and is respectful for stakeholders is accompanied, or even driven, today by destination management organizations (DMOs). DMOs manage, in collaboration with public administrations, the collective actions in their territory that are aligned, at least for some of them, within the logic of an "alternative tourism" (Botti and Le Roy 2021).

The current context of crises and uncertainties thus leads to a series of questions in the field of tourism. This book explores many of these fundamental questions and seeks to answer them holistically using several theoretical and methodological frameworks in order to better understand the driving elements and subtleties of an "agile" approach in tourism, its transformations and impacts. It therefore proposes a pathway of theoretical benchmarks, analyses and case studies on tourism agility, at varied scales and contexts, to consider contemporary changes and contribute to their understanding in an increasingly complex environment. It thus examines the relationships between crises and tourism, territorial, organizational agility, etc., including perspectives from diverse and complementary disciplinary fields: planning, economics, urban studies, geography, management and marketing, information and communication, language and literature, sociology, etc.

This book is structured in four parts and two volumes.

The first volume, focusing on the themes of uncertainties, technologies and societies, is divided into two parts. The first part lays the groundwork for understanding the discourse around the concept of a major crisis, potential agile responses and the question of a destination resilience. Diwersy, Gay, Magri and Vanni examine "tourism in the local and national press: study of the impact of the pre- and post-Covid discourse". Martin-Colonna and Kadri complement this work with an analysis on the "Covid-19 health crisis and tourism: perceptions and analyses in Francophone scientific literature 2020–2022". Spindler and Huron question the potential outcomes of the crisis: "Towards a different tourism? Theoretical solutions to consider, avenues to explore". Concluding this first part, Fabry and Zeghni present the "resilience of a tourist destination in the post-Covid era: the case of Val d'Europe Agglomération". The second part explores tourism agility between technology and society. Regarding questions related to technology, Regalado-Pezúa, Toro and Sosa Varela first extend the geographical scope of the analysis to Latin America and to the "identification of digital skills: a study of Peruvian tourist businesses". Bories and Pichon then study the critical point connecting "artificial intelligence and the search for meaning in support of marketing agility in tourism". Focusing on the societal and social approach to tourism agility, Laudati, Batazzi and Alexis examine the "relationship to otherness: the role of interactions between tourists and the inhabitants of a territory". Finally, Annes, Bessière and Ravas look at how to reconcile tourism and agricultural agility, envisioning "farm hospitality as a transitional process from the perspective of agritourists".

The second volume focuses on the relationships between tourism agility, attractiveness, marketing and sustainability. It is composed of two parts. The first part of the book addresses the question of marketing and communication at the heart of tourism agility, stories of actors and territories. First, Sotiriadis and Shen consider "the agility of the tourist-consumer: a framework for tourist marketing". Christofle and Fournier analyze "online communicational agility of international tourist destinations: Cannes, Nice, Monaco". Férérol focuses her work on "the Accros du Peignoir (Massif Central): Proof of the agility of French spa environment". Marsat and Polge examine the "intertwined attractions and destinations: The case of the UNESCO site of the Chaîne des Puys-faille de Limagne". Finally, Fournier studies the "collective agility at the heart of enhancing tourism in Hauts-de-France during the Covid period". The second part looks at sustainability as a challenge to tourism agility. In this regard, Hatt and Clarimont envision how to "manage attendance: a challenge to public policies to preserving and enhancing natural heritage" and

Decoupigny analyzes "metropolitan spaces and proximity tourism". Frochot, Mondou and Violier then propose a reflection on "hyper-mobility in light of environmental and social challenges". Finally, Hue and Herbert share a "return on experiences of eco-friendly mobility and sustainable tourism in Côte d'Opale: the bicycle as a vector of agility".

References

ADEME (2021). Bilan des émissions de gaz à effet de serre du secteur du tourisme en France. Report, ADEME, Paris.

Blanc, E. (2016). Une communication des organisations comme facteur des risques psychosociaux liés à l'acculturation au numérique (Groupe La Poste). *Communication & Organisation*, 49, 191–201.

Botti, L. and Leroy, C. (2021). De l'impact à la performance environnementale du tourisme : mesurer pour piloter durablement les territoires. In *Organismes de gestion de destination. Stratégies et pratiques pour un management responsable et durable des territoires touristiques*, Botti, L. and Spindler, J. (eds). L'Harmattan, Paris.

Bourdieu, P. (1979). *La distinction. Critique sociale du jugement*. Minuit, Paris.

Briant, E., Bechet, M., Machemehl, C., Suchet, A. (2020). Utopies d'un tourisme en re-nouvellement. *Téoros*, 39(3) [Online]. Available at: http://journals.openedition.org/teoros/7312.

Christofle, S. (2023). Tourism and meeting incentive convention event (MICE) tourism in Europe, systemic shock, structural transformations and resilience. In *Resilience and Regional Development: New Roadmaps*, Pascariu, G.C., Kourtit, K., Nijkamp, P., Ţigănaşu, R. (eds). Edward Elgar Publishing, London.

Christofle, S., Papetti, C., Fournier, C. (2019). Tourisme, trajectoires et images : les média socionumériques, outils contemporains d'adaptation communicationnelle de destinations ? Une voie de recherche en devenir. In *Tourisme et adaptations*, Tritz, C., Cholat, F., Uppen, J., Gwiazdzinski, L. (eds). Éditions Elya, Paris.

Davezies, L. (2008). *La République et ses territoires : la circulation invisible des richesses*. Le Seuil, Paris.

Debos, F. and Boillot, F. (2014). Communication des organisations, territoires et TIC au coeur du changement et du développement durable. *Les Cahiers de la SFSIC*, 10, 164–169.

Delaplace, M. (2021). Après la crise, un tourisme durable ? *L'Economie politique*, 91(3), 8–22.

Dubuc, A. (2020). Prévoir l'imprévisible ? *Gestion*, 45(2), 40–43.

Esnault, L., Zeiliger, R., Vermeulin, F. (2006). On the use of actor-network theory for developing web services dedicated to communities of practice. In *Proceedings of the EC-TEL06 Workshops*, Crete.

Falk, M.T. and Hagsten, E. (2022). The uneven distribution of fees for virtual academic conferences. *Journal of Convention & Event Tourism*, 23(3), 189–208.

Fialaire, J. (2018). La nouvelle régulation des activités touristiques en France : entre innovation et réformes territoriales. In *Le tourisme : un domaine de compétence partagé*, Fabry, N. and Spindler, J. (eds). L'Harmattan, Paris.

Gourlay, F., Maheo, C., Marinos, C., Pasquer-Jeanne, J. (2024). Espaces de coworkation et nomades numériques : des objets touristiques non identifiés. *Teoros, Revue de recherche en tourisme* [Online]. Available at: https://hal.science/hal-04384727.

Guetchouli, M., Lechalard, P.P., Miranda, S. (2020). Innovation ouverte et smart tourism : quand les acteurs d'un territoire s'unissent pour un tourisme intelligent et durable. *Gestion*, 37(4), 43–68.

Homburg, C., Theel, T., Hohenburg, S. (2020). Marketing excellence: Nature, measurement, and investor valuations. *Journal of Marketing*, 84(4), 1–22.

Kalaignaman, K., Tuli, K.R., Kushwaha, T., Lee, L., Gal, D. (2021). Marketing agility: The concept, antecedents, and a research agenda. *Journal of Marketing*, 85(1), 35–58.

Kemps, S. (2023). Digital 2023: Local Country Headlines Report [Online]. Available at: https://datareportal.com/reports/digital-2023-local-country-headlines.

Kerleo, J.-F. (2020). L'administration de projet : pérenniser le provisoire et l'agilité dans les structures publiques. *Revue Française d'Administration Publique*, 175(3), 721–734.

Lenzen, M., Sun, Y.Y., Faturay, F., Ting, Y.P., Geschke, A., Malik, A. (2018). The carbon footprint of global tourism. *Nature Climate Change*, 8, 522–528.

Mandal, S. and Dubey, R.K. (2020). Role of tourism IT adoption and risk management orientation on tourism agility and resilience: Impact on sustainable tourism supply chain performance. *International Journal of Tourism Research*, 22(6), 800–813.

Martin, J. (1991). *Rapid Application Development*. Macmillan, New York.

Musso, P., Ponthou, L., Seuillet, E. (2007). *Fabriquer le futur 2*. Le Village Mondial/Pearson Education, Paris/London.

Paris, T. (2015). L'agilité. *Le journal de l'école de Paris du management*, 111(1), 3.

Pélissier, N., Coutant, A., Domenget, J.-C., Rasse, P. (2015). *Analyzing Uses and Devices Together: The Interest of Sociotechnical Approach.* IAMCR World Congress, Montreal.

Pellegrin-Romeggio, F. (2020). Une nouvelle compétence d'assembleur pour une gestion dynamique du tourisme local. *Revue d'économie régionale et urbaine*, 2, 289–310.

Roesch, A. (2003). *L'écocitoyenneté et son pilier éducatif : le cas français.* L'Harmattan, Paris.

Sauvé, L. (2007). L'éducation relative à l'environnement et la globalisation : enjeux curriculaires et pédagogiques. *Revue education relative à l'environnement, Regards –Recherches – Réflexions*, 6. doi: 10.4000/ere.3894.

Spindler, J. (2019). Tourisme et management public. In *La recherche en management du tourisme*, Clergeau, C. and Peypoch, N. (eds). Vuibert, Paris.

Thoenig, J-C. (2014). *Dictionnaire des politiques publiques*, 4th edition. Presses de Sciences Po, Paris.

Thomas, B., Faye, D., Berry, F. (2020). Strategically marketing Florida's cities: An exploratory study into how cities engage in public marketing. *American Review of Public Administration*, 50(3), 275–285.

Veltz, P. (2017). *La société hyper-industrielle. Le nouveau capitalisme productif.* Le Seuil, Paris.

PART 1

Marketing and Communication at the Heart of Tourism Agility: Stories from Actors and Regions

1

Tourist Consumer-driven Agility: A Framework for Tourism Marketing

1.1. Introduction: marketing environment and consumer behavior in the digital era

Advancements in digital technologies have created a user-friendly interactive market and social environment for tourist consumers to more easily and efficiently create relationships, access information, complete transactions, and engage and interact online with tourism destinations and suppliers (Gretzel 2018; Morrison 2019). This convenience and efficiency radically transformed tourists' consumption behavior, creating challenges and opportunities for involved stakeholders (Cohen et al. 2014; Sotiriadis 2017). Business reports and intelligence suggest that tourism and digital technologies are fashioned for each other. These technologies can add value to all stages of the tourism experience by offering interactive, supportive and engaging information (OECD 2018; Deloitte Access Economics 2019; Reportlinker 2020). Consumers of all age groups were found to use SM platforms for all digital activities throughout their customer journey (World Economic Forum 2019, 2021; Reportlinker 2020). Likewise, tourist consumers constantly evolve, being influenced by and more dependent on social media (SM), digital platforms and user-generated content (UGC) by other individuals, and simultaneously influencing market trends, aspirations and expectations (Sigala et al. 2016; Park et al. 2019; Pop et al. 2021).

Chapter written by Marios SOTIRIADIS and Shiwei SHEN.

For a color version of all figures in this chapter, see www.iste.co.uk/christofle/tourism2.zip.

Undeniably, tourists of all age groups increasingly rely on digital platforms, SM and mobile systems for their tourism activities (Srivastava 2019). Given the experiential nature of tourism, it is believed that digital platforms and SM will continue to strongly influence tourists' decision-making (Cohen et al. 2014; Gretzel 2018; Lu et al. 2018; Liu et al. 2020). SM, mobile devices and travel apps with blogging, live-streaming and picture sharing, in turn, exert considerable influence on the decision-making of tourists and play an important role in supporting tourism-related activities (Dimitriou and AbouElgheit 2019; Park et al. 2019; Pop et al. 2021). Tourism destinations and suppliers are increasingly utilizing the same platforms and channels to connect and engage consumers for various management and marketing purposes (Sotiriadis 2017; Morrison 2019). In this regard, designing and implementing appropriate and suitable marketing strategies remains challenging, requiring in-depth knowledge of consumers. Tourism managers and marketers must better understand tourists' behavior, modify and even revolutionize their communication and marketing strategies to co-evolve with digital technologies (Font and McCabe 2017). The agile methodology is regarded as a valuable approach to addressing the related issues in a digitalized market environment. The present conceptual paper constitutes an endeavor to suggest a workable and implementable framework interrelating the tourists' requirements and expectations to the actions of marketing communications through the agile marketing approach.

The study aims to answer the question, "How can agile marketing be used more effectively in obtaining a mutually beneficial balance between the visitors' expectations and the tourism suppliers' offering of experiences?". To address this question, a conceptual model is suggested, drawn on the theoretical basis of the consumer decision journey (CDJ) (Hudson and Thal 2013; Yachin 2018; Pop et al. 2021) and of the model of 8Ps for integrated services marketing strategies (Kotler et al. 2019; Morrison 2019). It is posited that the agile approach is the bridge/link between the requirements of destinations' visitors through the four stages of CDJ and the marketing activities based on the 8Ps model. This conceptual paper contributes to the literature on the implementation of agility in the field of tourism marketing. From a theoretical perspective, it develops a framework linking the two poles (tourists and suppliers of tourism services) in the digital marketing environment. The ultimate aim is to guide marketers in designing and implementing communication and marketing strategies flexibly and adaptively.

1.2. Theoretical framework: agile marketing

According to Homburg et al. (2020), marketing excellence is a strategy focused on achieving organic growth by executing priorities related to the marketing ecosystem, end user and marketing agility, the latter being an approach to achieve excellence in marketing. Marketing agility is the extent to which an organization/company rapidly iterates between making sense of the market and executing marketing decisions to adapt to the market (Kalaignanam et al. 2021). Nowadays, digital technology allows marketers to engage in innovative new ways to meet consumers' needs far more effectively. To take advantage of the new possibilities enabled by digital, marketers have to become agile (Edelman et al. 2016). Agile, in the marketing context, means using data and analytics to continuously source promising opportunities or solutions to problems in real-time, deploying tests quickly, evaluating the results, and rapidly iterating.

Agile marketing is very useful in managing the uncertainty around complicated knowledge work. At its core, it is a tactical marketing approach in which marketing teams collectively identify high-value projects on which to focus their collective efforts, use sprints (short, finite periods of intensive work) to complete those projects cooperatively, measure their impact and then continuously and incrementally improve the results over time. The agile methodology is an iterative, incremental process, constantly working with customer feedback; hence, it is regarded as a valuable approach to addressing and responding quickly to changes in the market. Agile strives for simplicity, releasing things early and often, and iterating based on market reactions. Agile marketing aims to improve the speed, predictability, transparency and adaptability to change the marketing function (Agile Marketing 2017).

Agile marketers follow a process called Scrum, designed to increase alignment with the organization's business aims, improve communication both within and outside the marketing team, and increase the speed and responsiveness of marketing. This process is iterative, allowing for short marketing experiments, frequent feedback, and the ability to react to changing market conditions. Agile marketing can help marketing departments of just about any shape and size be more efficient, serve their customers better and be more fully integrated into the work of the business as a whole. AM involves anticipating and responding to early signs of change and turning them into an opportunity to either tap into the new market or expand the share in the existing market. Therefore, this approach enhances the ability to quickly adapt and respond to the market, identify and prioritize high-impact activities, and deliver customer-centric outcomes.

The principles and values of agile marketing methodology are as follows: (i) Priority is customer satisfaction through marketing, which solves problems and creates value; (ii) interaction and close engagement with customers; (iii) experimentation and learning through a feedback loop; (iv) encouragement of new ideas for messages and channels as well as processes aiming at continuous improvement; (v) prioritization of actions based on resources available and suitable allocation; (vi) measurement and accountability: monitoring progress and measuring results; (vii) driving long-term marketing strategies with short-term, focusing on customers and improving responsiveness and relevance: generate faster creative ideas, do more testing, work on smarter improvements, and achieve better results; and (viii) sustainable marketing keeping a constant pace and pipeline. All of these principles stand for effective tourism marketing.

As Edelman et al. (2016) underline, there are some prerequisites for agile marketing to work. An organization must have a clear sense of what it wants to accomplish with its agile initiative (e.g. which customer segments it wants to acquire or which CDJs it wants to improve) and have sufficient data, analytics and the right marketing–technology infrastructure. This technology component helps marketers capture, aggregate and manage data from disparate systems; make decisions based on advanced propensity and next-best-action models; automate the delivery of campaigns and messages across channels; and feed customer tracking and message performance back into the system. While these elements are crucial for success, the most important factor is the people – bringing together a small team of talented people who can work together quickly. They should possess skills across multiple functions (both internal and external). The team itself needs to be small enough for everyone to remain accountable to one another – 8–12 is the maximum size. Jeff Bezos famously referred to "two-pizza teams", that is, teams no bigger than can be fed by two pizzas (Edelman et al. 2016).

Agile methods can improve direct-response marketing activities and the performance of product development, marketing mix and brand marketing by providing more frequent feedback, allowing for testing and iterating of ideas and communications in the market, and accelerating the process for delivering impact from brand efforts. The main means is analyzing the data to identify the opportunities to develop insights based on targeted analytics. The insights should identify anomalies, pain points, issues or opportunities in the DCJ of key customer or prospect segments. By properly adopting agile practices, marketers can transform their organizations into fast-moving teams that continually drive growth for the business (Edelman et al. 2016). However, organizations should know the issues and challenges in implementing the agile marketing approach. Kalaignanam et al. (2021) highlight the organization's challenges in executing marketing agility, including ensuring brand consistency, scaling agility across the marketing ecosystem, managing data privacy concerns, pursuing marketing agility as a fad and hiring marketing leaders. The authors caution that marketing agility may only be well-suited for some firms and all marketing activities.

Strategic agility comprises three interrelated dimensions: customer agility, partnering agility and operational agility. A recent study by Hadjielias et al. (2022) explored how strategic agility underpins digitalization and customer value outcomes in tourism and provides context-based theorization of the utility of strategic agility. Their study's findings highlight the role of three interrelated agility capabilities – customer (to source and test ideas), partnering (to establish and coordinate partnerships) and operational (to support operations) – in enabling tourism organizations to leverage digital technologies to produce and deliver customer value, while responding to tensions inherent within each agility dimension.

Based on the above synoptic discussion, this chapter discusses that AM is an adequate approach in the field of tourism marketing.

1.3. A blended approach: a framework based on two models

As indicated, this conceptual paper proposes a framework for implementing the agile marketing methodology in tourism. This framework was drawn on two models – the customer decision journey (CDJ) and the 8Ps of services marketing, which is briefly presented in the following sections.

1.3.1. *Consumer/customer journey in the digital era*

As already highlighted, digital platforms and SM have been gamechangers in consumer behavior in all domains and, more particularly, in the tourism field. These digital platforms play a critical role in decision-making in the general social and market environment (Cohen et al. 2014; Sotiriadis 2017). They are used by tourists as decision-support tools in selecting the various components of their trips/holidays (Liu et al. 2020). In temporal terms, these choices occurred through the CDJ (Hudson and Thal 2013; Yachin 2018).

	Digital platforms' influences and consumers' actions
Consider	Initial consideration set: tourist consumers consider an initial set of destinations based on perceptions and exposure to various media and digital platforms and channels (including SM). Their perceptions are created by campaigns or UGC on platforms. At this stage, consumers are also searching for inspiration or getting inspired from UGC by other consumers.
Evaluate and buy	Information search, gathering and shopping on platforms: tourist consumers adopt a set of criteria and evaluate the various options. Then, they purchase by selecting a tourism destination/supplier. Booking and shopping through digital platforms.
Enjoy the experience	Ongoing exposure on and through digital platforms and channels. Tourists are enjoying the experience itself at the destination. The actual trip and visit of a place (activities and sightseeing) and platforms affect the choices and decision-making related to on-site activities.
Advocate and Bond	Post-consumption experience: they share their experiences and reviews, become supporters/advocates and spread positive or negative comments on various digital platforms. Tourists build expectations based on experience to inform the next decision journey, make recommendations and provide support.

Table 1.1. *The consumer decision journey and influence by digital platforms*

Literature suggests that the CDJ consisted of four main stages: (i) consider, (ii) evaluate and buy, (iii) enjoy the experience and (iv) post-consumption with support/advocate and bond. This study applies the above model and focuses on implementing marketing activities by tourism destinations and suppliers when they are going through their decision-making process through the whole CDJ (pre-trip, during and post-trip). The CDJ model has been adapted because tourism is an experience, not a product. It consists of four phases/stages: consider, evaluate and buy, enjoy (the experience itself) and resulting satisfaction, and advocate and bond (post-experience behavior). Table 1.1 (Edelman 2010; Hudson and Thal 2013; Varkaris and Neuhofer 2017; Dimitriou and

AbouElgheit 2019) depicts the four stages, the consumers' actions and digital platforms' influences. According to Hudson and Thal (2013), SM make the "evaluate" and "advocate" stages increasingly relevant for both tourism destinations and suppliers in a digital-dominated market environment.

Pop et al. (2021) used the CDJ model to explain the impact of social media influencers' (SMI) trust on tourists' decision-making. They focused on evaluating the role of CDJ constructs (including desire, information search, evaluating alternatives, purchase decisions, satisfaction and experience sharing) in mediating the interrelation between SMI trust and the dimensions of CDJ. The study by Liu et al. (2020) examined the roles of SM – need generator, supporter, guider and approver – in tourists and their choices regarding each tourism component. Previous studies also highlighted the inter-influence/interrelationship between the various stages.

From a marketing perspective and consumer behavior, tourism destinations and suppliers' designed and implemented actions (strategies and tactics) essentially aim to communicate and influence consumers' above digital activities through the four stages of CDJ (Kotler et al. 2019).

1.3.2. *Marketing implementation: the marketing mix*

The approach of destination/tourism supplier marketing planning involves setting marketing objectives, crafting a marketing plan, monitoring the implementation of the plan and reporting on progress (control), evaluating the effectiveness of the marketing plan and measuring the performance (Morrison 2019; Sotiriadis 2021). DMOs and suppliers use the marketing plan as a guide for implementing their selected marketing activities and programs. All tourism marketers have an arsenal of tools to use in appealing to visitors (existing and prospective). These tools are the "Ps of marketing". The initial model of the 4Ps was extended into an 8Ps model to address the unique aspects of marketing tourism and hospitality services (Morrison 2010; Kotler et al. 2019).

The principal tools/media are product, price, place, promotion, packaging, programming, partnership and people. The marketing plan describes in detail how each of the 8Ps of marketing (marketing mix) will be used for each target market to achieve that market's objectives for the upcoming period.

– *Product*: the destination product is multi-dimensional. It includes physical elements (attractions, facilities, transportation and infrastructure) but also has a human dimension (people). The destination also offers many packages and arranges events and festivals (programming). A DMO is concerned about and monitors the quality of visitors' experiences within the destination.

– *Price*: price is a multi-faceted concept, considering internal and external factors. Prices also tend to attract certain markets and repel others. Additionally, price levels influence value-for-money perceptions.

– *Place*: in tourism marketing, the component "place" represents distribution/access to services and the online and traditional travel trade channels used to draw visitors to the destination. It is worth noticing the significance of digital platforms and the predominant role of digital distribution channels.

– *Promotion*: promotional mix elements include advertising and sales (personal selling), public relations, sales promotion and merchandising. Now, DMOs are heavily involved with digital marketing techniques. All promotions are types of communications, and a DMO must integrate promotions to be consistent. This process is known as integrated marketing communications (IMC). It is worth underlying two specific approaches. Digital marketing uses digital-format information and communication technologies (ICTs) to liaise with audiences, provide destination information and promote the destination through various digital channels and techniques. The most important techniques and venues include websites (unquestionably the principal communications platform for DMOs and suppliers), email, SM, social network sites, traveler review sites, blogging, mobile phones and smartphones. IMC is the second approach. It is the coordination and integration of all DMO's external communications and promotions to increase their effectiveness and consistency. The basic idea behind IMC is that promotions are a type of communication, and an organization/company must integrate all types of promotions, ensuring they are consistent. Significant benefits such as greater consistency in communication messages and greater effectiveness (Sotiriadis 2021).

– *Packaging*: packaging in tourism constitutes a key tool for the DMO in customizing the destination product for specific target markets. Packaging is the combination of related and complementary tourism services and facilities into a single-price offering (Morrison 2019). This marketing element could take the precise form of a series/range of experience opportunities.

– *Programming*: there are many opportunities for destinations and big resorts to arrange special activities or programs – such as events and festivals – that are attractive/appealing to visitors. Many DMOs and tourism organizations worldwide have implemented this component efficiently and effectively.

– *Partnership*: over the last two decades, we have witnessed an increasing activity in building marketing partnerships and emphasizing tapping into the power of combining forces with other tourism actors and stakeholders. Partnerships are very important due to the composite nature of tourism experiences.

– *People*: the personal and visitor-minded service encounters within a destination and the various suppliers providing tourism services greatly impact the visitor's experience and satisfaction. Every destination and supplier's ultimate and strategic aim is to offer a valuable experience and delight their guests.

The marketing mix's above components are critical in achieving the related objectives. Therefore, there is an imperative for control/monitoring and evaluation procedures and measurements. An agile marketing plan must include specific control and evaluation procedures and measurements for the activities. In this field, adequate evaluation measures or metrics, milestones and performance standards are very important. This crucial consideration leads us to our suggested framework.

1.4. Proposed framework for implementing marketing agility in tourism

This section briefly presents the suggested framework for designing and implementing the approach of agile marketing in tourism experiences. This framework comprises two pillars – consumer behavior and marketing mix – linked by the agile marketing approach. The focus and beginning point are on the left side (the tourist) for one simple reason: tourism is a consumer-driven activity. Tourist consumers (various market segments) have their requirements and expectations regarding tourism experiences; these demands are precisely expressed through the digital activities performed through their CDJ (Sotiriadis 2017; Varkaris and Neuhofer 2017; Wong et al. 2020; Sotiriadis et al. 2023).

	Activities on digital platforms
Consider	Looking at/searching on digital platforms and social networks for tourism destinations/suppliers. Looking for inspiration. Making suggestions to and considering suggestions from friends and peers. Determining the choice set of tourism destinations and businesses.
Evaluate and buy	Identifying attributes to include in the selection criteria. Preferences for tourism destinations and suppliers/services. Willingness to pay a premium price for higher value/services.
Enjoy the experience	Using platforms as a learning tool about the visited places. Digital platforms as an assisting tool. Digital platforms as motivating/recommending guides to the tourism experience (doing activities during the visit).
Advocate and bond	Sharing experiences, recommendations and support to destinations/ suppliers. Sharing online reviews, good and bad experiences, as well as positive and negative practices in persuading and motivating other tourists. Recommending to relatives, friends and peers.

Table 1.2. *Digital activities performed by tourists through the four stages of CDJ*

Tourism destinations and suppliers should meet and address the expectations and requirements by designing and offering the appropriate experience opportunities and attempting to influence the tourists' digital activities by designing and implementing suitable marketing strategies and adequate tools.

The communication and promotional actions should consider all available tools, based on the 8Ps model, and in an integrated manner (integrated communications marketing).

The main focus is on tourists, so the proposed framework is named tourist-driven marketing agility. The reason is simple: the needed input to perform efficient and effective marketing activities comes from consumer feedback, and a tremendous amount of consumer data and analytics are provided on digital platforms.

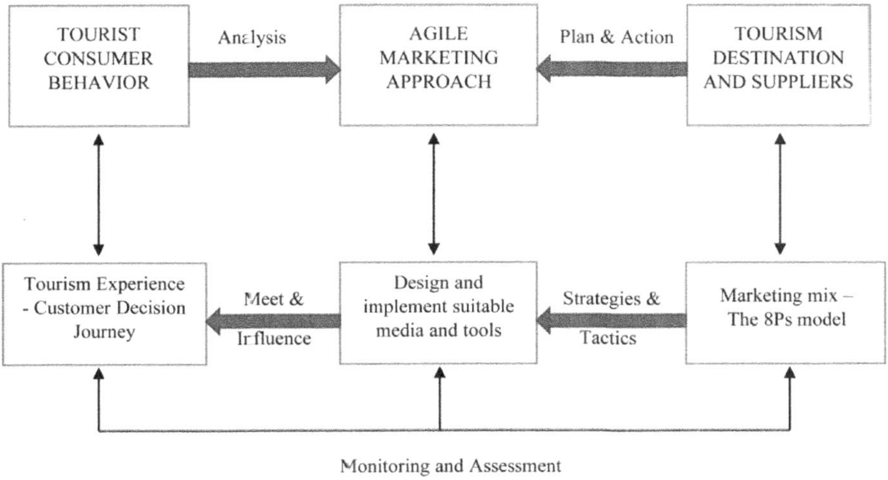

Figure 1.1. *Suggested framework for tourism marketing agility: a tourist-driven approach*

Last but not least, there is an imperative for controlling/monitoring the progress of marketing mix implementation and evaluation of performance based on continuous feedback from tourists (data analysis). All of the above digital activities should be monitored and properly analyzed; digital technologies now provide the tools and the potential to do so. The approach of agile marketing is about working faster, smarter and more efficiently.

1.5. Conclusion

In the 21st century and digitalized business and marketing environment, everything changes extremely fast; it is essential to be flexible and adaptable to market changes and to focus on business value and consumer needs productively and cost-effectively. The main underlying idea is flexibility and adaptability; agile allows companies to be on the move, follow new trends and do exactly what is in demand, considering consumers' and market needs.

Within this context, tourism destinations and suppliers have an unprecedented need for speed and flexibility. Those two factors in today's always-on, always-connected markets equal a tremendous competitive advantage. With the pace of change in consumer needs, they must be responsive to outperform in their markets. Nowadays, there is no more time to waste, and with easy access to data, DMOs and suppliers have a choice: be agile and use data to inform quick test-and-learn activities and rapidly adjust to the market or follow the status quo and "wait for perfect".

In this era of disruption, tourism destinations (DMOs) and suppliers should develop the people, process and marketing technology to adopt and implement agile marketing to improve the effectiveness of all elements and tools used. The agile approach is about implementing tactics and media flexibly and adaptively to increase efficiency and improve effectiveness. The suggested framework considering the topic of agility in the marketing field is a conceptual endeavor contributing to linking/connecting the two poles/sides (demand/consumer and supply/destination) through marketing actions. However, it is merely a theoretical framework; it should be implemented, tested and assessed for its value and utility. Some empirical investigation is needed with research projects in various contexts (countries) and settings (tourism industries).

1.6. References

Agile Marketing (2017). What is agile marketing? [Online]. Available at: https://agilemarketingalliance.com [Accessed 10 March 2022].

Cohen, S.A., Prayag, G., Moital, M. (2014). Consumer behaviour in tourism: Concepts, influences, and opportunities. *Current Issues in Tourism*, 17(10), 872–909. doi: 10.1080/13683500.2013.850064.

Deloitte Access Economics (2019). Technology disruptors in tourism. Deloitte, Canberra [Online]. Available at: www.deloitte.com/au/deloitte-access-economics.

Dimitriou, C.K. and AbouElgheit, E. (2019). Understanding generation Z's social decision-making in travel. *Tourism and Hospitality Management*, 25(2), 311–334. doi: 10.20867/thm.25.2.4.

Edelman, D. (2010). Branding in the digital age. *Harvard Business Review*, 88(12), 62–69.

Edelman, D., Heller, J., Spittaels, S. (2016). Agile marketing: A step-by-step guide. Guide, McKinsey [Online]. Available at: https://www.mckinsey.com/business-functions/marketing-and-sales/our-insights/agile-marketing-a-step-by-step-guide [Accessed 15 March 2022].

Font, X. and McCabe, S. (2017). Sustainability and marketing in tourism: Its contexts, paradoxes, approaches, challenges and potential. *Journal of Sustainable Tourism*, 25(7), 869–883. doi: 10.1080/09669582.2017.1301721.

Gretzel, U (2018). From smart destinations to smart tourism regions. *Journal of Regional Research*, 42(1), 171–184.

Hadjielias, E., Christofi, M., Christou, P., Hadjielia Drotarova, M. (2022). Digitalization, agility, and customer value in tourism. *Technological Forecasting and Social Change*, 175, 121334. doi: 10.1016/j.techfore.2021.121334.

Homburg, C., Theel, M., Hohenberg, S. (2020). Marketing excellence: Nature, measurement, and investor valuations. *Journal of Marketing*, 84(4), 1–22. doi: 10.1177%2F0022242920925517.

Hudson, S. and Thal, K. (2013). The impact of social media on the consumer decision process: Implications for tourism marketing. *Journal of Travel & Tourism Marketing*, 30(1–2), 156–160. doi: 10.1080/10548408.2013.751276.

Kalaignanam, K, Tuli, K.R., Kushwaha, T., Lee, L., Gal, D. (2021). Marketing agility: The concept, antecedents, and a research agenda. *Journal of Marketing*, 85(1), 35–58. doi: 10.1177/0022242920952760.

Kotler, P., Bowen, J.T., Baloglu, S. (2019). *Marketing for Hospitality and Tourism*, 8th edition. Pearson, Hoboken.

Liu, X., Mehraliyev, F., Liu, C., Schuckert, M. (2020). The roles of social media in tourists' choices of travel components. *Tourist Studies*, 20(1), 27–48. doi: 10.1177/1468797619873107.

Lu, Y.T., Chen, Z.W., Law, R. (2018). Mapping the progress of social media research in hospitality and tourism management from 2004 to 2014. *Journal of Travel & Tourism Marketing*, 35(2), 102–118. doi: 10.1080/10548408.2017.1350249.

Morrison, A.M. (2019). *Marketing and Managing Tourism Destinations*, 2nd edition. Routledge, New York.

OECD (Organization for Economic Cooperation and Development) (2018). *OECD Tourism Trends and Policies 2018*. OECD, Paris. doi: 10.1787/tour2018-en/.

Park, O.J., Kim M.G., Ryu, J.H. (2019). Interface effects of online media on tourists' attitude changes. *Tourism Management Perspectives*, 30, 262–274. doi: 10.1016/j.tmp.2019.03.005.

Pop, R.-A., Săplăcan, Z., Dabija, D.-C., Alt, M.-A. (2021). The impact of social media influencers on travel decisions: The role of trust in consumer decision journey. *Current Issues in Tourism*, 25, 823–843. doi: 10.1080/13683500.2021.1895729.

Reportlinker (2020). Global business travel market size, trends and insights [Online]. Available at: https://www.reportlinker.com/report-summary/Tourism/3288/ [Accessed 28 April 2022].

Sigala, M., Christou, E., Gretzel, U. (2016). *Social Media in Travel, Tourism and Hospitality: Theory, Practice and Cases*. Routledge, London.

Sotiriadis, M. (2017). Sharing tourism experiences in social media: A literature review and a set of suggested business strategies. *International Journal of Contemporary Hospitality Management*, 29, 179–225. doi: 10.1108/IJCHM-05-2016-0300.

Sotiriadis, M. (2021). Tourism destination marketing: Academic knowledge. *Encyclopedia 2021*, 1(1), 42–56. doi: 10.3390/encyclopedia1010007.

Sotiriadis, M., Koufopoulos, D., Zhou, Q. (2023). Social networking sites' influence on consumer decision-making within the context of smart tourism. *International Journal of Hospitality & Tourism Management*, 7(1), 1–10. doi: 10.11648/j.ijhtm.20230701.11.

Srivastava, S. (2019). Gen Z and millennial travel: The wanderlust generations. Deloitte [Online]. Available at: https://www2.deloitte.com/ [Accessed 10 May 2022].

Stylos, N. (2019). Technological evolution and tourist decision-making: A perspective article. *Tourism Review*, 75, 273–278. doi: 10.1108/TR-05-20190167.

Varkaris, E. and Neuhofer, B. (2017). The influence of social media on the consumers' hotel decision journey. *Journal of Hospitality and Tourism Technology*, 8, 101–118. doi: 10.1108/JHTT-09-2016-0058.

Wong, J.W.C., Lai, I.K.W., Tao, Z. (2020). Sharing memorable tourism experiences on mobile social media and how it influences further travel decisions. *Current Issues in Tourism*, 23(14), 1773–1787.

World Economic Forum (2019). Social media by generation [Online]. Available at: https://www.weforum.org/agenda/2019/10/social-media-use-by-generation/.

World Economic Forum (2021). Social media global usage [Online]. Available at: https://www.weforum.org/agenda/2020/11/social-media-global-usage-philippines-uk-usa-china/.

Yachin, J.M. (2018). The 'customer journey': Learning from customers in tourism experience encounters. *Tourism Management Perspectives*, 28, 201–210. doi: 10.1016/j.tmp.2018.09.002.

2

Online Communication Agility for International Tourist Destinations: Cannes, Nice, Monaco

Nice, Cannes and Monaco are historic tourist destinations that are known and frequented internationally (Reclus 1864; Observatoire du tourisme Côte d'Azur 2020). Through the online communication of destination management organizations (DMOs) via digital social networks (DSNs) (Facebook, Instagram, etc.), these tourism, leisure and events territories constantly convey images of practices and locations (Christofle and Fournier 2020).

Our research hypothesis concerns the ability of Nice, Cannes and Monaco to adapt, or even transform, their territorial tourism communication, both rapidly and sustainably, in a world that is undergoing both structural (increased consideration of sustainability principles, accelerating digitization, etc.) and economic change (geopolitical and health crises, etc.). We propose to examine how agile communication strategies can be implemented by destinations.

We postulate that the spatiotemporal tourism agility of these territories can be measured and analyzed comparatively, through a diachronic study of the use of social networking sites, by means of the following major elements: dates of tool adoption, the rhythm of publication, DMO/tourist interfacing, use or non-use of influencers, content (photos, speeches, etc.), etc.

Chapter written by Sylvie CHRISTOFLE and Carine FOURNIER.

Positioning our work within the geographical approach of spatial analysis, we consider that a municipality with an international reputation, measured by the number of tourists it receives, will have greater communication agility than a lesser known locality receiving fewer tourists. At the same time, we believe that destinations that are geographically close to each other, or that are part of the same tourist area and that face similar problems, will tend to develop similar communication strategies, or even to be included in similar circles of reflection or public policies, as part of more global destination management bodies.

2.1. Theoretical framework

Within the dual paradigm of competition in globalization and “glocalization” (Roudometof 2016; Arkhipov and Yeletsky 2021), territorial communities “face the challenge of having to strategically differentiate themselves from their peers to attract opportunities” (Thomas et al. 2020). Various marketing tools associated with an events policy and the staging of locations are used to create and consolidate a tourist image (Buhalis and Amaranggana 2013; Bernadou 2017; Thomas et al. 2020). Public players, particularly DMOs, which includes tourist offices, convention bureaus, etc., promote their territory through communication channels. This is traditional communication through brochures, audiovisual media advertising, hosting journalists, etc., or more contemporary communication through digital media platforms, DSN, partnerships with influencers, etc. (Buhalis and Law 2008; Navío-Marco et al. 2018; Jimenez-Barreto et al. 2020). Fundamental transformations in the game of territorial tourism communication, associating DMOs, tourists and even residents, are questioning our societies, our changing territories and research into the multiple effects (economic, marketing, geographical, sociological, etc.) of the Internet and digital social media (Dhiratara 2016; Minseong and Jihye 2020; Christofle and Fournier 2024). This object of study, which is still a developing field in social sciences and geography, has come about in order to better understand the strategies implemented by communities to develop the attractiveness of locations (Volo 2010; Christofle et al. 2019). In a post-Covid-19 tourism environment, in the midst of structural and economic upheaval, the agility of territories to adapt quickly to change, and even to transform themselves sustainably, is becoming essential. However, there is a lack of theoretical knowledge and empirical research on the use of social media and the role of content in the adaptability of destinations (Ghorbanzadeh et al. 2022). Agile methods, however, would consolidate the sector's ability to cope with crises and periods of uncertainty. A number of studies have highlighted theories associating marketing and agility (Kalaignanam et al. 2021). Researchers identify agile marketing as a key aspect of marketing excellence (Homburg et al. 2020).

In the article "Co-creating social media agility to build strong customer-firm relationships", Chuang (2020) considers "social media agility to be a key commercial imperative" (p. 202). The author adds that a company's communication with customers using social media is crucial to create and share social information associated with information processing capabilities (Chuang 2020, p. 202). This article, taken from the *Industrial Marketing Management* journal, applies to firms of all kinds, without specifically mentioning tourism organizations.

We assume, however, that DMOs fall into this category, as they respond to comparable imperatives: to "sell" a destination as well as possible, in order to give visitors complete satisfaction, so that they talk about it to those around them and make others want to visit, thus creating a virtuous circle.

Chuang identifies five hypotheses linking business, agility, social media and customers. In our work, we will retain three of them, thus adapted to our research theme:

– The use of social media would enable DMOs to react with agility and speed to changes in the market/customer behavior (ability of DMOs to process social information).

– Co-creation with visitors would be positively linked to social media agility.

– Levels of social media use would have a positive moderating influence on the relationship between social media agility and the strength of visitor/DMO relationships.

Furthermore, the hypothesis that a municipality with a high international reputation, measured by the number of tourists it receives, would have greater communication agility than a lesser known locality receiving fewer tourists, requires the use of control variables, such as tourist numbers.

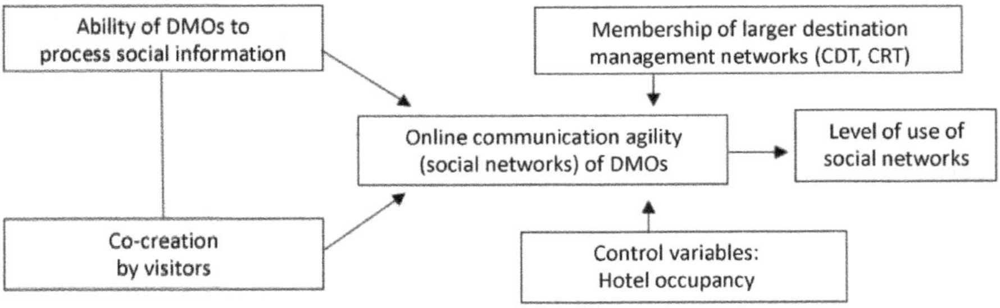

Figure 2.1. *Online communication agility of DMOs (authors: Christofle and Fournier, according to Chuang (2020, p. 103))*

2.2. Methodology

Among existing social media, Instagram, an application, DSN, and photo and video sharing service created in 2010, has become a major tool for the exchange of information between Internet users and for destinations wishing to get to know their target markets. Indeed, Instagram is ranked as the third favorite social media platform and the fourth most-used platform in the world (Kemps 2022a).

Instagram's potential advertising audience, in relation to the total population aged 13 and over, is 47.6% (versus 43.3% in 2021), with a 10% increase compared to 2021 (Kemps 2022b, p. 55). Instagram's popularity, massive usage and audience thus justify its use in this research as a territorial image analysis tool (Jansson 2020).

We chose to work from the official Instagram accounts of the tourist offices of the Nice Côte d'Azur metropolis, Cannes and the Principality of Monaco. The DMO publications on this social network were extracted using a dedicated application (PhantomBuster). They were then statistically processed and analyzed using textual data analysis software (Iramuteq).

Figure 2.2 shows the data retrieved via PhantomBuster, an application that automatically collects data from all types of DSNs. The information includes the date of the post, its location (where available), the number of likes received by the publication, the number of comments and its description.

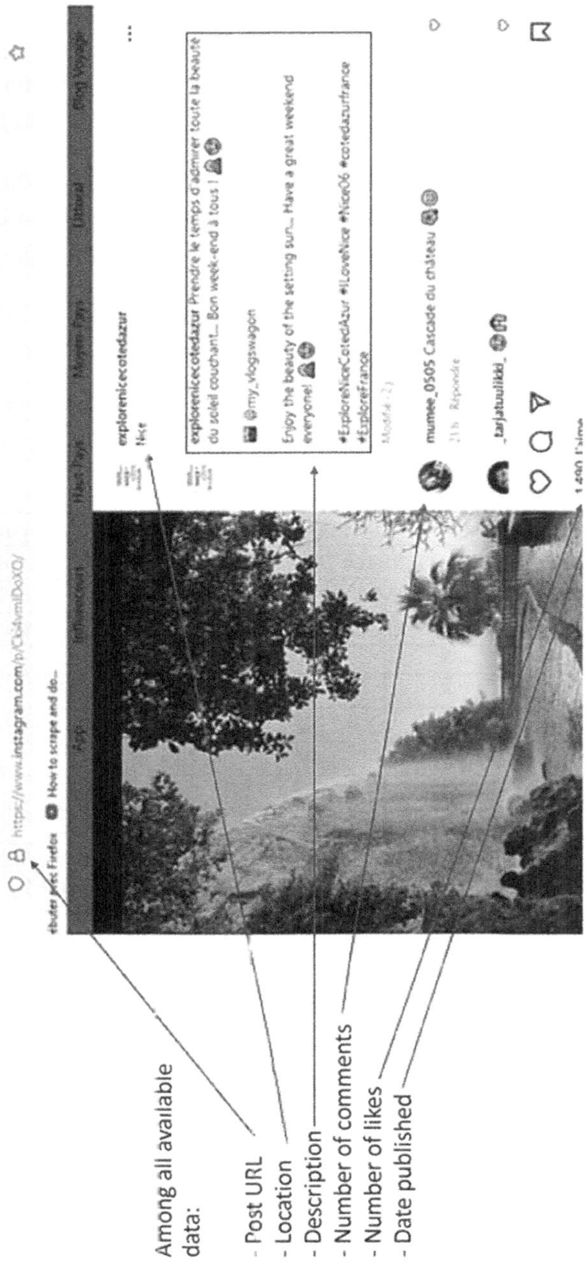

Figure 2.2. *Data from Instagram accounts using PhantomBuster (screenshot). For a color version of this figure, see www.iste.co.uk/christofle/tourism2.zip*

From these elements, we can assess, for example, the speed of appropriation of the tool (thanks to information on the date of first publication), the rhythm of publication, the types of spaces represented (thanks to localization) and the ability to engage and interact with an audience (thanks to the study of the number of comments and likes).

There are, however, difficulties: a lack of geolocation either by the community manager or by the Instagrammers, hashtags with little or no indication of localization, problems linked to different spellings of place names with accents or hyphens in their names. In these situations, checks are then carried out to identify the location of the photos presented.

2.3. Results and discussion

2.3.1. *Are DMOs early adopters?*

DMO	Facebook	Twitter	Instagram	YouTube
NCA	February 2011	March 2011	August 2013	October 2011
Cannes	June 2011	May 2010	May 2013	August 2011
Monaco	January 2009	February 2009	July 2012	April 2008

Social network	Launch date
Facebook	February 2004
Twitter	March 2006
Instagram	October 2010
YouTube	February 2005

Table 2.1. *Date of the first post on the Nice Côte d'Azur, Cannes and Monaco DMO accounts on the main social networking sites, and the launch date of the various networks (authors: Christofle and Fournier)*

Table 2.1 summarizes the dates of account creation on the various DSNs of the three DMOs studied. The second table shows the launch dates of the different platforms, so as to facilitate comparative analysis. We note that the Nice Côte d'Azur (NCA), Cannes and Monaco DMOs are not early adopters of social networks. They were perhaps waiting until the tool had sufficiently penetrated society to seize it. Indeed, for tourism communications to have an effective impact, they need to reach as many people as possible. It is worth noting, however, that Monaco was quicker to make use of all DSNs compared to Cannes or Nice Côte d'Azur.

Does this foundation on DSNs imply that DMOs have immediately appropriated the platforms from their launch, with, for example, regular publications since the date of account creation, or was there a period of adaptation to the tool before full appropriation?

First of all, acquiring the tool and mastering it takes time. Indeed, the graph (Figure 2.3) shows a period of adaptation, with irregular years in terms of the number of publications, until the tool is finally fully integrated into tourism communication and used on an almost daily basis. There is a question of the decline for 2023. This drop in the number of posts is the same for all three DMOs, whereas for several years, a minimum of one publication per day was posted. The explanation may lie in the presence of Instagram's new reel tool, which takes the form of ephemeral videos that are popular with the public (Kemps 2022b), but do not appear in the publication feed. Instagram's decision to develop the reel tool corresponds to the platform's need to compete with TikTok, the DSN that is very popular with young people, by adapting to the contemporary desires of Instagrammers who are fond of these very short videos. It is worth noting the flexibility, speed and responsiveness of the three DMOs, who have responded to this new format by integrating it into their communications.

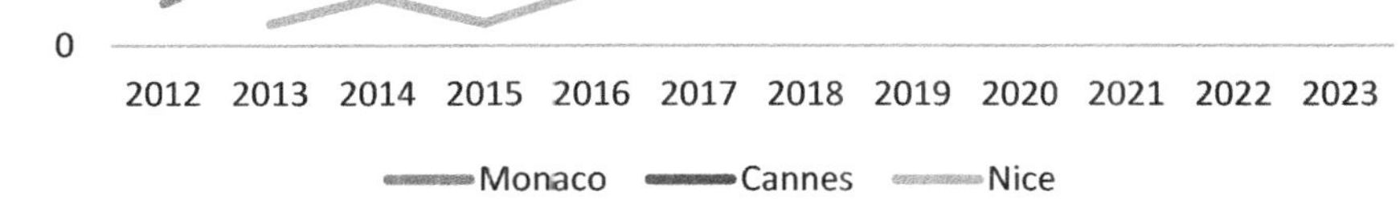

Figure 2.3. *Annual change in the number of posts on Instagram by the DMOs of Nice Côte d'Azur, Cannes and Monaco (authors: Christofle and Fournier). For a color version of this figure, see www.iste.co.uk/christofle/tourism2.zip*

After an initial analysis of the reactivity, or even flexibility, of DMOs, based on account creation dates, appropriation of DSNs and adaptability to new formats, our fundamental interest is in the images projected by DMOs.

Tourism agility can, in fact, be assessed in terms of the locations represented by discourse and photography: off-the-beaten-track spaces, traditional tourism images, etc.

2.3.2. *What publications?*

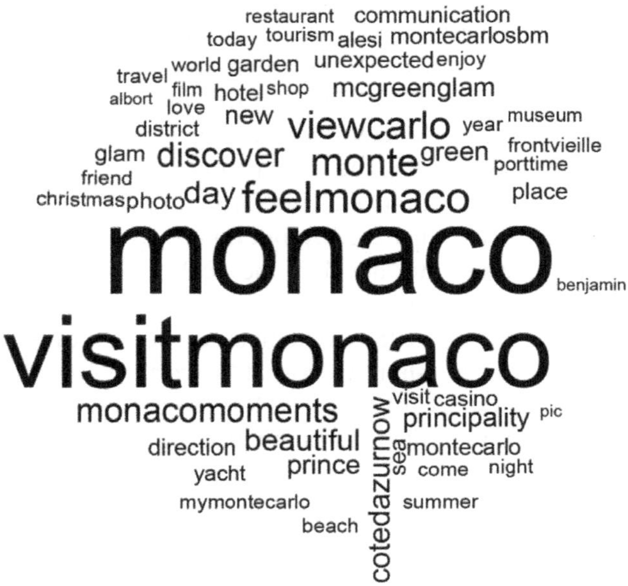

Figure 2.4. *Terms that appear at least 100 times in Monaco's DMO posts on Instagram, November 22, 2023 (authors: Christofle and Fournier)*

As a first step, let us take a look at hashtags, imposed by Instagram's search mode, which are a key element in locating posts on this social network. A hashtag is a "word or phrase preceded by the symbol # that classifies or categorizes the accompanying text" (Merriam-Webster). Consequently, there are a large number of hashtags that appear in three-word clouds, obtained by textual analysis of the content of posts from the three DMOs analyzed. On the basis of a minimum of 100 occurrences on the Instagram accounts of the three DMOs, we obtain a good, central position, in addition to the name of the destination, for the three-word clouds represented here (Figures 2.4–2.6), for visitmonaco (the Principality's official tourism hashtag) or explorenicecotedazur for its neighboring Alpes-Maritime region, with Cannes having no official hashtag. The hashtag for the Provence-Alpes-

Côte d'Azur region (onatousbesoindusud) is also present on the Nice Côte d'Azur's Instagram account, as is that of the RTC of Côte d'Azur, cotedazurnow. The latter, launched in the wake of the July 14, 2016 attack, therefore continues to be used.

While hashtags largely dominate the composition of these word clouds, we also note the presence of emblematic locations for each destination: Fontvieille and Monte-Carlo for Monaco, Cours Saleya, Place Masséna and the Promenade des Anglais for Nice Côte d'Azur, and the Croisette and Palais des Festivals for Cannes.

There are also recurrent references to beaches (either in French or English), ports, sunshine and vacations.

Figure 2.5. *Terms that appear at least 100 times in Nice Côte d'Azur DMO posts on Instagram, November 22, 2023 (authors: Christofle and Fournier)*

Figure 2.6. *Terms that appear at least 100 times in Cannes DMO posts on Instagram, November 22, 2023 (authors: Christofle and Fournier)*

2.3.3. *What mutual recognition? Measuring interaction*

Recognition of an DMOs investment can be gauged by four indicators: a large number of followers, likes of each DMO publication, comments on each DMO publication and use of the destination's official hashtag by Instagrammers. On the DMO side, interaction with Instagrammers is in the form of reposts on the official website.

All three destinations are trying to win the loyalty of Instagrammers, but they do not have nearly as many followers as film or soccer stars. For example, in October 2023, the most followed personality on Instagram was Cristiano Ronaldo, with over 607 million followers. All things considered, and remaining within the framework of subscribers to the DSNs of famous destinations, it is worth noting that in 2023, Paris had 663,481 followers (Christofle and Fournier, in press). This information puts the near 65,000 subscribers to the Cannes account into perspective with the 77,100 subscribers to the Monaco account.

DMO	Number of subscribers (in thousands)	Average number of *likes*	Average number of comments	Number of *likes* for the most liked publication	Number of comments on most commented publication
NCA	67.7	1,257	15.2	8,123	534
Cannes	64.9	777.2	12.2	17,804	756
Monaco	77.1	435	5.6	5,759	88

Table 2.2. *Number of subscribers, average number of likes and comments, number of likes and comments on most popular posts, November 22, 2023 (Christofle and Fournier)*

The average number of likes is measured in the hundreds: an average of 435 likes per post for Monaco, 777 for Cannes and up to 1,257 for Nice. There seems to be an established but relatively limited interaction between web users and destinations on Instagram. While leaving a like is as simple an act as pressing a button, leaving a comment is a more time-consuming and therefore less developed action. Indeed, an average of 5.6 comments per publication is recorded for Monaco, and even Nice Côte d'Azur, which is more dynamic, gets no more than 15.2 comments on average per post. However, it is worth noting that a number of publications were enthusiastic about each of the three destinations studied. For Nice Côte d'Azur, the maximum of 534 comments was obtained for a competition post relating to the first edition of "Garden Live", "on Wednesday August 18, 2021 from 6:30 p.m. in the gardens of Château de Crémat". On Monaco's account, a quiz post garnered 88 comments: it offered two tickets for the Formula 1 Grand Prix. For Cannes, there was no quiz, but the following post, listing a series of locations and players in tourism and local life:

> #Cannes, in Wes Anderson mode by @onmetlesvoiles! Here are Adeline and Tony's favorite spots: The steps of the @palaisdesfestivals, The beaches, La Suquet, La Croisette, The Cannes Town Hall, The Noailles Media Library – Villa Rothschild, The @carltoncannes, The @martinezhotel, A boat tour with @canneswaterworld.

In terms of the most liked publications, Internet user opinions vary. In Cannes (Figure 2.7), the most popular video was shared with the Carlton when the luxury hotel reopened after a two-year renovation.

Figure 2.7. *Most liked publication in Cannes, November 2023 (screenshot). For a color version of this figure, see www.iste.co.uk/christofle/tourism2.zip*

Figure 2.8. *Monaco's most-liked publication, November 2023 (screenshot). For a color version of this figure, see www.iste.co.uk/christofle/tourism2.zip*

For Monaco (Figure 2.8), the most liked publication is a promotional video for the Principality.

Lastly, for Nice Côte d'Azur (Figure 2.9), it is a view of the Promenade des Anglais, with the Negresco in the center of the photograph. As a result, Internet users have a very positive view of DMOs' projection of images that are aesthetically pleasing, traditional and even anticipated. In short, destination "must-sees".

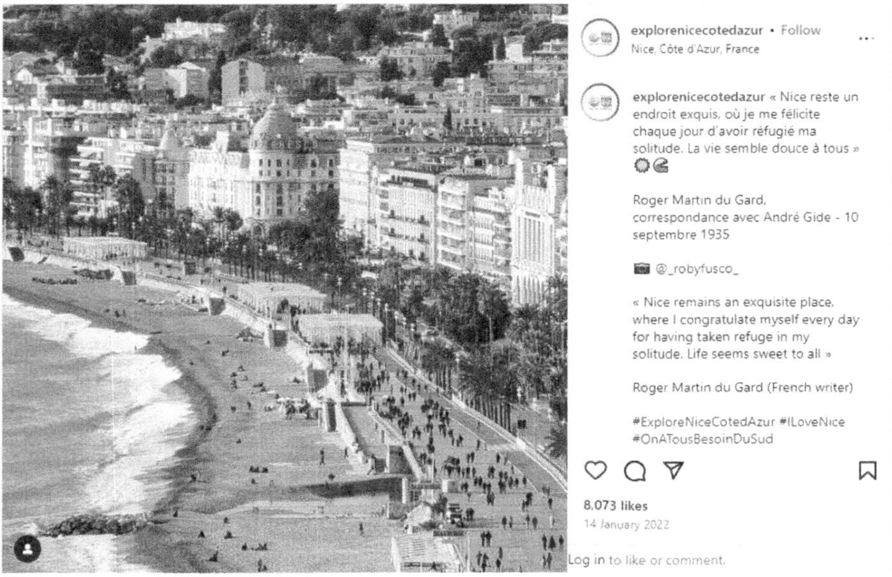

Figure 2.9. *Nice's most liked publication, November 2023 (screenshot). For a color version of this figure, see www.iste.co.uk/christofle/tourism2.zip*

Following these major elements in estimating the interaction between Instagrammers and DMOs, to assess the latter's agility in satisfying demand, we will now analyze the positioning of Instagrammers through their appropriation of the destination's hashtag. Let us first recall that, of the three DMOs studied, only two have opted for an official hashtag: Monaco with #visitmonaco created in 2018 and Nice Côte d'Azur with #explorenicecotedazur since 2021.

Note that the departmental capital had a different hashtag before 2021; the Alpes-Maritime metropolis has decided to propose a new one in relation to the name of the territorial authority expanding the Nice territory to 51 communes: Nice Côte d'Azur.

Once a hashtag has been suggested, do Instagrammers use it? At present, the most popular hashtag is Monaco, with just over 145,000 uses. The Nice Côte d'Azur hashtag is however found in just over 87,000 posts.

DMO	Number of posts using the official *hashtag*
NCA	87,633
Cannes	–
Monaco	145,013
Nice: #explorenicecotedazur, since 2021 Cannes: no official *hashtag*, use #Cannes Monaco: #visitmonaco, since 2018	

Table 2.3. *The official hashtag used by Instagrammers (authors: Christofle and Fournier 2023)*

DMOs have understood the value of involving Instagrammers. Organizations like to repost posts on their own accounts in order to raise their profile on Instagram. Monaco has even made this a principle. Indeed, the Monaco account clearly states: "Use #VisitMonaco and we will repost you on our social media channels". In this way, the account offers itself the publications of well-known Instagrammers, or even influencers, who then appear as "best publications" on the social network when the hashtag visitmonaco is searched.

DMO	Number of Instagrammer publication reposts on the DMO account
NCA	1,861
Cannes	1,609
Monaco	2,036

Table 2.4. *Reposts of Instagrammer publications on the DMO account (authors: Christofle and Fournier 2023)*

What are the locations posted online by Instagrammers using the destination's official hashtag? Here again, we considered our research on the scale of the Nice metropolitan area and the Principality of Monaco. We selected the last 1,000 posts using the official hashtag. Internet users understood that the Nice Côte d'Azur hashtag was that of the metropolis and not of Nice alone, because metropolitan communes appear in addition to the central city. Thus, Saint-Martin-Vésubie in the hinterland, Auron, a mountain resort, and coastal areas such as Beaulieu-sur-Mer, Menton and Villefranche-sur-Mer are among the most shared locations. The Promenade des Anglais and the Hotel Le Méridien were also posted. A less expected presence is the Mirabelle restaurant in La Gaude, in the middle country. There was also an "intruder" in this top 10: the beach at Villeneuve-Loubet, even though Villeneuve-Loubet does not belong to the NCA metropolitan area: was this a web user's error or a way of giving greater visibility to this resort?

Location	Number
Nice	227
Saint-Martin-Vésubie	70
Beaulieu-sur-Mer	22
Auron–Saint-Étienne-de-Tinée	20
Menton	19
Villefranche-sur-Mer	16
Le Méridien Nice	14
Restaurant Mirabelle, La Gaude	12
Nice ville–Promenade des Anglais	17
Plage des Bouches du loup, Villeneuve-Loubet	8

Table 2.5. *The top 10 locations from the last 1,000 posts using the hashtag explorenicecotedazur as of November 22, 2023 (authors: Christofle and Fournier 2023)*

On Monaco's Instagram account, the Monte-Carlo district is first, followed by Monaco, with no further details. As this scale is small, the locations within the territory are highlighted: high-end hotels (Hôtel de Paris, Fairmont), the casino, the Prince's Palace of Monaco, a restaurant of the Société des bains de mer de Monte-Carlo (Mada One) and a contemporary art exhibition space: *Espace 22*.

The main locations represented by Instagrammers are therefore not, on the whole, fundamentally different from those presented by DMOs, with the addition of places to eat (restaurants) or to go out.

Location	Number
Monte-Carlo, Monaco	199
Monaco	150
Hôtel de Paris, Monte-Carlo	32
Espace 22	24
Fairmont, Monte-Carlo	22
Casino of Monte-Carlo	18
Mada One	15
Monte-Carlo Bay Hotel & Resort	14
Hôtel Hermitage, Monte-Carlo	13
Prince's Palace of Monaco	12

Table 2.6. *Top 10 locations from the last 1,000 posts using the hashtag visitmonaco as of November 22, 2023 (authors: Christofle and Fournier 2023)*

Having judged agility in terms of the three DMOs' appropriation of the Instagram tool, and then reported on the modes of interaction between the tourist office account and Instagrammers, we will now lay the foundations for a composite index, so as to measure online communication agility.

2.3.4. *Producing a composite index measuring online communication agility*

The production of a composite index to measure online communication agility could enable us to compare destinations. In our opinion, it should take the following criteria into account: rapidly create an account on a new social network, appropriate this new social network (publish regularly), propose a unifying hashtag and succeed in imposing it on Instagrammers, interact with Instagrammers and whether they are influencers or not (average number of likes received by official publications, but also number of comments received by each official publication). Furthermore, with regard to interaction, the aim is to identify whether there are any ongoing exchanges between the DMO (via its official account) and Instagrammers.

Let us take a look at each of the components of this index:

– The ability to quickly create an account on a new social network. This is measured in terms of the number of months elapsed between the creation of the social network (here, Instagram, 2010) and the opening of an account by the DMOs being studied. The closer the ratio is to 1, the more responsive the DMO is. The closer it is to 0, the longer it takes the DMO to invest in the new social network. The results for the three destinations show a gradient from Nice to Monaco.

– The ability to appropriate this new social network and therefore to publish regularly. This is measured in terms of the number of posts published in year n on the DSN, divided by the number of days in a year (Table 2.8).

– The ability to propose a unifying hashtag and impose it on Instagrammers. This is measured by the ratio between the number of DMO publications and the number of publications using the official hashtag on Instagram (Table 2.9).

– The ability to interact with Instagrammers, whether they are influencers or not. This is measured by the ratio between the average number of likes obtained by the DMO's publications and the number of reposts from the DMO (Table 2.10).

DMO	Number of months between account creation and social media creation	Result
NCA	34	0.029
Cannes	31	0.032
Monaco	21	0.047

Table 2.7. *Assessing the speed of creating an Instagram account (authors: Christofle and Fournier)*

DMO	Number of posts published in 2021	Result
NCA	287	0.78
Cannes	561	1.53
Monaco	146	0.4

Table 2.8. *Number of posts in 2021 divided by the number of days in a year (authors: Christofle and Fournier)*

DMO	Number of DMO posts	Number of publications using the official hashtag	Result
NCA	2,023	87,633	43.31
Cannes	–	–	–
Monaco	2,570	145,013	56.42

Table 2.9. *Number of publications using the official hashtag divided by the total number of DMO posts (authors: Christofle and Fournier)*

DMO	Average number of likes	Number of reposts from DMO	Result
NCA	1,266	1,861	0.68
Cannes	757	1,609	0.47
Monaco	437	2,036	0.21

Table 2.10. *Ratio between the number of reposts from the DMO and the average number of likes obtained by DMO publications (authors: Christofle and Fournier)*

To measure the composite index, we add the four elements defined above, and divide them by four (Table 2.11).

DMO	Result
NCA	11.19
Cannes	0.508
Monaco	14.26

Table 2.11. *Composite index (authors: Christofle and Fournier)*

Overall, the results confirm our initial hypotheses. The use of Instagram enables the DMOs being studied to react with agility and speed to market changes and consumer habits (the DMO's ability to process social information). Co-creation with visitors is positively linked to social media agility, and levels of DSN use appear to have a positive moderating influence on the relationship between platform agility and the strength of visitor/DMO relationships.

We have created a composite index to bring together important results and facilitate comparisons.

Destination	Number of stays in millions
NCA	4.2
Cannes	1.7
Monaco	0.45

Table 2.12. *Control variable: number of stays (average 2018–2019) (Observatoire du tourisme Côte d'Azur 2020)*

There are, however, limits to our research: the index needs to be refined. Indeed, this first test of an index measuring online communication agility could take more elements into account. At the same time, the value of each element could be measured, for example, the fact of having or not having an official hashtag. In addition, the consequence of a late account creation date seems to have less of an impact once the tool is used and fully mastered. Similarly, innovative practices based on social networks could be considered in agility, such as the creation of a store on a social network (as in the case of Cannes, which sells products on the Facebook platform).

2.4. Conclusion

An analysis of Nice Côte d'Azur, Cannes and Monaco DMO publications on Instagram showed a persistence of communication, based on the must-see locations of each destination associated with traditional activities (catering, accommodation and outings), with a few exceptions. The contemporary nature of the tools used therefore does not really change the content of tourism communication. That being said, the publications posted by Internet users, in addition to the egotistical glorifications of selfies, generally follow the "what to see/do" approach, in a race for the best shot to get noticed on the web.

In a move that is becoming the norm, DMOs are now integrating publications by web users into their accounts. Internet users are gradually succumbing to it, through the use of official hashtags, to massively disseminate regional images to their subscribers.

The construction of a composite index is essential when comparing destinations. Though, at present, Nice Côte d'Azur, the largest and most touristic territory in terms of number of stays, appears to lag behind Monaco in terms of communication agility, this can be explained by recent changes in terms of proposing a unifying hashtag. The hashtag explorenicecotedazur was launched in 2021, four years after the Monaco hashtag. As a result, it took some time for the new hashtag to catch on with Instagrammers. Cannes here is suffering from the absence of an official hashtag.

This study would benefit from a consolidation of research, using a more traditional methodology – sociological interviews with DMO resource people and Internet users – in order to discuss practices and choices, as well as to better understand the strategies that have been implemented. Another extension of the survey would be an in-depth analysis of the comments left by Internet users on DMO publications, as well as the number of times their publications were liked or commented on.

Lastly, to overcome some of the problems encountered, which led to long processing times and limitations in the study (visuals without captions, inaccurate hashtags and lack of geolocation of photographs), it would be interesting to develop a methodology based on artificial intelligence and image recognition, as part of the processing of big data. As it stands, the study has enabled us to use a quantitative methodology based on Big Data to gain a better understanding of the digital communication strategies implemented by three major international tourist destinations in the Côte d'Azur Alpes-Maritime region.

2.5. References

Arkhipov, A.Y. and Yeletsky, A.N. (2021). Modern globalization: Development of glocalization and fragmentation of the world economy. *International Journal of Sociology and Social Policy*, 41(1/2), 224–238.

Bernadou, D. (2017). Construire l'image touristique d'une région à travers les réseaux sociaux : le cas de l'Émilie-Romagne en Italie. *Cybergeo: European Journal of Geography*, 826. doi: 10.4000/cybergeo.28481.

Buhalis, D. and Amaranggana, A. (2013). *Smart Tourism Destinations. Information and Communication Technologies in Tourism*. Springer, Cham.

Buhalis, D. and Law, R. (2008). Progress in information technology and tourism management: 20 years on and 10 years after the internet – The state of eTourism research. *Tourism Management*, 29(4), 609–623.

Christofle, S. and Fournier, C. (2020). Marques territoriales et communication sur Instagram, enjeu contemporain de grandes destinations touristiques françaises : analyse comparée Côte d'azur France et Provence enjoy the unexpected. In *Marques et labels touristiques, leurs contributions au développement des collectivités territoriales*, Salvador, M. and Spindler, J. (eds). L'Harmattan, Paris.

Christofle, S. and Fournier, C. (in press). Métropole parisienne et communication numérique touristique : images territoriales médiatisées sur Instagram par l'office du tourisme et des congrès et par les instagrameurs. In *Tourismes à Paris*, Gravari-Barbas, M., Jacquot, S., Fagnoni, E. (eds). L'Harmattan, Paris.

Christofle, S., Papetti, C., Fournier, C. (2019). Tourisme, trajectoires et images : les médias socionumériques, outils contemporains d'adaptation communicationnelle de destinations ? Une voie de recherche en devenir. In *Tourisme et adaptations*, Tritz, C., Cholat F., Tuppen, J., Gwiazdzinski, L. (eds). Elya, Paris.

Chuang, S.H. (2020). Co-creating social media agility to build strong customer-firm relationships. *Industrial Marketing Management*, 84, 202–211.

Dhiratara, A., Yang, J., Bozzon, A., Houben, G.-J. (2016). Social media data analytics for tourism – A preliminary study. *CEUR Workshop Proceedings*, 12(1748), 1–12 [Online]. Available at: http://ceur-ws.org/Vol-1748/paper-12.pdf.

Ghorbanzadeh, D., Zakieva, R.R , Kuznetsova, M., Ismael, A.M., Ahmed, A.A.A. (2022). Generating destination brand awareness and image through the firm's social media. *Kybernetes*, 52(9), 3292–3314.

Homburg, C., Theel, T., Hohenburg, S. (2020). Marketing excellence: Nature, measurement, and investor valuations. *Journal of Marketing*, 84(4), 1–22.

Jansson, A. (2020). The transmediatourist: A theory of how digitalization reinforces the de-differentiation of tourism and social life. *Tourist Studies*, 20(4), 391–408

Jimenez-Barreto, J., Rubio, N., Campo, S., Molinillo, S. (2020). Linking the online destination brand experience and brand credibility with tourists' behavioral intentions toward a destination. *Tourism Management*, 79, 104101.

Kalaignanam, K., Tuli, K.R., Kushwaha, T., Lee, L., Gal, D. (2021). Marketing agility: The concept, antecedents, and a research agenda. *Journal of Marketing*, 85(1), 35–58.

Kemps, S. (2022a). Global digital yearbook, global digital statshot – We are social – Hootsuite. Report, DataReportal, Singapore [Online]. Available at: https://datareportal.com/reports/digital-2021-april-global-statshot.

Kemps, S. (2022b). Digital 2021 – France, global digital statshot. Report, DataReportal, Singapore [Online]. Available at: https://datareportal.com/reports/digital-2020-france?rq=France.

Koens, K., Postma, A., Papp, B. (2018). Is overtourism overused? Understanding the impact of tourism in a city context. *Sustainability*, 10(12), 43–84.

Minseong, K. and Jihye, K. (2020). Destination authenticity as a trigger of tourists online engagement on social media. *Journal of Travel Research*, 59(7), 1238–1252.

Navío-Marcoa, J., Ruiz-Gómez, L.M., Sevilla-Sevilla, C. (2018). Progress in information technology and tourism management: 30 years on and 20 years after the internet – Revisiting Buhalis and Law's landmark study about eTourism. *Tourism Management*, 69, 460–470.

Observatoire du Tourisme Côte d'Azur (2020). Chiffres clés 2020. CRT Côte d'Azur France [Online]. Available at: http://www.cotedazur-touriscope.com/pdf/chiffres/2020/chiffres-cles-fr-2020.pdf.

Reclus, E. (1864). *Les villes d'hiver de la Méditerranée et les Alpes Maritimes : Hyères, Cannes, Nice, Monaco, Menton, Sanremo*. Hachette, Paris.

Roudometof, V. (2016). Theorizing glocalization: Three interpretations. *European Journal of Social Theory*, 19(3), 391–408.

Thomas, B., Faye, D., Berry, F. (2020). Strategically marketing Florida's cities: An exploratory study into how cities engage in public marketing. *American Review of Public Administration*, 50(3), 275–285.

Volo, S. (2010). Bloggers' reported tourist experiences: Their utility as a tourism data source and their effect on prospective tourists. *Journal of Vacation Marketing*, 16(4), 297–311.

3

"Les Accros du peignoir" (Massif Central): Proof of the Agility of the French Spa Scene

3.1. Introduction

Until the 1930s, French spas, at least the most significant ones, were true pleasure resorts where well-being, leisure and the right to do nothing were openly sought (Grenier 1984; Carribon 2001; Penez 2005; Jazé-Charvolin 2014):

> Without ever renouncing their primary therapeutic vocation, even in large cosmopolitan spa towns, French spas are, in restricted times and places, characterized by the concentration of a wide range of activities and entertainment for spa-goers. Visitors' attention can be focused on several areas: the spa park, a place to relax and socialize, offering pleasant walks in a natural setting that has been recomposed and mastered; the casino – which is too often only remembered for its gaming rooms – offering a plethora of daytime and evening activities; and lastly, sporting activities, all of these were booming at the beginning of the 20th century. (Carribon 2014, p. 90)

However, by 1947, the recreational and hedonistic practices of the social thermalism of the Belle Époque and the Roaring Twenties were a thing of

Chapter written by Marie-Ève FÉRÉROL.

the past. Crenotherapy changed aspects and became a purely curative practice, reimbursed by health insurance. This social thermalism certainly contributed to a boom in clientele (Figure 3.1), but as Jamot (2008) points out, it also had adverse effects that were disastrous in terms of visitors of establishments and the maintenance of spa resorts as major tourist centers:

> The victory won by the resorts' new medical corps and the elected representatives who support them is, in fact, a Pyrrhic victory, as its implications are double-edged. Admittedly, the decision to erase all references to any kind of leisure or fitness system and, beyond that, the desire to break off with all forms of tourism is logical in a scientistic and medical spirit. However, to do so is to limit the possibilities of using thermal water and to totally ignore the role of the environment (accommodation, entertainment, etc.) in restoring health [...]. It took a good dose of social optimism not to realize that a total change in clientele was going to completely overturn the reception system: the resort. (Jamot 2008, p. 10)

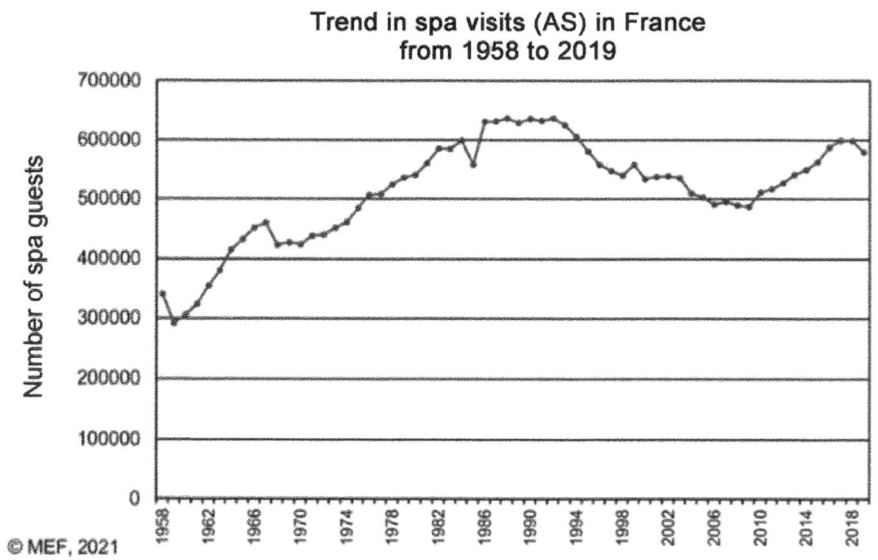

Figure 3.1. *Trends in spa visits (sources: (Jamot 1988) until 1982, then CNETh and RVE). Please note, for 1985, there is likely a typing error in the statistics, as there was no economic crisis in that year, unlike the three previous ones (1959, 1968 and 1977)*

The fragility of the new model can be seen as early as the late 1980s. In fact, from 1988 onward (the peak of the spa industry), the decline of the contract spa sector began (Figure 3.1). Between 1988 and 2009, the number of spa-goers fell from 630,000 to 480,000, a decline of 23.5%. Furthermore, the influx of socially insured spa-goers, coupled with excessive medical care and a total absence of wellness offerings, is driving away moneyed customers (Authier and Duvernois 1997), not to mention the fact that French thermalism lives, as it were, on state perfusion (Weisz 2002). On the one hand, it is heavily dependent on the behavior of spa-goers with regard to reimbursement by social security; and on the other hand, it is fragile with regard to public policies (Conseil National du Tourisme 2011).

Surprised and interested by the success of the fitness industry, which was developing at the same time, a number of spas gradually began to enter this niche. However, doctors' reluctance about the practice considerably hindered and delayed the process (Jamot 1996). Its redevelopment came far too late: 10 years late! In the late 1990s and early 2000s, any reference to the thermalism of the past and hedonistic pleasures was banned for fear of discrediting purely medical thermalism. Thalassotherapy, on the other hand, has no such qualms. "The thread between the hedonic and medical aspects has been renewed through thalassotherapy, which masterfully combines curative practice and the pleasure of water. Being a recent creation (1980s), the therapeutic argument here is a pretext for well-being and fitness" (MIT Team 2011, p. 56).

In addition to increasing competition from thalassotherapy, several factors explain the structural and cyclical crisis of the 1990–2000 period: the disappearance or decline in certain illnesses (notably those contracted in the colonies), increasingly strong competition from drugs, patients' reluctance to take three weeks off work for a cure (even if it was reimbursed), insufficient renewal of the patient base, the abolition of university courses in crenotherapy, the hyperspecialization of French resorts and the appeal of foreign resorts with modern, open-minded fitness complexes (Tunisia, Italy, Israel, etc.).

In 2011, the CNT was alarmed by this situation and published a detailed report on the spa industry, including suggestions for diversification:

– a medical axis, with new services (therapeutic education, ageing well) aimed at the traditional customers of conventional cures;

– tourism, based on a range of uses for water and spa treatments, including thermoludism and the idea of moving past single activities.

That said, the CNT are aware that many challenges lie ahead for resorts. In particular, it calls for a specific marketing approach to be implemented:

> The marketing of open-air cures represents a real challenge for former spa operators, who have to appeal to a new clientele that is nowhere near as loyal as their traditional clientele. It is all about marketing to win over new customers, which is necessarily more costly. (Conseil National du Tourisme 2011, p. 36)

Ten years after the CNT report, in the face of an unprecedented crisis, how have spa operators risen to the challenge of diversification? How have spa players reinvented and rethought the spa industry in the post-2000 era? How agile have they been? What strategy have they employed to communicate more effectively? This question is all the more pressing, given that the sector was hit hard by the Covid crisis in 2020–2021, when it was in remission. Let us take a closer look at the case of Massif Central spas.

3.2. Methodology

The choice of the Massif Central as a study area is justified by the presence of old water cities (Vichy, La Bourboule, Le Mont-Dore, Royat, Châtel-Guyon)[1], which suffered the most from the crisis of the 1990s. Even today, they are struggling to make a comeback. Their decline explains, among other things, the drop in the share of spa visitors to Massif Central resorts in total French visitor numbers: from 20% in 1983 to just 12% today (Figure 3.2).

NOTE.– This chart does not show the administrative breakdowns in order to highlight the decline of large spa areas such as Auvergne, or on the contrary, the emergence of new spa destinations (Charente resorts, in particular). The Nouvelle-Aquitaine region has also been divided in two, so as to distinguish the South-West around the Dacquois system.

In addition to classic documentary work, this research is above all exhaustive, since all of the directors of tourist offices (TO) and spa resort

1 By 1914, they were among France's leading spas (Authier and Duvernois 1997).

managers (at least those who agreed to be interviewed) were questioned during the winter of 2019–2020. It is also based on a series of interviews conducted on a regular basis (and for a very long time) with the staff of the Route des villes d'eaux (RVE)[2], an association grouping together the 17 resorts of the Massif Central, whose creation in 1998 under the aegis of the DATAR was intended to lead to an overhaul of local thermalism and a change of image (Férérol 2015)[3]. Lastly, a meeting with the deputy director of the Comité régional de développement touristique (regional tourism development committee) (September 6, 2019) was also deemed necessary to gain perspective and gather testimony from outside of the spa sector.

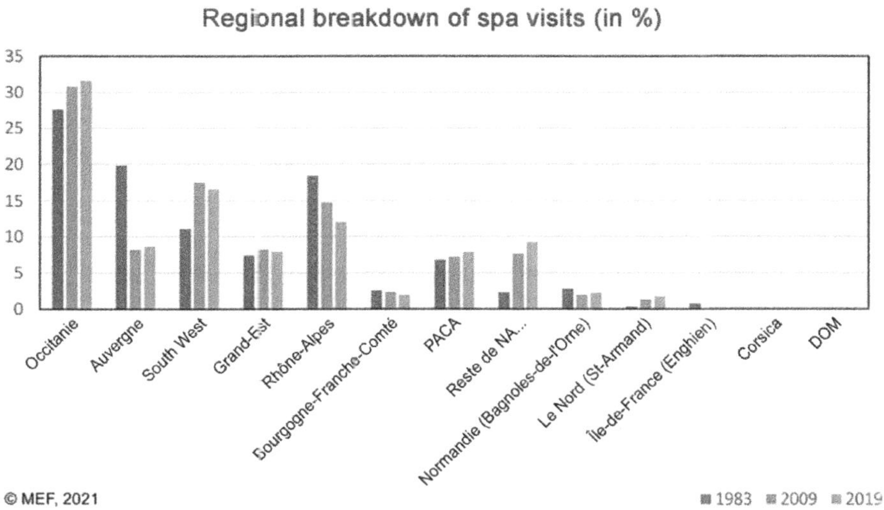

Figure 3.2. *An Auvergne spa (heart of the Massif Central) struggling to regain its place (source: CNETh; personal regional groupings). For a color version of this figure, see www.iste.co.uk/christofle/tourism2.zip*

Before going any further, let us recall the definition of thermalism as we understand it (Férérol 2022). For us, spa health tourism is divided into two branches: medical (healthcare) tourism and wellness tourism. The former,

2 É. Brut, General Manager, S. Huin, Communications and Development Director and L. Lemoine, Heritage and Digital Project Manager.

3 This article from 2015 shows the organizational agility shown by spa players in the Massif Central, who joined forces to form an association, fighting the crisis together rather than side by side.

based on scientific studies to prove the validity of treatments, encompasses preventive medical tourism (when you are in good health, you do what it takes to stay healthy), curative medical tourism (when you learn to live with a chronic illness, such as asthma, in resorts specializing in the respiratory tract) and post-operative medical tourism (the phase of physical and moral repair after surgery). The latter is more akin to wellness tourism, where spa water is used for recreational and sensory purposes.

3.3. Contextualization: the decline of the Massif Central's flagship resorts

Like the rest of France, and a few years ahead of schedule, the resorts in central France have been hit hard by the structural and cyclical crisis (Figure 3.3). It is quite a dramatic situation: between 1988 and 2009, visitor numbers fell by 54%[4], compared with 23.5% at national level, and dropped below the 100,000 mark. Jamot (2003, p. 307) cannot describe the situation harshly enough: "from supremacy to anonymity", "Massif Central bled dry".

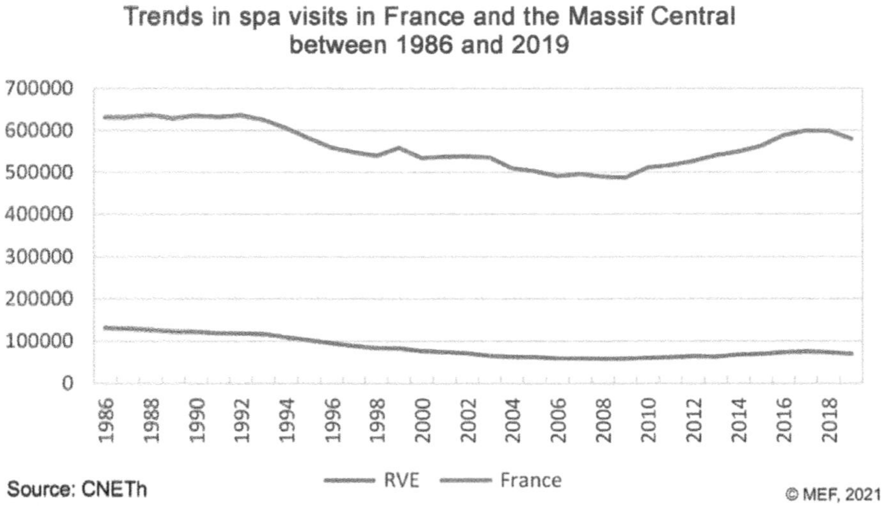

Figure 3.3. *Trends in spa visits in France and the Massif Central between 1986 and 2019. For a color version of this figure, see www.iste.co.uk/christofle/tourism2.zip*

4 Since 2003, one of La Bourboule's spa establishments, which is now closed, has not been reporting its figures; that being said, the 5,000 or so people not counted have little impact on the percentage.

The most important resorts are the hardest hit: La Bourboule is down 83%, Châtel-Guyon 79%, Royat and Vichy 65%, and Le Mont-Dore 53%. Although these five Auvergne resorts received 12.6% of the national clientele in 1988, they only got 4.5% ten years later.

There are several reasons for this decline. Some are the same as at national level (see above), while others are regional: highly medicalized conception of thermalism, non-existent heliotropism, insufficient investment to renovate spa and hotel facilities, neglected media, etc. (Jamot 2008).

Since 2009, as on a national scale, visitor numbers have been on the rise. From 57,654 to 72,623 visitors in 2018, an increase of 26%, slightly higher than the national average. However, visitor numbers are still below the 100,000 mark reached in the 1980s.

The second problem is the image that French spa resorts, particularly those in the Massif Central, still project: an "old-fashioned" image, where nothing happens and medicalized thermalism dominates.

However, since the 2000s, the Massif Central resorts, supported by the Route des villes d'eaux association (Water cities route association), have been moving toward wellness thermalism and, more broadly, toward tourism diversification based on their spa heritage (Férérol 2015, 2019):

> Spa resorts need to rediscover their ability to seduce. Our option is to introduce tourism with the development of fitness and fun. Fitness has been poorly exploited by spa establishments because it is still too medicalized. We have been robbed by thalassotherapy by leaving the doors wide open. (J.-F. Béraud, former director of RVE, president of the Fédération thermale et climatique since 2015)

In order to give resorts back their appeal (see previous quote), to make their activities better known and to attract new customers, a solution has been found by the players in the field: a territorial brand, called Les Accros du peignoir (AP)[5].

5 For those who are interested, an educational case focusing on spa communication using the example of "Les Accros du peignoir" has been submitted to the Centrale de cas et de médias pédagogiques (case studies and teaching media center) by M.-N. Rimaud and ourselves.

3.4. The remedy for the crisis: a territorial brand based on humor, inclusivity, experience and openness to the cultural world[6]

According to its creators, the ambition of the brand, registered with INPI (Institut national de la propriété intellectuelle) in 2017, is to revamp the image of the resorts, deploying new communication codes to erase clichés and combat prejudices, in order to facilitate the arrival of new clientele, notably generation X (born in the 1960s and 1970s) and Y (1980s). To achieve this, a four-pronged approach was adopted.

3.4.1. *A reflective work on the identity to be given to the Massif Central's water towns*

During a series of workshops and brainstorming sessions, players from the spa community (RVE staff, elected representatives, tourist office technicians, etc.) began by reflecting on the identity of a spa town. This work on identity is indeed essential in a territorial marketing process (Rebillard 2007, 2012); this led to the distinction of six "identity" categories: physical, personality/character, cultural world, reflection of yesterday to today, climate and mentalization. Several terms emerged, but only the most prominent were retained for future promotion campaigns: elegant, spectacular, restful, artists, a break from the everyday, etc.

Professionals are concluding that spa resorts are in tune with the times, reinforcing their efforts to promote these original tourist sites. For them, spa towns correspond to the fashion for retro, old-fashioned locations and, above all, to the need for wellness, whether it be physical or moral[7]. The call for papers for the Astres conference[8] held in Nice in 2022 sums it up well:

> Body maintenance has become a market that is truly linked to body standards of 'being healthy and beautiful' (Queval 2008). The challenge is to act on one's body to take care of one's appearance: nutrition, jogging, body care, cosmetics, aquagym,

---

6 For the organizational and financial model, please refer to our contribution to the book coordinated by J. Spindler and M. Salvador entitled *Marques et labels touristiques* (2020).

7 RVE marketing study and digital strategy (2015).

8 Conference on "Tourism agility in times of crisis: replications, accelerations, reinventions, etc.".

balneotherapy-thalassotherapy, bodybuilding, medicine and cosmetic surgery (Boltanski 1974; Le Breton et al. 2013). From this perspective, the post-Covid traveler would be looking for a tourist experience that is both unique and allows him or her to optimize his or her sense of wellness. (Tan et al. 2014)

3.4.2. *Choosing humor and self-mockery*

The strength of Les Accros du peignoir (AP) lies in its choice of humor and self-mockery, both in visuals and writing. This kind of communication is rather incongruous in a spa environment that has long been under the under the supervision of doctors, who felt it was inappropriate to laugh at an activity that deals with sick people.

Today, however, the situation is reversed in the Massif Central: elected resort officials (including doctors) no longer hesitate to put on a show and walk around in bathrobes, right in the middle of Paris, for the promotion of thermalism!

The APs are based on derision. This is not a neutral semantic choice; it is second-degree: Les Accros refers to junkies (we are addicted to bathrobes). The brand's charter, on the other hand, is aimed at slow-life, pleasure-seeking and good-life enthusiasts. The AP preserves its health capital, and seeks resourcefulness in places it admires, both architecturally and culturally.

Humor has also entered the field of communication around the many tourism products created by RVE[9]. The Les Accros du peignoir brand, for example, has revitalized the creative process.

In 2021, a number of products were put together, directly linked to the region and, if possible, in keeping with the humor of Les Accros. Saint-Nectaire, in reference to the filming of Kaamelott at the Château de Murol, has offered a tow-year "Arthurian ride to well-being" holiday (Figure 3.4).

9 In 2002, RVE worked with just two tour operators (TO) for five products; today, this is a sign of the success of this association in revitalizing the spa business, with more than 200 products on offer and 40 national TOs being partners.

Texte accompagnant la photo, Site Auvergne Destination, site officiel du tourisme en Auvergne, consulté le 20/09/2022.

Figure 3.4. *Example of a product marketed by RVE and promoted with the humor of Les Accros*[10]*. For a color version of this figure, see www.iste.co.uk/christofle/tourism2.zip*

---

10 Figure translation: "Why did *Les Accros du Peignoir* [a French marketing campaign focused on promoting the spa towns in the Massif Central region of France] choose **Saint-Nectaire** for their 'Arthurian' ride to well-being? Firstly, this exceptional village is named after a French cheese, which promises a good feast for all Caradocs present. And secondly, with over 2,000 years of balneology, it's the perfect place to relax between two stages of the quest for the Holy Grail.

The *Mercure Les Bains Romains* hotel offers the ultimate luxury! A hot stone massage and private Jacuzzi for two: the perfect combo for clearing the mind and getting back into shape before trying to pull King Arthur's Excalibur from its rock.

Just a short ride away, visit Murol chateau, an emblematic site where Lord Leodagan lived... But first, enjoy a feast in the tavern, after, of course, trying the Holy Grail at *Les Mystères de Farges*.

"Odi panem quid Meliora: this doesn't mean anything to us, but it does have a nice ring to it".

Texte accompagnant la photo, Site Auvergne Destination, site officiel du tourisme en Auvergne, consulté le 20/09/2022: Text accompanying photo, *Site Auvergne Destination*, official website for tourism in the Auvergne region [Accessed 20/09/2022].

3.4.3. *More punchy, inclusive and experiential communication*

The RVE attributes three objectives to communication around Les Accros: to set the tone (personify the conversation through the brand, set a playful and cheeky tone, stage the destination through experiential immersion), inspire (animate its communication channels in a seductive, engaging way and share customer stories/photos/videos) and convert/build loyalty (have a surprising editorial approach all year round and occasionally talk about its products and offers)[11].

Figure 3.5. *The use of different communication channels. For a color version of this figure, see www.iste.co.uk/christofle/tourism2.zip*

To reach them, RVE has opted for storytelling. What do we mean by storytelling? The art of telling stories, on innovative media, through a scenario with an offbeat tone. For Blancherie (2011, p. 10), "storytelling brings concreteness, situations and experiences. It relies on symbolism and imagination", while for Durand (2011, p. 17), "in the age of Web 2.0, this communication technique makes it possible to involve customers and 'fans' of a brand. Tourism, with its close proximity to the public, is a sector that is

11 RVE marketing study and digital strategy (2015).

particularly well-suited to storytelling. The upstream and downstream stages of a trip, from preparation to memory-making, are an integral part of the adventure. That is why e-tourism (websites and social networking sites) considerably expands the opportunities for creating and receiving stories".

The storytelling of Les Accros will be equally as "reflexive" (once upon a time) as it is "projective" (there will be). To illustrate the "once upon a time", a great deal of work has been done in advance to bring the story to light. Indeed, since 2008, the RVE has been working to make elected representatives and the general public aware of the rich heritage of their commune, and to promote it (by drawing up inventories, organizing exhibitions, etc.).

As for the "there will be" theme, Les Accros places particular emphasis on experiential stimulation. Future customers need to be able to project themselves through interviews and videos. In fact, democratization requires experiential stimulation, on the one hand, to show the inside of the buildings and detail what the treatments consist of, in order to reassure the future customer; and on the other hand, of course, to create desire. However, this experiential communication is double-edged. "The operator states in its communication that it is committed to providing the consumer with an experience whose positioning is clearly announced. Such a form of commitment is risky, as it must not disappoint" (Petr 2014, p. 39). Customers, especially "elusive discoverers" (those who explore a new destination every year) (Évin-Leclerc 2010, p. 22), can be doubly disappointed, and can potentially spread the word about it, now on a much larger scale via social networks.

Regular visitors are also likely to abandon the resort of their dreams if the care and surroundings no longer live up to their expectations. The result would then be disastrous, undoing the efforts made to improve the image. There must be no disconnect between the products, the ideals promised by the brand and the offer delivered in the area.

The storytelling of Les Accros will be deployed across several communication channels (web, radio, print media, flyers, etc.) (Figure 3.5):

– creation of a multimedia platform dedicated to Les Accros du peignoir in 2018;

– broadcasting of a four-episode comedy web series in 2018–2019, with a 40-something active male protagonist in a couple, who is a little overweight, sympathetic and funny, so that he is easy to identify with (videos still available on Les Accros website);

– radio show on France Bleu from 2019 to 2021;

– collaboration in 2021–2022 with local journalist Fanny Agostini for the web series *Buée et Claquettes*, designed to showcase the richness of each resort and the benefits of water;

– regular flagship events such as afterworks to initiate a community of ambassadors to spread the word via social networks.

Figure 3.6. *An inclusive and deliberately wacky universe. For a color version of this figure, see www.iste.co.uk/christofle/tourism2.zip*

The aim of Les Accros du peignoir is to attract a new clientele, both for medical thermalism and for wellness, and this means democratizing the activity. To break down the image of treatments reserved exclusively for women, for a rather well-off, white social class with an impeccable physique, visuals are very important.

From now on, burly women, black women, men and homosexual couples will be featured on advertising posters (Férérol 2023).

Wacky images also populate the annual magazines, showing resort life (Figure 3.6).

3.4.4. *Water cities: creative and innovative*

While the aim of the operations prepared by the RVE's heritage officer is to highlight the wealth of the spa towns in an artistic and offbeat style, the underlying aim is to rediscover the creative function that the resorts had in their heyday, and ultimately to change the public's view of them, all financed in large part by the Commissariat général à l'égalité des territoires (CGET Massif Central) and the regions concerned as part of the "Telling the story of spa heritage through storytelling and digital technology" project[12]:

> Our aim is to recapture the DNA of the Massif Central spas, which have been important cultural centers since the 19th century, attracting artistic and political figures from all over Europe. We felt it was important to reconnect our region with this somewhat forgotten past. One of our objectives is to make a lasting impression and change their image, while at the same time seeking to rejuvenate our audiences, notably through the mediation and dissemination of artist residencies to schoolchildren. We are convinced that young regulars can

12 Back in 2013, RVE teamed up with the European Historic Thermal Towns Association to help people discover Europe's shared cultural heritage, through an interactive novel via Facebook, revolving around four fictional characters gravitating around the cultural environment (past and present) of thermal spas. This project, under the aegis of Mr. Thomas-Pénette, then Director of the European Institute of Cultural Routes, was a failure. The very (overly) erudite content excluded a large part of the public. Since then, the RVE has always been committed to combining digital tools with basic content.

become ambassadors for the region, and even bathrobe enthusiasts. (Léa Lemoine, RVE)

In 2016, the Route des villes d'eaux (Water cities route) began working with "notebook artists", connected artists with an international following. They were asked to reinterpret the cultural and tourist assets of the Massif Central's 17 spa towns in their own contemporary style.

Figure 3.7. *Opening up spas to the contemporary cultural world. For a color version of this figure, see www.iste.co.uk/christofle/tourism2.zip*

At the end of their work in the field, the "notebook artists" saw their drawings put to good use, notably through the production of a manual for the "Accros du peignoir" (Figure 3.7). This may seem a trivial operation, but its value lies in its resonance on social networks.

> The question is no longer whether or not it is worth launching a social media presence: you have to be where the audience is. [...] They enable tourism regions and businesses to develop their brand awareness, unite a community around their brand, recruit fans and share their emotions with Internet users in real time[13].

The "Voyages artistiques avec les Accros du peignoir" (Artistic journeys with the Bathrobe addicts) operation also testifies to the very strong link between the spa and its territory. This three-pronged communication campaign gave rise to numerous exhibitions, press kits, etc.

– For two years, from 2019 to 2021, RVE entered into a partnership with the École supérieure d'art et de design de Saint-Étienne (Saint-Étienne School of Art and Design). Seventy students gave free rein to their imagination, while being subjected to a constraint: their work must have a link with water, thermalism and the resort. Their creations ranged from visual arts (graphic arts, street art, videos) to object design. They were shown to the public as part of the "Culture bains" touring exhibition (2022–2023):

> The challenge was to come up with a way of thinking about space that would be common to all water cities, and that would give rise to a medium that could be easily promoted on social networks. The idea was to project ourselves into the future to tell different stories. In 2050, Les Accros du peignoir have become an influential community. What for? Why? In the end, the students were able to weave three fictional scenarios, all of which take us back to a very important relationship of meaning and ritual in relation to water. One, in the form of a dystopia set in a period of dictatorship, projects water as an element of power, even of mass manipulation. Another, more melancholic, proposes

13 Fabry (2011). [Online]. Available at: www.tourisme-tic.com/les-reseaux-sociaux-et-le-tourisme/#more-1103 [Accessed on January 21, 2020].

> a mythology of paradise lost through artifacts and pilgrimages following the disappearance of spa water. The last, more optimistic, develops a spiritual relationship with the resource, which has become scarce and therefore in need of preservation, and with which we had to imagine a more qualitative relationship. (L. Grégori, ESAD teacher, as reported by RVE)

> The 'Villes d'eaux et design d'espace' project was an opportunity to better understand the culture of spa towns, which for many of us was unknown, and to identify the difference between the care aspect and the wellness aspect. (L. Bouyssou, ESAD student)

– At the same time, the spa towns of the Massif Central have been used to support the creativity of a particular artist, with Vichy, Royat, Châtel-Guyon, Cransac and Bourbon-Lancy each hosting an artist-in-residence for two weeks (Figure 3.7). Each new residency is an opportunity for the artists to produce a work inspired by spa culture and positioned in a more global context: the presence of thermal springs and access to water, living conditions and the environment, spa town architecture and the notion of the ideal town, spa wellness and the relationship with everyday life, etc. Their stay was fruitful, as evidenced by the creation of street art frescoes and digital works. These works will be showcased as part of Clermont-Ferrand's bid to become the European Capital of Culture 2028:

> Street art is developing a great deal today in contemporary art, with artists of many influences using walls as a space for suggestive expression, a common thread running through the project. Their work is helping to change the image of spa resorts, which are finding it hard to shake off an aesthetic associated with their past. The aim is to rejuvenate the image of spa resorts by playing the card of a new kind of itinerant cultural tourism. (A. Squizzato, street art consultant)

– Lastly, the Route des villes d'eaux (Water cities route) contacted the Cité internationale de la tapisserie d'Aubusson (Aubusson International Tapestry City) to take part in this artistic journey of Les Accros du peignoir. This institution has been invited to choose three works from its collections featuring the theme of water, to be installed temporarily in 2022 in three spa establishments (Le Mont-Dore, La Bourboule and Saint-Nectaire).

More than a significant increase in spa visitor numbers, the aim of Les Accros was to get people talking about spa resorts in ways other than negative ones ("old people's towns", "where you get bored", "where everything is run-down" (in reference to the many wastelands that may exist)). The RVE was pleased with the coverage in the local, regional and national press (news briefs, articles, etc.) and on social networks. Here, for example, is a testimonial from a blogger responsible for the www.nouveautourismeculturel.com website:

> This week, I received a magnificent press kit from the Massif central, and the more I read it, the more I thought that everything was great: the press kit, clear and graphically perfect; the artistic program of Les Accros du peignoir, with its funny name; the artists used, not chosen because they are "friends of the mayor", as is too often the case. Les Accros du peignoir have revisited all the cultural traditions of the Massif central water routes [blogger error], from the famous bathrobe (1900) to the street art of today's artists! Let us therefore go and visit these water cities and the creative itineraries they offer, which have become or will become a new wealth of cultural tourism in France![14]

3.5. Conclusion

Since 2009, the French spa industry has been regaining a certain dynamism (Revue Espaces 2019). The context is favorable: mistrust of drugs in the wake of the Mediator scandal, renewed interest in natural treatments as part of sustainable development, the wellness craze, not to mention a demographic that favors thermalism. According to INSEE forecasts, France will have 20 million people over 65 by 2050. Aging well will therefore be a major factor in the years to come. It will be necessary to prevent all age-related illnesses.

Nevertheless, this is a fragile sector, and not all spas are benefiting from this exceptional upturn. Furthermore, Covid has left resorts drained of

14 See: www.nouveautourismeculturel.com/blog/2020/11/05/les-accros-du-peignoir/ [Accessed on October 1, 2023].

customers. The sector's strong momentum has come to a screeching halt in 2020 and 2021:

> The tourism sector was one of the first and most severely affected sectors by the health crisis, which had a major impact on the spa industry. In 2020, a 68% drop in visitor numbers was recorded at national level among spa-goers under contract, due to the imposed closure periods, and numerous cancellations in view of the general health context.[15]

The Massif Central, one of the world's longest-established spa regions, has had to revamp its communications. It has partly opted for a humorous approach. As Meyronin (2015) has shown, the use of humor, self-mockery and contrast is omnipresent in territorial marketing. However, the danger of such a bias is that humor becomes trivialized and toned down over time. It is very hard to renew ourselves whilst keeping our DNA.

On the other hand, more inclusive communication campaigns are attempting to democratize spa practices, often internalized as elitist activities or reserved for perfect figures. One of the scriptwriters who helped formalize the brand regrets, however, that we are reverting back to "supermodel" images, far removed from the "jolly good fellow" aspect of the first communication campaigns. Lastly, the "water cities" have reconnected with their history by offering a cultural and creative face to the entire population, and not just to an erudite public.

All of these communication campaigns were a daring but successful gamble for a rather tight-lipped sector, that is permanently under the social security gaze, always looking for a pretext to no longer reimburse treatments.

Henceforth, spa resorts no longer hesitate to present themselves as touristic sites in their own right, fulfilling the wish of Dr. Christian Corne (2006)[16], former Vichy councilor and president of the RVE: "We are proud of thermalism, proud to take care of it; thermalism must not make us lower our heads as has often been the case for too many years".

---

15 See: https://www.economie.gouv.fr/stations-thermales-plan-soutien-developpement-gouvernement# [Accessed September 20, 2022].

16 Speech given at the First European Thermal Heritage Event in Aix-les-Bains in 2006.

3.6. References

Authier, A. and Duvernois, P. (1997). *Patrimoine et traditions du thermalisme*. Privat, Toulouse.

Blancherie, J.M. (2011). Le storytelling ne raconte pas d'histoire. *Espaces*, 298, 10–16.

Boltanski, L. (1974). Les usages sociaux du corps. *Annales économies, sociétés, civilisations*, 26(1), 205–233.

Carribon, C. (2001). Du thermalisme mondain au thermalisme social : les villes d'eaux françaises dans l'Entre-deux-guerres. PhD Thesis, Université de Bordeaux, Bordeaux.

Carribon, C. (2014). Villes d'eaux, villes de Loisirs. L'exemple des stations thermales françaises de la fin du XIXe siècle aux années trente. *Histoire urbaine*, 41(3), 83–103.

Conseil National du Tourisme (2011). *La diversification des stations thermales*. Ministère de l'Économie, Paris.

Durand, S. (2011). Écrire des histoires pour changer le monde. *Espaces*, 298, 17–19.

Évin-Leclerc, A. (2010). La gestion de la relation-clients. In *Le marketing touristique des collectivités territoriales*, Debarge, S., Druhen, X., Évin-Leclerc, A., Van Houtte, F. (eds). Territorial Éditions, Voiron.

Férérol, M.E. (2015). La revitalisation des stations thermales du Massif central français par *la Route des Villes d'Eaux* : entre mémoire et innovation. In *Les Routes Touristiques*, Marcotte, P. and Bourdeau, L. (eds). Édition des Presses de l'Université de Laval, Québec.

Férérol, M.E. (2019). La valorisation numérique du patrimoine thermal du Massif central. In *Thermalisme et patrimoines dans les zones de montagne en Europe du XVIIIe au XXIe siècle*, Jalabert, L., Meynen, N., Castaner, E. (eds). Presses Universitaires de l'UPPA, Pau.

Férérol, M.E. (2020). Les Accros du peignoir : la marque qui dépoussière le milieu thermal du Massif central. In *Labels, marques touristiques et développement des collectivités territoriales*, Salvador, M. and Spindler, J. (eds). L'Harmattan, Paris.

Férérol, M.E. (2022). Entrée "Thermalisme". In *Encyclopédie scientifique et technique du tourisme et des loisirs*, Gay, J.C. (ed.). GIS Études Touristiques/ Université d'Angers, Angers.

Férérol, M.E. (2023). La représentation des sexes dans le milieu thermal. *Mondes du Tourisme*, 23 [Online]. Available at: http://journals.openedition.org/tourisme/6046.

Grenier, L. (1984). Les villes de santé. In *Villes d'eaux en France*, Grenier, L. (ed.). Institut Français d'Architecture, Paris.

Jamot, C. (1988). Thermalisme et villes thermales en France. PhD Thesis, Université de Clermont-Ferrand, Clermont-Ferrand.

Jamot, C. (1996). De la cure médicale au tourisme de santé : vers une reconversion fonctionnelle des stations thermales. In *2000 ans de thermalisme*, Jarassé, D. (ed.). Publications de l'Institut d'Etudes du Massif central, Clermont-Ferrand.

Jamot, C. (2003). Les stations thermales du Massif central en quête d'avenir. *Prace Geograficzne*, 111, 305–316.

Jamot, C. (2008). Les stations thermales à l'épreuve du thermalisme social. *Bulletin d'histoire de la Sécurité Sociale en Auvergne*, 8, 6–17.

Jazé-Charvolin, M.R. (2014). Les stations thermales : de l'abandon à la Renaissance. *In Situ*, 24 [Online]. Available at: https://insitu.revues.org/11123.

Le Breton, D., Pomarede, N., Vigarello, G., Andrieu, A., Aoetsch, G. (2013). *Corps en formes*. CNRS Éditions, Paris.

Meyronin, B. (2015). *Marketing territorial*. Vuibert, Paris.

MIT Team (2011). *Tourisme 3 : la révolution durable*. Belin, Paris.

Penez, J. (2005). *Histoire du thermalisme en France au XIXe siècle*. Economica, Paris.

Petr, C. (2014). Le tourisme expérentiel, ça n'existe pas… mais c'est utile à la réflexion marketing. *Espaces*, 320, 38–42.

Queval, L. (2008). *Le corps aujourd'hui*. Gallimard, Paris.

Rebillard, S. (2007). L'analyse identitaire, un enjeu pour les territoires. *Espaces*, 245, 20–23.

Rebillard, S. (2012). Marque de destination et identité territoriale : des destins liés. *Espaces*, 303, 13–14.

Revue Espaces (2019). Dossier Spécial : le renouveau du thermalisme. *Espaces*, 349, 57–115.

Tan, K., Luh, H., Kung, S., Shiann, F. (2014). A taxonomy of creative tourists in creative tourism. *Tourism Management*, 42, 248–259.

Weisz, G. (2002). Le thermalisme en France au XXe siècle. *Médecine/Sciences*, 18(1), 101–108.

4

Attractions and Interconnected Destinations: The Case of the Chaîne des Puys–Limagne Fault UNESCO Site

For those involved in tourism destinations, the issues of viability and development, which involve meeting demand as well as the expectations of other stakeholders, must be considered from a dynamic perspective, not only in terms of the "lifecycle" of destinations (Butler 2009), but also in terms of their resilience to environmental changes.

Destinations are local systems with more or less organized governance and management. The aim of this chapter is to take a closer look at the representation of a local tourism system in order to help structure and manage it. It is in line with the duality adopted by Botti (2010), who specifies that "while one of the factors of tourism lies in the attractions of the territory, another determinant involves all its stakeholders". This chapter therefore focuses on (1) the relationship between attractions, destinations and areas of governance, all of which can be interwoven and nested at several levels of the spatial scale; and (2) the roles played by the various stakeholders in terms of their functions, resources and intentions.

The aim is to contribute to "robust" site and destination management, in other words, management that is able to remain relevant under various assessments and environmental conditions (Roy 2002).

Chapter written by Jean-Bernard MARSAT and Étienne POLGE.

A case study illustrates this point by focusing on the interconnection of an emblematic natural heritage site, which acts as an attraction, and several destinations which may or may not overlap with the site.

A model of this interconnection will be suggested, as well as a representation of the system of multiple actors involved in the management of the site as a natural space and/or as an attraction, and thus in the management of the destinations concerned.

4.1. Issues, references and models

The problem addressed in this chapter is based on the type of case studied by the "Valo-Sites" research project, or "Methods for assessing the socio-economic effects of management and valorization policies for natural heritage sites", whose objective involves the study of tourism and site-related leisure activities.

The attractiveness of this type of heritage site, its extensive nature and, simultaneously, its limited accommodation capacity, mean that the boundaries of the tourist phenomenon linked to the site's visitor numbers have to be considered a priori as not known in advance and probably quite broad.

The study of the tourism system also focuses on the offer of services and their organization. One specific feature of this type of site lies in the fact that the public policies pursued there aim, alternatively or simultaneously, to preserve heritage and develop tourism: the search for a robust structurization of the system thus leads to a review of the particularities of the population of actors involved in one or both of these roles.

This means considering the following:

– the geography of the system, taking into account visitor numbers, the diversity of visitors, accommodation facilities and the various leisure practices of these visitors;

– the actors involved, taking into account the diversity of roles and scales of intervention.

4.1.1. *Spatial features of the local system*

4.1.1.1. *Framing the issue: tourist attraction and tourist destination*

A tourist attraction, in its primary sense, refers to one of the elements that "draws" the tourist (away from their usual place of residence) to their destination (adapted from Lew (1987)). In the extended sense, it includes organizational and cognitive elements (notably the "marker" system, which provides information on the attraction). A distinction is made between "primary" attractions, which alone motivate the choice of destination, and other types of attraction (secondary or tertiary) (adapted from Leiper (1990)).

The tourist destination, in its primary sense, is "where the tourist wants to go during [their] stay", what the tourist defines as their destination. This place generally includes accommodation and most of the tourist's activities. The minimalist definition is thus the geographical area that the tourist has identified and chosen as the place to stay and have activities (adapted from Laws (1995)). In the extended sense, it is the set of attributes and services involved in/contributing to the tourist's stay (adapted from Murphy et al. (2000)).

A substantial body of literature has focused on the relationship between attractions and destinations, notably under the (broader) theme of destination "attractiveness". The systemic nature of the principles of tourist attractiveness is highlighted by Badot and Lemoine (2015). It depends both on the strength of each of its attractions, but also on an overall effect that links the various accessible attractions in the mind of the potential visitor, and even other general attributes attached to the encompassing territory or country. This is in line with Violier (2009), who believes that a simple inventory of attractions is not enough.

4.1.1.2. *Distinctions between "destination-d", "destination-o" and "A-H area"*

We hypothesize that it is relevant and useful to distinguish between the destination perceived by the visitor before coming to the site, with the attributes that determined their choice, and the destination that has been identified by supply side actors, which the latter manage and promote. We will call the first "destination-d" (d for demand), and the second "destination-o" (o for offer, the scale here is collective). The latter may have been identified and delineated on the basis of a sum of accumulated individual demands and practices, or by other means and for other reasons (intention of an actor, administrative logic). We also assume that it is relevant and useful to consider the area over which an attraction (A) has an impact on accommodation (H), in other words, the location of all of the accommodation of A's visitors. We will call this the "A-H area". This notion of the relationship between attraction and accommodation is close to the considerations of Piriou (2011) on the "monotopic" or "polytopic" nature of a place, depending on whether it provides all of the necessary functions (recreation, accommodation, etc.) or "requires an association with other places due to a lack of functions". Similarly, De Grandpré's (2009) model of the regional tourism system distinguishes three main components, including "reception structures" (accommodation, catering, other) and "attractions".

4.1.1.3. *The various spatial configurations of leisure travel*

A number of authors have looked at the various types of global tourist trips, ranging from single destinations to itinerant tours. Lue et al. (1993) explore different travel patterns, possibly combining day trips with single or itinerant stays. Their aim is to help those involved in the supply side of the market to understand visitors' rationales when planning their trips. They identify five forms of travel that include a given attraction, noted as A. An extract is shown in Figure 4.1.

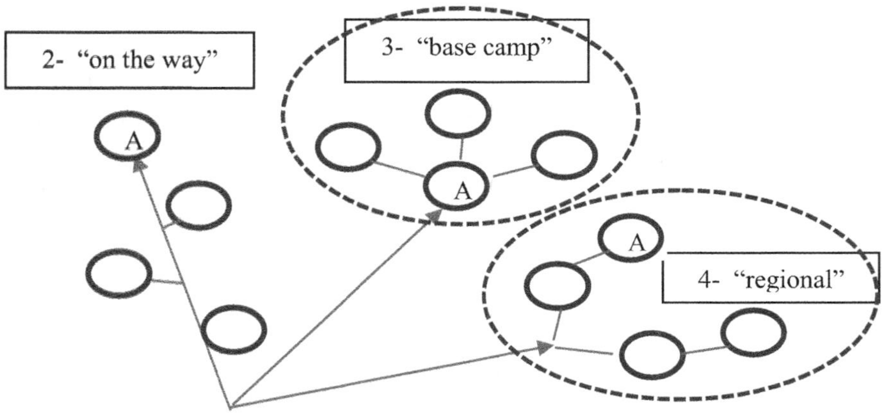

Figure 4.1. *Partial diagram of the various spatial forms of leisure travel (adapted from Lue et al. 1993; production: Marsat)*

According to the traveler, diagrams 3 and 4 may correspond to a global "destination-d" (dotted circle). In the same field, Lew and McKercher (2006) expand on their inventory of tourist trip types (clearly distinguishing between accommodation and points of visits). However, this literature does not clarify the transition from the typology of individual tourist behaviors to the identification of tourist destinations.

4.1.1.4. *Identification of destination-o, relationships between objects and between scales*

The challenge for supply-side and public policy actors is to identify the relevant destinations and the interrelationships between destinations. For example, Dredge and Jenkins (2003) point out that the process of differentiation between destinations is the result of complex interactions between considerations of place identity and the diverse logics of actors at different scales. In addition to this, there is a question of how to delineate the destination. Furthermore, some analyses, such as those carried out by Klarić et al. (2002), start from the resources available in a region/country and resources seen as possible attractions, either on a local scale (a spa) or as components of a product (thermalism in region X). This raises the question of scale, as well as the possible primacy of product appeal over local appeal.

Another issue that is sometimes highlighted in the literature is that of relationships between destinations-o. For example, Haugland et al. (2011) refer to links between destinations, as well as links between destinations and the "region", which are seen as resources.

4.1.1.5. *Relationships: attraction/location/destination-o*

One aspect of the problem involves looking more closely at the relationship between attractions and destinations by locating the place of accommodation: accommodation is a major item in tourists' budgets and therefore in supply-side economics; the place of accommodation may be distant from that of the attraction; it may influence the choice of attractions visited (distance criterion).

More generally, it is also necessary to verify the relationship between the geography of the overall tourism system and visitor motivations. One of the established factors is that of travel, but even so-called gravity models can be more complex (Morley et al. 2014).

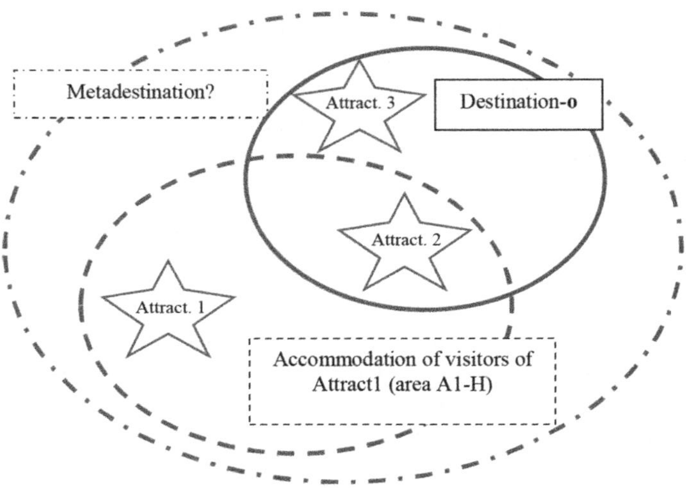

Figure 4.2. *Attraction/destination interconnection diagram (production: Marsat)*

The aim here is to better understand and describe the links between attractions and destinations, and to discuss not only possible overlaps, but also possible interconnected destinations to be promoted and managed (possible meta-destinations?), in order to jointly inform site management and tourism development management policies.

A theoretical diagram of the possible interconnection of attractions and destinations is shown in Figure 4.2.

4.1.2. *Management issues: stakeholder profiles, objects and scales of intervention*

The management of attractions and destinations is the other issue addressed in this chapter, with this particular question: how is the geography of the tourism phenomenon linked to attractions and "destinations-d" handled by the various actors who intervene in the system, in one capacity or another? At the very least, how is the management of "destination-o" and "independent" attractions structured? This question is linked to the previous one, as these various actors are also involved in the very identification of destinations-o.

We have proposed a heuristic model to characterize the actors involved in attraction and destination management in terms of the major strategic core functions (Flagestad and Hope 2001) and their actual roles (Marsat et al. 2010).

The usual actors in the local tourism system are local authorities, service-providing companies, DMOs (destination management organizations) and, in a diffuse way, the entire local population. Other local and nonlocal actors intervene in a variety of ways, notably as regulators, service providers, resource managers (specific infrastructures, assets shared with other uses, etc.) and so on.

We propose to examine the major basic strategic functions according to the following triple focus: "strategic marketing" in reference to the positioning school (Porter 1980), "resource and skills management" in reference to Wernerfelt (1984) and Barney (1991), and "stakeholder management" in reference to Freeman (1984) and Donaldson and Preston (1995).

The actors mentioned here are involved in these three families of functions in different ways. The "actors × functions" cross-reference table is an analytical tool to be used with three geographies in mind: that of resources (including the site); that of the tourism offer; and that of visitor numbers, profiles, behavior and spending. Strategic functions are also interdependent (Pearce 2016), and more generally, the "actors × functions" cross-reference allows us to question the coherence of the system.

4.2. Case study

The main site taken into account in the Valo-Sites project is the perimeter of the "Chaîne des Puys–faille de Limagne" (CPFL) property as inscribed on the UNESCO World Heritage list, including its "buffer zone". The central zone is a group of 80 dormant volcanoes, aligned from north to south over a length of 32 km and a width of 4 km, above a Hercynian base at altitudes of between 700 m and 1,000 m. The whole area borders the Clermont-Ferrand urban area, separated by the Limagne fault.

The site is intensively visited by tourists and excursionists. A number of major attractions are offered to visitors, either in the form of one-off natural sites (emblematic volcanoes such as the Puy de Dôme or Pariou), or in the form of visitor attractions built and/or managed by companies (Vulcania, Lemptégy volcano, Panoramique des dômes train, Volvic spring, Grotte de la Pierre, etc.).

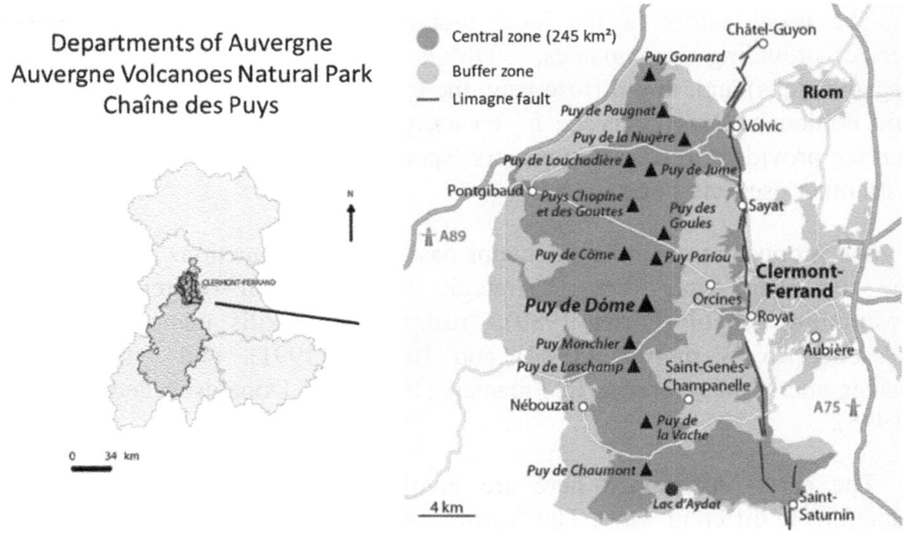

Figure 4.3. *Location of the Chaîne des Puys–faille de Limagne site and UNESCO listing zone*[1]*. For a color version of this figure, see www.iste.co.uk/christofle/tourism2.zip*

The sections of the Valo-Sites research project devoted to the tourism and leisure sector included (1) a study of visitor numbers, profiles, behavior and spending, with a major survey of visitors to the CPFL, and (2) an exploration of local tourism governance.

4.2.1. *Study on the visitors*

4.2.1.1. *Method*

The study was based on a face-to-face visitor survey, conducted at visit sites between May 2019 and February 2020. A total of 1,011 interviews

---

1 See: www.chainedespuys-failledelimagne.com.

were conducted, providing information on 2,894 visitors. The questioning focused in particular on their profiles, their behaviors (accommodation, activities and means of transport) and the geography of the latter (routes, places of accommodation and places of activities), their motivations and the part played by the CPFL in their choice of destination ("CPFL effect"), as well as the details of their expenses.

Estimating the CPFL's contribution to the reasons for tourist stays enables us to assess whether the CPFL is a primary, secondary or tertiary attraction for the tourist in question. We estimated a "CPFL effect coefficient in destination choices" (1, 0.75, 0.5, 0.25 or 0), depending on the visitor's answers to a direct question and a control question.

4.2.1.2. *Results concerning the nature and geography of visits and visitors*

Over 70% of annual visitors are tourists. Calculating the weight of the CPFL in tourists' choice of destination reveals a certain degree of dispersion: 63% of visitors chose their destination largely or mainly for the CPFL (coefficients greater than or equal to 0.5), and of these 27% chose their destination solely for the CPFL (case of so-called "primary attraction"). Note that 86% of these tourists stay in a single place. The proportion of short stays is quite high: 48% last from one to three nights. Two-thirds of tourists (66%) visit the site just once during their stay.

The geography of tourist activities is spread out over the entire site, from the major "one-off attractions" (Puy de Dôme summit, Vulcania, etc.) to the "secondary" volcanoes and other trails. The geography of accommodation shows that 90% of tourists stay in the Puy-de-Dôme county. This is the population that we are examining in greater detail.

We have chosen to refer to the territories of existing DMOs. There are eight in the county, five of which intersect with the site. The map (Figure 4.4) shows the contours of the *inter-municipalities* and the schematic contours of the site (dotted line).

The distributions of distances between tourist accommodation and the CPFL center (for illustrative purposes) are shown in Figure 4.5. The fact that more than 50% of visiting tourists stay more than 20 km, or even more than 40 km, from the site center, is significant.

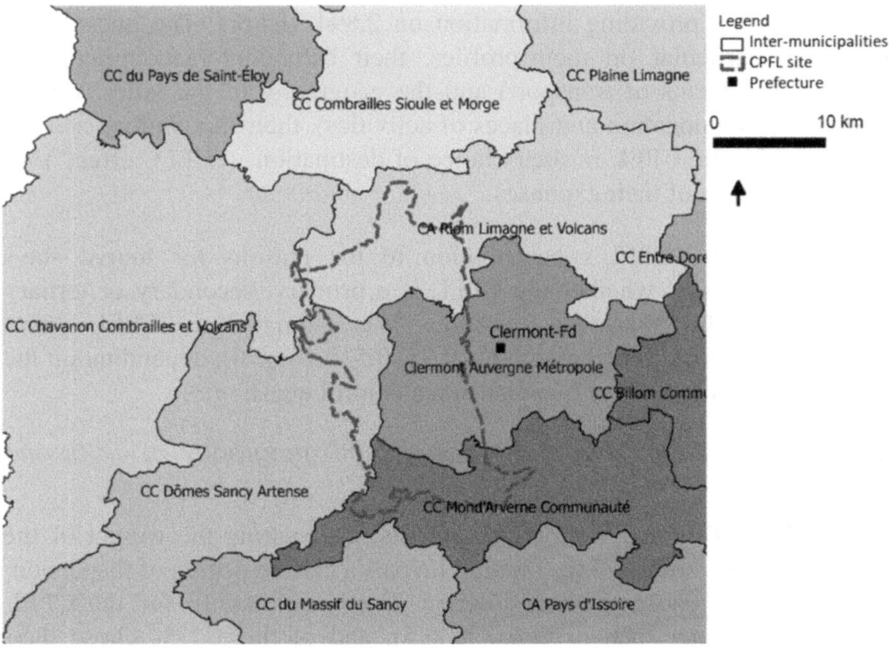

Figure 4.4. *Map of inter-municipalities and site outline, intersecting five of them. Production: Polge (sources: OpenStreetMap (inter-municipalities) and Puy-de-Dôme departmental council (UNESCO perimeter)). For a color version of this figure, see www.iste.co.uk/christofle/tourism2.zip*

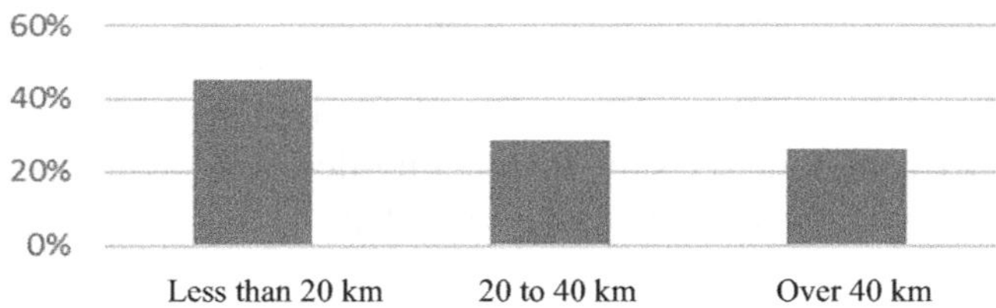

Figure 4.5. *Distribution of distances between tourist accommodation and CPFL center (source: authors)*

The distribution of places to stay is shown in Table 4.1, expressed either in number of tourists or in number of overnight stays.

We are concentrating our analysis on the two territories of Clermont Auvergne Métropole (CAM) and Massif du Sancy (Sancy), the main hosts for visitors to the CPFL. Each of these two areas has a wide range of attractions of all kinds and accommodation capacity. Ultimately, they see themselves as destinations-o in their own right.

DMOs (supporting intercommunities)	% of tourists	% of overnight stays
Clermont Auvergne Métropole (CAM)	36	25
CC of the Massif du Sancy	18	22
Itinerants	12	11
CA Riom Limagne and Volcans + CC Plaine Limagne	9	12
Three other DMOs intersecting with the CPFL	6	6–7
Other	7	10

Table 4.1. *Distribution of locations by DMO*

Estimating the share of visitors to the CPFL within the customer base of the destinations-o completes the analysis. For the CAM, this share, at 36% in 2019, is significant, given the many other attractions of this destination-o (business, culture, thermalism, etc.). For the Sancy, this share is 16% in 2021, but the Sancy includes three ski resorts. If winter is not taken into account, this share rises to 22%, making it very significant even though the CPFL does not intersect with this territory.

The particularity of the case study is as follows:

– The CPFL, as a whole, can be considered an attraction. For at least 27% of tourists visiting the area, it is a primary attraction in nature. It has little in the way of accommodation capacity, and this will not change much due to the site's protection.

– The CPFL intersects with the CAM area, but most of the accommodation noted in this area is not in the CPFL itself.

– The Massif du Sancy does not intersect with the CPFL, but still accounts for 22% of overnight stays by CPFL visitors.

– The CPFL is an attraction that needs to be strongly integrated into the strategies of the actors in these destinations-o, whether they intersect or not, as confirmed by the actors in the DMOs.

The diagram of possible configurations is shown in Figure 4.6.

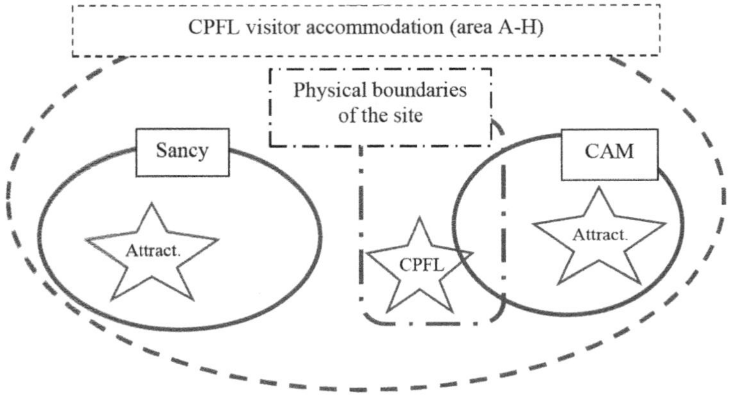

Figure 4.6. *Interconnection between the attraction of the CPFL site and the destinations-o of Clermont Auvergne Métropole (CAM) and the Massif du Sancy community of communes (Sancy) (production: Marsat)*

4.2.2. *The study of the management of the tourism system affected by attraction (the CPFL)*

The main functions involved in managing a tourist attraction or destination are identified here in simplified terms, with reference to the management of an economic organization. We will focus here on two main strategic functions: resource management and marketing.

4.2.2.1. *Managing resources and skills in the tourism system*

This function covers the following: (1) resources dedicated to tourism and leisure and (2) non-dedicated resources, shared with other purposes and uses. In the case of exceptional natural sites, the management of non-dedicated resources (space, landscapes, etc.) is essential for tourism. The site under study is protected by several systems, and its management is carried out according to the various features of these systems. In particular, a UNESCO "management plan" reflects the commitments and coordination of the main actors: the Puy-de-Dôme departmental council (CD63), the French government, the Auvergne Volcanoes Natural Park (PNR) and local authorities. It should be noted that (1) there is no single local actor responsible for overall management (such as a joint association) and

(2) three of the major actors involved in resource management operate on a territorial scale beyond the local level.

With regard to the collective management of resources dedicated to tourism and leisure, CD63 is involved in an unusual way, as owner of the Puy de Dôme volcano, developer of the volcano summit and owner of a cogwheel train to access it. The other facets of the management of dedicated resources are carried out by the DMOs, the PNR and the CD63, in particular to sensitize and train professionals, which has led to a specific action committing them to respect and promote the spirit of site management. In this way, a network can gradually be formed around these two site management actors, CD63 and PNR.

Lastly, interviews with all of the DMOs in the Puy-de-Dôme department confirmed that major tourist attractions other than the CPFL are present in the five territories intersecting with the site, and other tourist projects are logically in the process of being drawn up and developed. As far as tourism resources are concerned, each intercommunal territory is managed as a destination-o, with its own attractions and projects.

4.2.2.2. *Territorial and tourism marketing*

The UNESCO listing is generally recognized in terms of brand awareness and potential tourism promotion for listed sites, even though tourism development is not one of UNESCO's objectives. The CD63, which spearheaded the listing process, is de facto a major actor in this aspect of marketing. This contribution also comes under the heading of territorial marketing. Listing can benefit the image of the entire department, helping the area to attract residents and businesses and, for companies, helping them to recruit.

When it comes to marketing, there are several scales to consider. The 2019 visitor survey included a question: "where would you say you actually spend your [vacations]?", which was asked to the first half of the sample (500 responses). The results are only indicative, but show the following hierarchy (in number of responses): "Auvergne", "Puy-de-Dôme" and then "local name" (either of the DMOs/inter-municipal territory, or even of the accommodation commune).

At their own scale, the DMOs practice operational and more or less strategic marketing. The promotion of their territories highlights their various attractions, including the CPFL natural site (and also attractions in neighboring territories). A significant development in recent years has been the emergence of networking between DMOs. This collaboration involves joint marketing initiatives, customer observation and other exchanges of expertise. This marketing function also reflects the interconnection of different scales, with actions at local, network, departmental and interdepartmental levels.

4.2.2.3. *The multi-scale tourism management hypothesis: arguments and limitations*

The results outlined above suggest the possibility of tourism management, with certain functions carried out on a supra-local scale. This is already the case in terms of site management as a resource not dedicated to tourism. In the field of marketing, Auvergne's reputation and the role of the county are also noted. The interviewees expressed the wish to draw up a strategy encompassing several DMOs and the site, to look at whether an ad hoc structure is needed, etc.

However, formalizing this shift in scale in the form of an ad hoc structure would come up against another facet of the interconnection of attractions/sites-destinations-o: what has been observed for the Chaîne des Puys site can just as easily be observed around another major attraction. The result may even be a continuous paving of interconnected links. Which structures would satisfactorily encompass these overlaps? The answer depends on each case. Networking (Lazzeretti and Petrillo 2006; Pupion 2010) should also be considered as an alternative or as a complement, but this does not deter us from thinking about the design of the network.

4.3. Discussion – conclusion

The case study and the system formalization work together to shed light on a search for the best overall structuring and organization of tourism systems. The formalization we have suggested has two foundations: (1) spatial analysis, positioning places of practice (around attractions) and places of accommodation, then examining the areas defined by the actors as destinations; (2) analysis of the functions to be carried out for the management of a tourist destination, as for the management of an isolated attraction, examining the management of resources and their actors, and marketing and its actors, without forgetting the tourist.

This twofold approach highlights the theoretical possibility of overlaps between the areas concerned, at the local level, and the important interplay of actors from different scales. In many simple cases, a primary or secondary attraction is located within a destination-o, and the gradients of intensity (motivations, concerted action) as a function of distance, in particular, make it possible to neglect overflows between A-H areas and destinations-o. However, the case study of the CPFL site is particularly illustrative of overlaps, since the site is not a destination in itself, and its management – like certain tourist functions themselves – involves the county, the PNR and the state. Complex cases where several overlaps are juxtaposed in an even more extensive manner cannot be ruled out. Overall structuring and management must therefore combine the management of attractions, the boundaries, organization and management of destinations-o, and the art of multi-scale networking.

Various continuations are possible, such as the following:

– An in-depth study of the relationships between motivations for one or more attractions, practices (activities and accommodation) and their locations.

– Contributions to the supply-side approach, down to the level of tourism service providers, for example, by situating each service provider (especially accommodation providers) in relation to the attractions that "concern" them to varying degrees (their "attractions capital").

– All extensions on multi-sector (tourism, heritage and others) and multi-scale governance.

4.4. References

Badot, O. and Lemoine, J.-F. (2015). Élargissement des principes de l'attractivité commerciale à ceux de l'attractivité touristique : le cas de La Vallée Village à Marne-la-Vallée. *Management avenir*, 3, 187–203.

Barney, J. (1991). Firm resources and sustained competitive advantage. *Journal of Management*, 17(1), 99–120.

Botti, L. (2010). Pour une gestion de la touristicité des territoires : stratégie collective et management de l'attractivité. PhD Thesis, Université Montpellier-I, Montpellier.

Butler, R.W. (2009). Tourism destination development: Cycles and forces, myths and realities. *Tourism Recreation Research*, 34(3), 247–254.

De Grandpré, F. (2009). Modélisation du système touristique régional (MTR) : application québécoise. *Tourisme et territoire*, 1(1), 6–66.

Donaldson, T. and Preston, L.E. (1995). The stakeholder theory of the corporation: Concepts, evidence, and implications. *Academy of Management Review*, 20(1), 65–91.

Dredge, D. and Jenkins, J. (2003). Destination place identity and regional tourism policy. *Tourism Geographies*, 5(4), 383–407.

Flagestad, A. and Hope, C.A. (2001). Strategic success in winter sports destinations: A sustainable value creation perspective. *Tourism Management*, 22(5), 445–461.

Freeman, R.E. (1984). *Strategic Management: A Stakeholder Approach*. Pitman, Boston.

Haugland, S.A., Ness, H., Gronseth, B.-O., Aarstad, J. (2011). Development of tourism destinations – An integrated multilevel perspective. *Annals of Tourism Research*, 38(1), 268–290.

Klarić, Z., Weber, S., Marušić, Z. (2002). The use of regional analysis of tourism resources for destination zone identification in Croatia. *Tourism*, 50(2), 157–164.

Laws, E. (1995). *Tourist Destination Management: Issues, Analysis, and Policies*. Routledge, London.

Lazzeretti, L. and Petrillo, C.S. (2006). *Tourism Local Systems and Networking*. Elsevier, New York.

Leiper, N. (1990). Tourist attraction systems. *Annals of Tourism Research*, 17(3), 367–384.

Lew, A.A. (1987). A framework of tourist attraction research. *Annals of Tourism Research*, 14(4), 553–575.

Lew, A.A. and McKercher, B. (2006). Modeling tourist movements: A local destination analysis. *Annals of Tourism Research*, 33(2), 403–423.

Lue, C.-C., Crompton, J.L., Fesenmaier, D.R. (1993). Conceptualization of multi-destination pleasure trips. *Annals of Tourism Research*, 20(2), 289–301.

Marsat, J.-B., Guerra, F., Lépinay, T. (2010). Management stratégique de destination touristique et management territorial – Le cas du massif du Sancy. In *XLVIIè Colloque de l'Association de Science Régionale de Langue Française (ASRDLF)*. ASRDLF, Aoste.

Morley, C., Rosselló, J., Santana-Gallego, M. (2014). Gravity models for tourism demand: Theory and use. *Annals of Tourism Research*, 48(0), 1–10.

Murphy, P., Pritchard, M.P., Smith, B. (2000). The destination product and its impact on traveller perceptions. *Tourism Management*, 21(1), 43–52.

Pearce, D. (2016). Interdependent destination management functions. *Tourism Recreation Research*, 41(1), 37–48.

Piriou, J. (2011). Le haut-lieu touristique : un cadre d'analyse de l'excellence d'une destination. *Téoros – Revue de recherche en tourisme*, 30(1), 25–32.

Porter, M.E. (1980). Industry structure and competitive strategy: Keys to profitability. *Financial Analysts Journal*, 36(4), 30–41. doi: 10.2469/faj.v36.n4.30.

Pupion, P.C. (2010). Tourisme durable et valorisation de l'environnement du littoral aquitain : diversité et stratégies des acteurs. *Management & avenir*, 34(4), 289–305.

Roy, B. (2002). Robustesse de quoi et vis-à-vis de quoi mais aussi robustesse pourquoi en aide à la décision. *Newsletter of the European Working Group Multicriteria Aid for Decisions*, 3(6), 1–6.

Violier, P. (2009). Proposition pour un modèle d'analyse dynamique des lieux touristiques. In *Destinations et territoires*, Lemasson, J.-P. and Violier, P. (eds). Presses de l'Université du Québec, Quebec.

Wernerfelt, B. (1984). A resource-based view of the firm. *Strategic Management Journal*, 5, 171–180.

5

Collective Agility at the Heart of Tourism Development in Hauts-de-France During the Covid Period

The Hauts-de-France (HDF) region's tourism economy is a major fact, with almost 21.3 million visitors expected to visit the region's tourist attractions in 2022 (according to the Hauts de France tourism 2023 report), and a wide range of tourist attractions, products and services on offer, including the Parc Astérix, Louvre-Lens, Château de Chantilly, listed seaside resorts on the Côte d'Opale, the Baie de Somme and the Great War sites. The region boasts a total of 1,000 cultural and leisure sites, including 84 museums, five UNESCO World Heritage sites and 134 classified sites, five national monuments, five regional nature parks and two "grands sites de France". During the pandemic, the HDF region maintained its local appeal, according to data from the Comité régional du tourisme et des congrès (CRTC). Tourism attractiveness will be defined here both by the HDF's ability to retain its own inhabitants as tourists, and by its ability to attract tourists from other French regions. The region ranks second out of thirteen in terms of tourist attractiveness – national and inter-regional tourism – with major direct and indirect economic benefits, that is to say, 6.2 billion euros in tourist consumption and 4% of regional GDP (CRTC 2023 numbers).

The aim of this chapter is to understand how institutional and noninstitutional players in the tourism sector were able to innovate and/or

---

Chapter written by Sandrine FOURNIER.

rethink the tourism offer to maintain the HDF's attractiveness during the pandemic in a collective agile approach that promoted the region.

To do this, we looked at a large panel of companies (489) in the region's five departments over a pre-containment and post-containment period. The tourism activities selected fell into three main categories: category 1: hotels and restaurants; category 2: museums and historic sites; category 3: parks, nature reserves and recreational activities.

To complete this first stage, direct observations at the facilities were carried out, combined with additional interviews after the complete reopening in April 2022, so as to observe the various operational and organizational practices and solutions for relaunching business.

We will present this work based on the following points:

1) enhancing the value of the "HDF" destination;

2) agility for tourism players: adapt, develop, innovate;

3) digital enhancement and agility;

4) promotional synergy between official operators/professionals and tourism and citizens/tourists;

5) three-party promotion by official and unofficial players via digitalization.

5.1. Promoting the "HDF destination" in the region

The question of the HDF region's attractiveness to tourists is particularly topical. Indeed, the region is said to suffer from a "nontourist vision of Northern France", or even a negative image due to a lack of knowledge of the area or a climate deemed less attractive than that of other French regions. On the contrary, we believe that the HDF's attractiveness is based on three pillars: the productive aspect, the residential aspect and the tourism aspect, all of which are gradually being enhanced by institutional bodies.

Since the new territorial organization of the management of tourist areas (NOTRe law 2015), the various local players have become major stakeholders in the communication of destinations to be promoted as resources (Gundolf et al. 2006). They work to promote tourism and support the appeal of the HDF destination, including on a local scale (Perrat and Zimmermann 2003). They have considerable resources and scope for action, enabling them to pursue an efficient enhancement strategy – infra-regional and extra-regional image – through the implementation of targeted and varied promotional tools.

With the creation of the *Mission attractivité* in 2017, entitled "la Mission attractivité Hauts-de-France-Comité régional du tourisme et des congrès" (Hauts-de-France regional committee of tourism et congress attractiveness mission), the territory is seen as a "marketing" product (Papadopoulos and Heslop 2002). The mission is tasked with supporting the attractiveness and outreach policy by integrating a cross-functional approach to improve assets and advise the region's professional players. The region's marketing strategy involves providing assistance and advice to local authorities, so that they can promote their assets.

Since the July 1, 2019 regulations – Articles L.133-11 and L.133-12 of the Tourism Code – every local authority can apply for a "tourist commune" or "classified tourist resort" label with a five-year validity by prefectoral decree. Selection criteria take into account innovations and new tourist needs, including new technologies and activities. Using the interactive map on the website of the French Ministry of Economy, Finance and Economic Recovery, we have identified 29 resorts or towns in the HDF region that have been awarded the tourism label, out of 400 nationwide: Pas-de-Calais (18 sites), Somme (seven sites), Nord (three sites) and Oise (one site).

After this overview of the "world just before" the pandemic, we will be looking at the "world after" (Davezies 2021), with a particular focus on the use of digital technology to enhance tourism value.

5.2. The agility of tourism players: adapt, develop and innovate

Many terms are used to explain the notions of internal and external flexibility, adaptability, agility and innovation (Barrand 2006). These are strategic and organizational responses to change.

In the wake of the Covid-19 shock, uncertainty and turbulence have demanded a high degree of adaptability from tourism players in the face of unprecedented urgency (Dautun et al. 2006). To operate as normally as possible, companies need to adopt proactive behaviors (Mikušová and Horváthová 2019) and combine agile practices (Deharo 2018). Thus, levels of flexibility, anticipation or adaptation (Marchais-Roubelat and Lengagne 2021) will correlate with the manager's creative behaviors (Powell and Baker 2011).

It is about creating new capabilities or opportunities (Altintas 2020) to differentiate ourselves from the competition. This capacity for innovation primarily depends on the agility of unit managers. After absorbing the shock of the pandemic, companies in the tourism sector were able to partly renew themselves.

Some absorbed the shock without making substantial changes to the structure or organization, through passive behavior, while others adapted through active behavior (Akgun and Keskin 2014) and proactive innovation through anticipation (Hamel and Välikangas 2003).

Choosing to remain a player in the tourism ecosystem during this period of crisis depended on a combination of variables. Cash reserves, financial capacity and/or subsidies all play a part in a company's level of adaptability. The personalities of managers, their values such as attachment to their business and the relationship with their territory through heritage, traditions, the expression of its culture and its identity to be defended (Batat 2016), are all part of the conditions for remaining players in tourism, through the adoption of more or less agile behaviors.

The Covid crisis has modified the notion of agility. While previous research allowed us to model this agility (Marchais-Roubelat and Lengagne 2021) in a process of anticipation, the pandemic required rapid, unplanned reactions. We could associate the ability of organizations to survive, remain flexible and adapt quickly with strategic agility (Shams et al. 2021).

5.3. Adding value and agility through digitalization

To promote and enhance a region as a tourism offering, integrating digitalization is seen as enriching factor in the value of the offer. We distinguish three stages: upstream, in other words, when choosing a destination; during the stay, with the evolution of digital tools during visits; and lastly, downstream, to remember the trip.

Digitalization is perceived as an aspect of the value of the tourist site, the local private offer and the interaction between tourists. The potential tourist, or tourist, integrates the use of digital tools before, during and after in their choice process. According to Neuhofer et al. (2012), the user integrates this triple-aspect into the perception and value of the tourism offer.

Three approaches can be identified here:

– The first focuses on length-of-stay forecasting (Arnould et al. 2002).

– The second focuses on the use of digital tools to enrich the customer experience (Rivière and Bourliataux-Lajoinie 2017).

– The third relates to digitization during the stay (Kim and Law 2015) or even after the stay by recalling the experience. This approach is directly in line with a B to C (business to consumer) logic.

The use of tourism applications such as “Somme en poche” facilitates the customer experience. The numerous QR codes on the sites offer contextual content to enrich the tourist experience without generating visual pollution.

The second approach focuses on providing tools for destination management organizations (DMOs) and local authorities. This B to B approach provides local stakeholders with a range of digital resources such as information platforms (Molinillo et al. 2018), reporting tools and tourist tracking. These tools analyze habits via smartphones and are used to share high value-added information (e.g. sending a personalized destination offer based on searches performed). The use of these practices has given rise to the concept of smart tourism, a form of tourism that combines digital solutions and eco-responsible values based on customer experience and virtual and augmented reality. Although the latter has been criticized (Femenia-Serra and Ivars-Baidal 2021), it remains a fundamental tool for enhancing the value of tourist sites and optimizing costs.

The last approach formalizes the use of digital technology to deal with a crisis situation. This last case is particularly important in the context of this study. The opportunistic reaction may be linked to an exogenous variable (as in the case of a pandemic), and corporate reactions are more often than not focused on managing communication and promoting services. In our case, we were able to observe tourist sites developing digital communication on social networks to highlight their offers or propose new services, such as online booking or real-time information.

5.4. Promotional synergy between official operators/tourism professionals and citizens/tourists

The issue of co-constructing tourism promotion (Clergeau and Violier 2013) is strategic for a destination, with impact on transport, hotels and restaurants, culture, leisure activities and so on (Delaplace 2021).

When it comes to promoting a territory, we need to take a broader view and see it as a place of life (Chamard and Schenkler 2017), of projects, of individual and personal experiences, of a collective identity co-constructed by all: its users and stakeholders. The promotion of a tourism offering or destination uses a range of private (the various tourism sites and monuments, accommodation providers, etc.) and public (the CRTC, tourist offices, DTCs) companies that intervene in a complementary way and cooperate to offer a homogeneous benefit to future tourists.

As the tourism offer evolves into the era of hyper-connectivity, new player profiles (entrepreneurs and start-ups) emerge, bringing about new interactions and organizational practices (Zaoual 2008), notably with a national network of incubators and accelerators dedicated to supporting digital tourism start-ups. In addition to these new entrants – the providers of digital tourism offerings – there are also the online communities of tourists who contribute to the co-creation and co-design of destinations between clusters of travelers and visitors (Bourlon 2020), by publishing photos and feedback on their tourist destinations. The key to a destination's attractiveness lies in coordinating the actions of these heterogeneous players, structuring their interactions, fostering their complementarities and generating synergies (Haller and Aldebert 2019).

How can or should official structures or local authorities manage their exchanges and contributions in order to control the region's e-reputation and its attractiveness?

The question of collective, participative and collaborative co-constructed promotion arises. Internet users (citizens and/or tourists) produce a value, a resource, free of charge (Dimitrova 2015) and share their actions and data through a blog or social network (Cardon and Prieur 2021). This real-life sharing, known as collaborative tourism, is set to change the way a destination is promoted.

To conclude this section, we would like to point out that the co-construction and co-creation of content via digital tools by all stakeholders work to promote destinations as tourist destinations.

5.5. Methodology, results and discussion

5.5.1. *Methodology*

We took an interest in a large population of companies in the tourism sector in the HDF region. To build up the sample, the method of selecting items by a sub-sector of activity was used based on the central database of the Chamber of Commerce and Industry. For the sake of internal and external validity (Shadish et al. 2002), a homogeneous selection was made from all of the companies identified as being involved in tourism.

In the first stage, a semi-directive questionnaire was carried out by telephone interview, with the aim of identifying ways of reinventing (agility) and organizing. The interview guide consisted of open and closed questions, designed to ascertain the way in which the target establishments had or had not redeployed their activities.

In a second phase, additional face-to-face interviews were conducted in April 2022 with different professionals from the first phase, focusing on two main questions: have you considered a plan to revive your business? Which operational, organizational or commercial solutions have you modified? This was in two respects:

– internally: sequencing of activities, development of a new business or online activity;

– externally: call for solidarity from Internet users or friends, collaborative tools and platforms, maintaining links with customers.

Thirdly, we conducted interviews with our contacts, such as CRTC and tourist office managers, to integrate their strategies, which involved technical advice, marketing and technical assistance they provided to tourism players during the pandemic.

Lastly, for the duration of the pandemic, we monitored and analyzed the press, CRTC, RTC and Chamber of Commerce and Industry websites in order to keep as exhaustive a record as possible of tourism projects and innovations.

5.5.2. *The agility of professional players in HDF*

An analysis of the results reveals two categories of respondents: pessimists, representing 251 out of 489 establishments, and optimists, representing 238 establishments, with varying degrees of agility, resistance and proactive behavior in the face of the pandemic.

Among these two categories, we will focus on companies described as being optimistic, and distinguish three types of adjustment strategies, which we will present here:

– Those who have not implemented any changes and maintained their strategy or offer, in other words, a majority of 132 out of the 238 establishments: "we have tried click and collect, but it is not profitable, there is too much upstream work and new costs (packaging) to manage" (Brasserie, Nord, April 2021).

– Those that are holding out, with 68 out of 238 establishments. They plan ahead and restructure, temporarily adapting to the offer or undertaking diversification activities (inter-trade collaboration, takeaway sales on pitches offered by local authorities on local markets): "we offer an escape game on the site, which opens us up to new customers" (Campsite, April 2021).

– The fewest, with 38 out of 238 sites. These take advantage of the opportunity to rethink, transform and innovate by anticipating and implementing important changes: creating a website, purchasing bicycles and creating a book of available walks, often resulting in major renovation work, provided that financing is available. "We now use 'Hypolite' to manage online bookings, which is more convenient for customers".

We counted four changes of activity from the start of the Covid crisis, for example, the sale of the restaurant to buy a food truck, the transformation of a high-end establishment into a brasserie, including a takeaway option, or several end-of-career anticipations, passing the business on to children or through sales or definitive closures.

5.5.3. *The adaptability of official operators/tourism professionals and citizens/tourists*

The world of information monitoring we adopted throughout the pandemic enabled us to highlight changes, partnerships or business creations from private structures (for example, the creation of escape games for several towns: Dunkirk, Lille, Arras) or public ones with differentiated agile practices (deployment of QR codes on tourist sites).

We have identified several types of agility:

– institutional agility (site improvements, virtual games created by teams during confinements or imposed by the drop in activity);

– organizational agility from professionals (creation of their own websites or network accounts) and the advent of new businesses based on virtual offerings;

– agility from citizens (more and more people are creating accounts on networks, such as Wake up Amiens and Lille addict).

In this agility, each of the players or professionals plays a role in the digital attractiveness of the region (see Figure 5.1). Furthermore, a new role for tourism operators is emerging (monitoring and consulting strategy, see legend: dotted arrows). They have to deal with new entrants (tourism entrepreneurs), who offer their digital services directly via m-tourism (web and mobile).

In a bid to make the initiatives of private companies more visible, public institutional operators such as the Regional Tourism Committee (RTC), Departmental Tourism Committees (DTC) and Tourist Offices (TO) are progressively following the creation of digital concepts or virtual realities, in order to assist them and make them visible on their official sites or at points of welcome.

Examples include treasure hunts (Enigmamiens), the Instagrammable ephemeral museum at Westfield Euralille and the "Goya Experience" exhibition at the Lille Museum of Fine Arts.

We will now discuss the cumulative collective agility of citizens, tourists, professionals and official bodies.

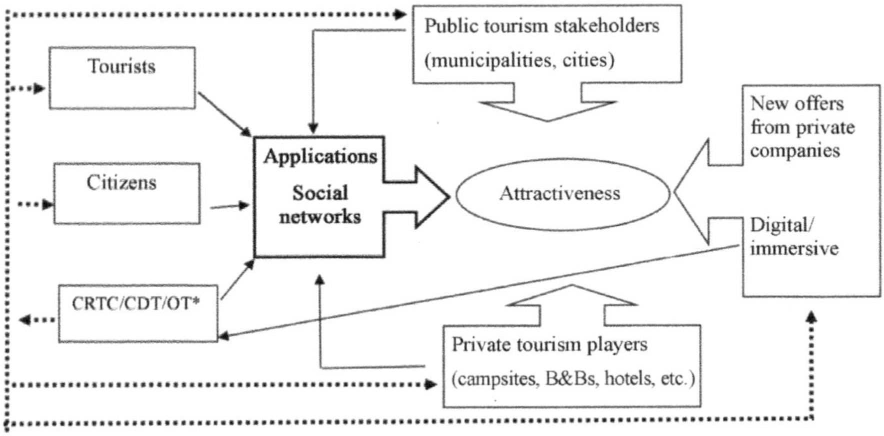

*Regional tourism committee, departmental tourism committee, tourist office

Legend: ···► *CRTC/DTC/TO network watch mode or application adapted to new behaviors (citizens/tourists/digital companies/communities) plus a guiding and advisory role*

Figure 5.1. *Collective agility and interrelations in stakeholder-driven tourism development (author: Fournier 2023)*

5.5.4. *Agility of regional, departmental and local tourism organizations*

As we saw in the previous section, the support strategies implemented by the HDF region's CRTC to maintain tourism attractiveness are multi-faceted and multi-level. The DMO has not only supported and guided professionals and local authorities (community of communes, communes, etc.) but has also adapted to their new targets of local tourists and new needs (wellness, nature, family) by adjusting and modifying its offers (sailing on the Somme, cycle routes, etc.).

The CRTC has stepped up its contacts with tourism professionals and players to support them and respond to their requests for change, including advising them on how to promote their tourism offers and/or services, notably with the contribution of a web marketer to facilitate the digital transition of professionals. The DMO's assistance has also helped guide the various players toward brand evolution, thanks to requests for certification, or toward digital openness through the creation or improvement of digital tools (creation of websites), or changes to offers in line with evolving expectations (development of unusual accommodation).

To give tourism players visibility and keep pace with the e-tourism trends expected by tourists, the CRTC's strategy has been to instill two parallel strategies: both digital referencing, with the assistance mentioned above, and ensuring the positioning of each player in the HDF "Haut et Fort" regional brand, by verifying marketing positioning with the help of DTCs and TOs. For example, on the "Hauts-de-France tourisme" website, tourists will be able to find all professionals by theme and sub-category. In the theme of well-being, tourists will find three sub-categories: sylvotherapy, sophrologie in the Somme Bay, sophrologie, and then in each of the windows, proposals with listings. During the pandemic, a huge amount of structuring work was carried out to promote the tourism industry and rethink its image.

Since the end of the pandemic in October 2022 (Figure 5.2), the marketing slogan for HDF tourism has evolved with a new brand: "Hauts-de-France tourisme, la générosité naturelle"[1], announced with a new name for CRTC "Hauts-de-France tourisme".

These operations were combined by areas with a verification and advice on how to join tourist labels (classified resorts and communes, towns and villages in bloom, tourism and disabilities), classifications (gîtes de France, Clévacances, ecolabels), various networks (SBP: Somme Battlefields' Partner; Accueil Vélo; Bistrot de Pays; etc.) and ensure visibility on the Internet.

In addition to logistical support for the digital transition and referencing on the CRTC platform, we have identified two types of additional public and private support:

– Public funding provided by local tourism development agencies supported by the region, and the creation of a tourism innovation accelerators in collaboration with France tourisme lab in 2020, or the creation of the "Tangente" project. This is a tourism innovation agency

1 Translation: "Hauts-de-France tourism, natural generosity".

subsidized by the Nord department to support the development of tourism microclusters. All of this public funding has contributed to the development of untapped areas such as river tourism, building restoration and the construction of an innovative 2.0 amusement park, "Picard IA" (opened in April 2022).

– Support for financing private entrepreneurial projects has been maintained despite the crisis, through the "Village by CA Nord de France" network. The plan is to imagine and set up local projects that are adapted, creative and innovative. Here are just a few examples: "Cocotte food tour", a gourmet adventure application with self-guided tours; the deployment of "Hootside" in the HDF region, an augmented reality experience based on the Asterix comic and linked with local tourist sites; or the eco-responsible "Setavoo" applications, which target natural areas and provide real-time information on beaches, with a focus on environmental protection.

5.5.5. *Interrelations between official operators/tour operators and citizens/tourists*

To boost attractiveness, official players are increasingly using digital tools or applications to distribute tourist information via mobile telephones (Petr 2010).

Mobile tourism (m-tourism) takes the form of scannable QR codes (documents, maps, images and videos for download), real-time content-sharing platforms via geolocated services and applications with informative content (maps, events and guides) and ratings (comments, 0–5 star ratings).

The longitudinal analysis of tourism operators has enabled us to observe the greater flexibility, anticipation and adaptation of the DTC of the Somme compared to other DTCs. The DTC has radically restructured its strategy, media and tools to create a shared digital offering, rethought by and for tourism players, tourists and citizens (web surfers, bloggers and others).

Certain additional agile capabilities (Mercanti-Guérin 2013) were required to adapt to the distance, new expectations and new typology of tourists as the pandemic progressed.

Figure 5.2. *Examples of logos (source: Somme tourisme). For a color version of this figure, see www.iste.co.uk/christofle/tourism2.zip*

A number of combined and interlocking strategies have been implemented, involving the deployment of digital interfaces on the Internet and on networks that are accessible and user friendly. One of the first steps in the move to e-tourism and social media was to recruit a community manager.

– The first strategy focuses on disseminating a strong brand image based on values and themes, using keywords and color codes (disconnect: blue; enjoy: yellow; contemplate: pink; remember: red; breathe: green), with the creation of logos (Go Somme). These graphic representations of brand recognition are to be used by all professionals and enthusiasts in publications (Figure 5.2).

– The second is focused on the policy of developing thematic tourism networks that are relayed to social networks, for example, "Somme digital" with the creation of several thematic accounts, such as a website (see: www.somme-tourisme.com), Instagram and Twitter accounts (Somme 14–18, Somme tourisme) and Facebook accounts (Somme tourisme with 98,000 fans, Great War Centenary in the Somme with 49,474 fans, etc.) to share and disseminate.

– The third is focused on social media, with a specific "pro" tab on the general DTC website, which was expanded during the pandemic. The organization offers technical assistance for professionals to create or improve their communication supports and master digital fundamentals with advice, a training offer (10€ for the year) to increase their readability via networks, or learn how to post podcasts.

– The fourth strategy focuses on collaborative tourism via citizen and tourist networks and blogs, with a strategic intelligence approach and contracting. In an attempt to control real-life sharing and collaboration by citizens and travelers, the DTC is proposing bipartite commitment agreements. Internet users (influencers) commit to publishing content (photo/video/story/post, etc.) on at least one of its RSNs per day of presence on the territory, with clear identification of the tourism markers (logos, goodies) and the partnership with Somme tourisme. In return, the DTC endeavors to cover expenses (accommodation, visits and travel) in the region during the blog trip, with the provision of a road book (the DTC retains the option of not publishing the content). Lastly, with regard to the management of citizen influencers, a manager pointed out during our discussions that some shots are so attractive that the DTC buys them and uses them for the tourist office websites in the area concerned, or to offer them as downloadable wallpapers.

5.5.6. *Discussion*

The health crisis seems to have been conducive to reflection and awareness, with a change in expectations, particularly among tourists, and the discovery or rediscovery of their tourist surroundings by local residents, with the development of local tourism.

For industry professionals, uncertainty initially dampened the desire to act, to adapt with a minimal level of agility and innovation. Gradually, and in response to the need for distance learning, professionals began to reconfigure their offers or supports through agile practices in response to the changing world (digital and more ecological tourism) with the support of the CRTC. A general policy of individual and collective rebuilding by public bodies and professionals was thus implemented, so as to face the crisis and anticipate new solutions. The "slack" period of the pandemic enabled tourism operators to rethink their offer to meet the expectations of tourists (new profiles and retention of old ones, etc.) through innovative (increased digitization) or more traditional motives for action (search for authenticity, care and ethical and unusual tourism). In other words, this study focused on the HDF region has enabled us to understand the innovative and digital cross-actions instigated by institutional bodies, professionals, citizens and tourists, which form a value chain (Fabry and Zeghni 2012).

The crisis has "imposed" an accelerated shift for many tour operators in the HDF region toward e-commerce practices (online reservations, use of digital interfaces) to maintain or boost the region's attractiveness. The tourism offer has also opened up to new entrants in the digital and augmented reality markets, thanks to private and public partnerships (Zaoual 2008). Ultimately, this study confirms the agility and flexibility of all stakeholders, including citizens and tourists, in times of crisis. We highlight the impact of online collaborative practices by citizens and tourists on networks as an additional challenge for the attractiveness of the region. We reveal the particularity of the new strategic role of supporting tourism operators (CRTC, DTC and TO) in the HDF region through the contract commitments of citizens and/or tourists.

5.6. Conclusion

By demonstrating their adaptability and agility, the players, service providers and professionals in the tourism industry have moved toward sustainable, collaborative digital tourism. They have been able to innovate and catch up with regions that are considered directly "touristic" in the collective minds of the public.

Thanks to support policies, private and public partnerships and the pooling of information (professionals, citizens and tourists), all stakeholders have been able to respond to the new types of tourist and changing expectations. The accelerated switch to digitalization during the pandemic ensured and enhanced the region's visibility and appeal.

5.7. References

Akgun, A.E. and Keskin, H. (2014). Organisational resilience capacity and firm product innovativeness and performance. *International Journal of Production Research*, 52(23), 6918–6937.

Altintas, G. (2020) . La capacité dynamique de résilience : l'aptitude à faire face aux événements perturbateurs du macro-environnement. *Management & avenir*, 115(1), 113–133.

Arnould, E.J., Price, L., Zinkhan, G.M. (2002). *Consumers*, 2nd edition. McGraw Hill, New York.

Barrand, J. (2006). *Le Manager agile, vers un nouveau management pour affronter la turbulence*. Dunod, Paris.

Batat, W. (2016). *Marketing territorial expérientiel*. Éditions Ellipses, Paris.

Bourlon, F. (2020). Quel tourisme pour les confins de nature dans un monde en crise ? Perspectives depuis la Patagonie chilienne. *Téoros*, 39(3) [Online]. Available at: http://journals.openedition.org/teoros/5572.

Cardon, D. and Prieur, C. (2021). La sociabilité peut-elle s'exhiber dans l'espace public numérique ? In *Les liens sociaux numériques*, Martin, O. (ed.). Armand Colin, Paris.

Chamard, C. and Schlenker, L. (2017). La place du marketing territorial dans le processus de transformation territoriale. *Gestion et management public*, 6(1), 41–57.

Clergeau, C. and Violier, P. (2013). Les enjeux particuliers des clusters tourisme. *Espaces*, 312, 15–24.

Dautun, C., Tixier, J., Chapelain, J., Fontaine, F., Dusserre, G. (2006). Le traitement de l'incertitude en gestion de crise : mise en place d'une veille stratégique du territoire. In *Colloque de maîtrise des risques et sureté de fonctionnement "risques et performances"*, Lille.

Davezies, L. (2021). *L'Etat a toujours soutenu ses territoires, sciences humaines*. Le Seuil, Paris.

Deharo, G. (2018). Le droit, un outil du management agile ? Une perspective juridico gestionnaire. *Revue française de gestion*, 272(3), 33–49.

Delaplace, M. (2021). Après la crise, un tourisme durable ? *L'Économie politique*, 91(3), 8–22.

Dimitrova, S., Cardon, D., Casilli, A.A. (2016). Qu'est-ce que le digital labor ? *Questions de communication*, 30(2), 407–409.

Fabry, N. and Zigani, S. (2012). Tourisme et développement local : une application aux clusters de tourisme. *Mondes en développement*, 1(157), 97–110.

Féminisa-Serra, F. and Ivars-Baidal, J.A. (2021). Do smart tourism destinations really work? The case of Benidorm. *Asia Pacific Journal of Tourism Research*, 26(4), 365–384.

Gundolf, K., Jaouen, A., Loup, S. (2006). Institutions locales et TPE dans le cas du tourisme. *Revue française de gestion*, 167(8), 141–155.

Haller, C. and Aldebert, B. (2019). Entrepreneuriat et tourisme : enjeux et perspectives. In *La recherche en management du tourisme*, Clergeau, C. (ed.). Vuibert, Paris.

Hamel, G. and Valikangas, L. (2003). The quest for resilience. *Harvard Business Review*, 81(9), 52–65.

Kim, H.H. and Law, R. (2015). Smartphones in tourism and hospitality marketing: A literature review. *Journal of Travel & Tourism Marketing*, 32(6), 692–711.

Marchais-Roubelat, A. and Lengagne, O. (2021). Pratiques de résilience organisationnelle et crise : anticipation ou adaptation ? In *XXXème conférence de l'AIMS*, Paris.

Mikušová, M. and Horváthová, P. (2019). Prepared for a crisis? Basic elements of crisis management in an organization. *Economic Research*, 32(1), 1844–1868.

Molinillo, S., Liebana-Cabanillas, F., Anaya-Sanchez, R., Buhalis, D. (2018). DMO online platforms: Image and intention to visit. *Tourism Management*, 65, 116–130.

Neuhofer, B., Buhalis, D., Ladkin, A. (2012). Conceptualising technology enhanced destination experiences. *Journal of Destination Marketing & Management*, 1(1/2), 36–46.

Papadopoulos, N. and Heslop, L. (2002). Country equity and country branding: Problems and prospects. *Journal of Brand Management*, 9, 294–314.

Perrat, J. and Zimmermann, J.B. (2003). Stratégies des firmes et dynamiques des territoires. In *Entreprises et territoires*, Dupuy, C. and Burmeister, A. (eds). La Documentation française, Paris.

Petr, C. (2010). E-tourisme : l'influence des technologies de l'information sur le consommateur. In *Le tourisme consommateur*, Decrop, A. (ed.). De Boeck, Brussels.

Powell, E.E. and Baker, T. (2011). Beyond making do: Toward a theory of entrepreneurial resourcefulness. In *Frontiers of Entrepreneurship Research*. Babson College, Wellesley.

Rivière, A. and Bourliataux-Lajoinie, S. (2017). Les effets des m-services touristiques sur la proposition de valeur d'une ville. *Décisions Marketing*, 85(1), 101–119.

Sham, R., Vrontis, D., Belvaeva, Z., Ferraris, A., Czinkota, M.R. (2021). Strategic agility in international business: A conceptual framework for "agile" multinationals. *Journal of International Management*, 27(1), 1–10.

Zaoual, H. (2008). Présentation générale : innovation et dynamiques de proximité. Une clef de lecture. *Marché et organisations*, 7(2), 5–16.

PART 2

Sustainability: A Challenge for Tourism Agility?

6

Managing Visitor Numbers: A Public Policy Challenge for Preserving and Enhancing our Natural Heritage

At a time when the space-time of tourists has changed, leading some to speak of a third tourism revolution[1] (Violier 2016), some tourist locations are experiencing high levels of tension. Various forms of opposition to tourism are emerging, revealing the disruption of the "inhabitants/tourists contract"[2] (Duhamel 2023) in these territories.

The democratization of a large number of outdoor activities, the development of local leisure activities and social networks, have all contributed to an increase in tourist and recreational uses[3] of certain protected natural sites. This increase in visitor numbers is disruptive to the

Chapter written by Émeline HATT and Sylvie CLARIMONT.

For a color version of all figures in this chapter, see www.iste.co.uk/christofle/tourism2.zip.

1 This is particularly characterized by strong growth in tourist mobility (driven by globalization and the emergence of new clienteles), a change in the "values" of the world and therefore in tourist attitudes/practices (with new expectations such as off-the-beaten-track forms of tourism) and a renewed quest for attractiveness.

2 This disruption is characterized by the emergence of tourism, aided by the digital revolution (development of the Internet and social networks), the seasonal adjustment of tourist practices (temporal extension) and increased proximity between residents and tourists ("living conflict").

3 We prefer to use the plural to express the diversity of "visitor number" modalities linked to the plurality of users (locals, day-trippers and tourists) and recreational uses (mountain biking, walking, hunting, fishing, etc.) in natural sites.

environment and raises a number of issues, including conflicts of use and how to anticipate or resolve them by regulating flows.

Strong media coverage of "over-tourism" and "over-visiting" of certain tourist locations, following a global health crisis which resulted in several periods of confinement, has led to this issue being placed higher on the political agenda. In June 2023, the French Ministry of the Economy, Finance and Industrial and Digital Sovereignty launched a plan to manage tourist flows, followed by a call for expressions of interest in October, issued by Atout France on the same subject.

However, flow management is particularly difficult to implement in open natural spaces (unlike museums, monuments or archaeological sites), with their multiple "entrances" rarely marked by physical boundaries, and which are also understood by their visitors as areas of free access.

This represents a major challenge for managers of natural areas, who are often protected under various laws (with a juxtaposition of protection figures on the same perimeter) and faced with an increase in visitor numbers, particularly in a post-Covid context, which means they need to adapt their practices. The PACA regional network of protected natural areas held a seminar on this topic in 2021, when many managers were initiating or developing policies to regulate visitor numbers with varying degrees of success. This raises the question of how to implement these public policies for managing visitor numbers on the scale of high-profile sites and natural areas, and the forms of tourist action developed by local players to deal with this (over)visiting.

Thus, while regulation is sometimes deemed necessary and put on the local political agenda, the question of how to implement it remains unanswered: who carries out these initiatives? What regulatory levers can be mobilized? What difficulties do managers encounter? How do residents and visitors perceive these regulatory measures, which are somewhat at odds with the idea of free enjoyment of the site?

We propose, on the one hand, to analyze the public policies implemented in natural areas to manage tourist and recreational frequentation (measures developed by public players to regulate the phenomena of heavy visitor numbers); and on the other hand, to shed light on the practices and representations of users confronted with the (over)visiting of sites (social acceptability of inhabitants, socio-professionals, visitors). This contribution is based on work carried out as part of two research programs. The first research, funded by the Plan urbanisme construction architecture[4] and conducted between 2015 and 2018, studied the visitor management policies developed by seven French natural sites, most of which are enrolled in the Grand Site operation approach (Vlès et al. 2017), based on some 20 semi-structured interviews with managers. This work also sheds light on how visitor numbers and management policies are perceived by users based on the analysis of 200 photo-questionnaires[5] submitted to users (residents and visitors) (Clarimont and Vlès 2017). A second channel of research focuses on the analysis of the load capacity management approach initiated by Port-Cros National Park, in 2016, and which led to the revision of the flow management policy, in 2021. It aims to trace the issues and methods of visitor regulation implemented in the territory (in particular, the governance approach adopted and the choice of regulation by marine shuttles) and to study the impact of these measures on visitor representations based on a dozen open interviews with managers and a comparative analysis of questionnaires sent to more than 1,000 visitors in 2018, and then in 2022.

The aim of this chapter is to highlight the challenges facing natural areas in terms of visitor flow management, the measures developed by public authorities to meet these challenges, the difficulties involved in implementing them, and visitors' perceptions of these flow-regulation measures.

6.1. Visits to natural areas with a high profile and major management challenges

6.1.1. *Large natural sites with high visitor numbers*

The relationship between tourism and the protection of major natural sites is ambivalent, to say the least (Vlès et al. 2017). Tourism has often been – and sometimes still is – at the origin of the protection and transformation of these territories. The first tourism associations, whether federative (Touring

4 PUCA is an inter-ministerial department dedicated to advancing knowledge of territories and cities and informing public action.

5 The questionnaire was administered in 2015–2016, face-to-face, in situ, to 300 visitors at three exceptional sites, either labeled Grands Sites de France (Sainte-Victoire) or in the process of being labeled (Pilat, Gavarnie).

Club de France, French Alpine Club) or local (tourist boards, professional groups, etc.), played a major role in institutionalizing protection rules for natural areas and places of interest (Gauchon 2002; Larrère et al. 2009). Tourism, however, quickly came to be seen as an activity that consumes space and disrupts natural ecosystems. In our urban and mobile societies, the advent of leisure activities has led to an increase in the number of visitors to natural areas where tourism and recreational activities take place. In high profile sites, management structures have been created to reconcile the joint (and paradoxical) issues of environmental preservation and public accessibility: the Grands Sites de France[6] (Duval and Gauchon 2007), some of which welcome over a million visitors a year (Baie de Somme, Camargue gardoise, Sainte-Victoire, Pont du Gard, Deux Caps (Blanc-Nez and Gris-Nez)).

When the sites are located in sparsely populated rural areas, there can be considerable pressure exerted by visitor flows, even if net visitor numbers can sometimes appear relatively modest, with a visitor/resident population ratio that can approach or even exceed 200: for example, for the Aven d'Orgnac, in the Ardèche, a site whose visitor numbers are nevertheless "only" 153,000 visitors/year, the Puy Mary volcano in the Cantal (500,000 visitors) where the ratio reaches a record 235 and the Pointe du Raz in Cap Sizun (800,000 visitors/year) (MEEM (Ministère de l'Environnement, de l'Energie et de la Mer) 2017).

Other emblematic protected natural areas, the national parks (Héritier and Laslaz 2007), are also faced with high visitor numbers, some of which are on the rise (Figure 6.1), which calls into question the ability of managers to simultaneously ensure the preservation of natural areas and the character of the site.

This challenge is particularly acute for natural sites located on the immediate outskirts of major metropolitan areas, which are subject to heavy local use, combining the recreational activities of local residents with the tourist activities of more occasional visitors. The pandemic of recent years has accentuated this phenomenon of local visitor numbers, which began several decades ago.

---

6 The Grands Sites policy was launched in 1979 by the French Ministry for the Environment and the Quality of Life to solve the problems of excessive visitor numbers and maintenance of certain well-known listed sites. The Grand Site de France label was created in 2000.

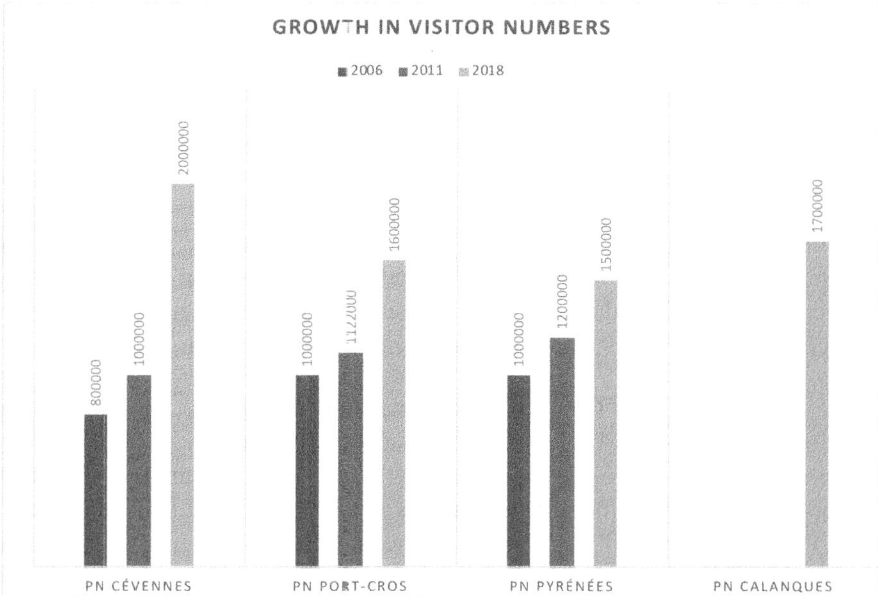

Figure 6.1. *Change in the number of visits to national parks located near cities between 2006 and 2018 (design: E. Hatt, based on CGDD – OFB (2021))*

This increase in visitor numbers, observed since 2006, seems to have been accentuated by the health crisis in certain national parks (particularly peri-urban parks). For example, in 2020, the Parc national des Calanques welcomed three million visitors between Easter and All Saints' Day, on 8,500 ha, representing a 40–50% increase in visitor numbers compared with 2018[7].

The attractiveness of well-known natural areas raises the question of how to manage visitor numbers. The terms "over-tourism", "over-visiting" and even "hyper-visiting" (used in the bill proposed by Senator Jérôme Bignon in 2019) are often used[8]. This plethora of designations emphasizing excess visitor numbers certainly raises questions about the scale of the phenomenon described, but also about the stigmatization of tourism that the use of the prefixes "over-" and "hyper-" implies. These superlative terms must be used with a lot of care, as social perception of excess is highly subjective, and

7 According to a representative of the Calanques National Park (April 2023).

8 Proposed law adopted by the senate, on various measures to regulate "hyper-visiting" of natural and cultural heritage sites.

largely depends on each individual's level of tolerance to co-presence in the same place. That is why we have opted here for the term "(over)visiting".

6.1.2. *(Over)visiting and visitor management issues*

The constant growth in the number of tourists visiting certain multi-functional natural sites raises a number of issues concerning the management of visitor numbers, which should be reviewed in order to ensure that recreational and productive uses coexist as effectively as possible, as well as other recreational uses (mountain biking, walking, hunting, fishing, etc.).

The managers of the Calanques National Park have noted an increase in anti-social behavior and the many impacts associated with high visitor numbers, including more traffic jams and illegal parking, damage to marine flora and waste management problems (interview, April 2023). The Director of the Port-Cros National Park also commented on the situation in an article published in *Libération* on September 25, 2020:

> We are in a quasi-industrial tourism business. It was an unusual summer. All along the French coast, we saw an increase in visitor numbers, with a public unaccustomed to respecting these natural spaces. There was a need to let off steam. A lot more anti-social behavior was observed. Music blasting, more litter than necessary. People smoking in the forest, where there is a high risk of fire. (Arnaud 2020)

The management of natural sites is faced with the difficulty of balancing between protection, preservation of the "spirit of the place" (the character of the site) and enhancement, elements that are essential to the local tourism economy; all this in an often-constrained context, marked by the vulnerability of sites to natural hazards and local pressures to urbanize or equip them (Vlès et al. 2017). The constant growth in the number of visitors to exceptional natural sites, whether Grands Sites de France or national parks, raises the issue of the impacts of this visitor number and its management, whether approached in terms of managing carrying capacities[9]

9 Tourism carrying capacity can be defined as "the number of tourists that a regional socio-economic system can sustainably accommodate without irreparably altering itself" (Cazes 1993, p. 139). The components of this acceptable level of visitation are as follows: infrastructure capacity, physical capacity of the territory (in terms of safety), ecological

(Chamberlain 1997; Navarro Jurado et al. 2013; Vlès 2018); or, as this concept has been the subject of a number of criticisms (Deprest 1997; Stock 2003), in terms of the limits of acceptable change (Broadhurst 2001). Taking note of these issues, in June 2023, the French Ministry of the Economy, Finance and Industrial and Digital Sovereignty launched a plan for the management of tourist flows, structured around four axes: understanding management, raising stakeholder awareness, measuring flows and impacts, and supporting territories[10]. In October 2023, this plan was supported by a call for expressions of interest led by Atout France, aimed at "increasing the quality and sustainability of the tourism experience through better flow management"[11].

Many managers of (over)visited natural areas are seeking to develop strategies for regulating visitor numbers and implement a certain agility in response to this challenge. In the following section, we offer an overview of the management systems adopted by a number of highly visited natural sites.

6.2. Managers of natural areas increasingly inclined to implement visitor management systems

6.2.1. *A variety of visitor management systems in natural areas*

To meet the challenges of high visitor numbers in natural areas, managers have implemented a wide range of flow management systems, including both tangible and intangible practices (Thoenig 2014). Based on the work of Deprest (1997), it is possible to draw up a panorama of flow management methods in tourist sites, aimed at acting on the volume of visitor numbers or their impacts (Table 6.1).

Extreme situations (site closures) are still uncommon in France. Most of the time, managers opt for strategies aimed at limiting or cushioning the impact of visitor numbers by regulating them, increasing the resistance of sites or modifying the nature of visitor numbers by raising awareness of "good practices" and "good gestures" (Figure 6.2).

---

capacity (availability and state of conservation of natural resources), psychological capacity of inhabitants and visitors (Audouit 2008).

10 See: https://www.economie.gouv.fr/tourisme-une-strategie-nationale-pour-gerer-les-flux-touristiques.

11 See: https://www.atout-france.fr/services/gestion-des-flux.

Reducing the volume of visitors		Limiting or lessening the impact of visitor numbers	
Stop visits	Close access to the site: integral nature reserves, decorated caves (Lascaux with the opening of Lascaux II in 1983; Niaux; Chauvet-Pont d'Arc with the opening of a Chauvet 2 replica, in 2015; Altamira, in Spain, partially reopened to the public as of 2014)	**Regulate visits**	– Spread out visitor flow to related sites (cirque de Gavarnie to cirques de Troumouse or d'Estaubé, Sainte-Victoire to massif de Concors, etc.) – Spread out over time: seasonally adjust visitor numbers or offer site visits outside peak periods (Dune du Pilat, Mont Saint-Michel) – Concentrate flows in time and/or space when visitor numbers are widespread (Dune du Pilat)
Limit visits	– Paid access – Limited accessibility by car (Pointe du Raz) – Introduction of visitor quotas (Ordesa National Park for the Ordesa cirque and Añiscló canyons, Calanques National Park for the Sugiton calanque since 2022) – Prohibition of certain practices (quad biking, motocross, mountain biking, paragliding, motorized and non-motorized flying, etc.) – Demarketing operations (Calanques National Park)	**Increase site resistance**	– Increase the capacity of infrastructures and services – Use resistant materials (Ordesa National Park: stone path in the cirque, footbridges to cross rivers)
		Modify the nature of visits	– Inform, raise awareness and educate visitors through campaigns (such as "Réussir ma rando", a post-Covid campaign run by the Conseil Départemental 64, or by the Parc National des Calanques) – Encourage practices that are less damaging to the environment (e.g. education in "good practices" in the Calanques National Park)

Table 6.1. *Types of flow management in tourist sites (design by Clarimont and Hatt (2023), according to Deprest (1997) and Clarimont and Vlès (2017))*

One way of doing this is to organize flows differently, so as to reduce their impact without reducing the level of visiting. Regulation allows flows to be spread out in space, dispersing them and thus lowering the pressure per square meter. The managers of the Gavarnie cirque, like those of the Grand Site Sainte-Victoire, have thus created other itineraries to offer a comparable view from the immediate vicinity, allowing them to spread flows across the area and generate economic benefits in less-frequented sectors. Managers have also been able to spread out visitor numbers with special offers (such as the "sunset" offer on Pilat) or by implementing dissuasive measures to discourage visitors, such as deliberately not maintaining access trails to the massif (Canigou) or limiting the capacity of parking lots (Sainte-Victoire, Bibémus access).

Figure 6.2. *"Good practice" signs at the start of a trail in the Calanques National Park (photo: Hatt 2023)*

Another strategy developed by managers to alter the nature of visitor numbers is to discourage visitors through strict control of information or the dissemination of "negative" information. For example, the Calanques National Park has decided to reduce the amount of promotion of its territory using a variety of levers: a "demarketing" campaign launched in conjunction with partners such as the Comité régional du tourisme Sud-PACA (French Regional Tourism Committee of the South), the removal of the exact geographical location of the Calanques from some of the department's beach maps, actions to raise awareness of environmental preservation among private influencers on social networks and the launch of a partnership with Waze to communicate poor access conditions to the site (traffic jams, parking difficulties, etc.).

Managers often combine these different levers to limit or cushion the impact of tourist and recreational activities. In recent years, experiments aimed at limiting the volume of visitors have also become more frequent.

6.2.2. *Experiments to limit visitor numbers in France*

While measures to reduce visitor numbers have been little used in France, or reserved for specific sites deemed particularly vulnerable and likely to suffer serious damage as a result of being open to the public (such as painted caves), they are now the subject of a greater number of experiments in natural areas.

Let us not forget that limiting access sometimes raises issues, particularly in terms of socio-environmental justice. For example, the introduction of a toll is a solution that promotes the idea that nature, or at least its development for the benefit of visitors, has a cost that the user must pay. While this practice is commonplace in North American national parks, it is not yet widely deployed in Europe, and raises the question of social justice in access to recreation and nature. Quotas (closure of the site when the daily visitor quota is reached: Font-de-Gaume cave, Ordesa valley, summer visit permit for Sugiton calanque) allow for a less targeted selection from an economic point of view, although it can be criticized by locals. This method, like the previous one, also implies being able to control all access sites, which is far from easy in natural areas, and can lead to significant costs for managers in setting up access points, monitoring them and, if necessary, punishing offenders.

Out of the seven natural areas studied in 2015–2016 (Vlès et al. 2017), the Ordesa and Mont-Perdu National Park was the only one to have defined a maximum visitor number threshold of "1,800 people simultaneously" present in the valley, accompanied by the development of a park-and-ride system with paid shuttles. The Park informed visitors that if this "maximum visitor capacity" was reached, "for the sake of the National Park, the public service will be temporarily halted".

A similar approach was implemented by Port-Cros National Park, which in 2016 launched a carrying capacity management initiative to better regulate visitor numbers and ensure the preservation of the Park's character[12] (Deldrève and Michel 2019). The Park has mobilized several research teams in a multidisciplinary approach, so as to conduct studies on the impacts of visitor numbers on flora and fauna (Iorio et al. 2020; Boudouresque et al. 2022) on the acceptability of salesmen and users (Van der Yeught 2018; Jungmann et al. 2021; Moisson 2023) or on the regulatory aspect of regulation (Boue 2022). It also called on a consulting firm to support the governance of this carrying capacity management approach and conduct participatory workshops with residents (Deldrève and Michel 2019). In 2021, this work led to the implementation of a regulation on the number of visitors accessing the island of Porquerolles. The threshold has been set at 6,000 visitors per day. The implementation of the regulation, while still raising certain questions, has been facilitated by the island nature of the territory and through working with the managers of the maritime shuttles to limit the number of passengers accessing the island of Porquerolles.

Another emblematic example of limiting the volume of visitors is Mont Blanc, access to which has been regulated in 2019 by a quota related to the number of places in the shelters. To this end, the Haute-Savoie prefecture (in partnership with the Fédération des clubs alpins and the peloton de gendarmerie de haute montagne) introduced a regulation requiring proof of a nominative reservation in one of the itinerary's shelters in order to make the ascent. This quota system was maintained when a decree protecting the natural habitats of Mont Blanc was adopted in October 2020, reinforcing measures to preserve the site. Last but not least, the Calanques National Park introduced a quota of 400 visitors for access to the Sugiton and Pierres Tombées creeks in 2022. To implement this quota, the Park introduced a free visitor permit (available on a digital platform) and continuous monitoring of the site's access points. The experiment, conducted for 45 days between June and August 2022, is scheduled to run for another five years, with an extension of the period of application, a reassessment of the number of visitors and a possible improvement in the booking system.

The acute nature of the issue of visitor management has led to a re-thinking of how the law should consider the issue of regulating visitor numbers, following on from the work undertaken by the Port-Cros National Park on managing the area's carrying capacity.

12 This research into the management of carrying capacity is a continuation of work begun in 2003, which led to the creation of a visitor observatory, Bountîles, in 2006 (Bergère and Le Berre 2011; Le Berre et al. 2013).

6.2.3. *Regulatory changes to support visitor number management*

Under French law, the mayor's police powers were limited and only concerned vehicular traffic in natural areas (the "4 × 4 law" did not apply to boats, pedestrians or cyclists). The work carried out by the Port-Cros National Park has enabled the park to collaborate with a legal expert on the issue of visitor management (Jolivet 2021) and to put this issue on the political agenda, with the support of the Senator for the Somme, Jérôme Bignon (author of a report on the regulation of "hyper-visiting" in 2019).

As a result of this work, Senator J. Bignon defended a draft law, adopted on first reading by the senate in November 2019, and finally incorporated into Law No. 2021-1104 of August 22, 2021 on combating climate change and building resilience to its effects. This law extends the police powers of mayors by introducing a new special administrative police force for access to protected natural areas (Article 231 of the law), extending the uses concerned and the possibilities for regulation (Jolivet 2021). Henceforth,

> access and circulation of people, vehicles and domestic animals in areas protected under [Book III] or Book IV may be regulated or prohibited, by substantiated decision, where such access is likely to compromise either their protection or enhancement for ecological, agricultural, forestry, aesthetic, landscape or tourism purposes, or the protection of animal or plant species (Law No. 2021-1104 of August 22, 2021).

While there is now a fairly broad consensus among site managers on the need for flow regulation, its implementation remains complex.

6.3. Visitor management systems: between concrete implementation difficulties and ambivalent social perceptions

6.3.1. *Challenges to the creation of operational management territories*

The practical implementation of visitor management can come up against a variety of challenges: financial, political (some elected representatives may be reluctant to commit to a strategy perceived as reducing the positive economic benefits of tourism) and organizational.

In fact, there are a number of obstacles to the creation of operational management areas. In particular, the fragmentation of local communities and the difficulty of finding a unifying structure make it difficult to integrate the project into a multi-communal territory. Examples of this in the 2010s include the fragile associative support for the Pôle d'excellence rurale (PER) project by the Néouvielle national nature reserve (Bessière et al. 2016) and the fragmented management of the Gavarnie-Mont-Perdu world heritage site. For this latter example, the international border and the lack of local consensus – on the French side – around the UNESCO World Heritage listing defended by an associative structure and development logics that are still strictly local have made it difficult to design a territorial project.

In the case of the Port-Cros National Park, the complexity of managing visitor numbers is due in particular to the diversity of the players responsible for managing the island of Porquerolles, part of which is located in the heart of the Park, but another part (the village) in the adhesion zone, requiring collaboration between the National Park, the commune of Hyères and Toulon Provence Métropole (port management) when choosing for measures to be implemented.

Another difficulty involves land ownership, which is often poorly controlled, with the prevalence of private ownership on certain sites (such as Sainte-Victoire) or the importance of undivided ownership in the Pyrenean mountains, where mountain pastures are, more often than not, privately owned by communes who have come together in board commissions to manage these high-altitude rangelands, which are now used for a variety of purposes.

Land acquisition policies by public institutions are sometimes not well received locally, as was the case for the Conservatoire du Littoral in the Dune du Pilat sector in 2016–2017 in order to reduce land fragmentation and base site management on publicly owned plots.

In parallel with these governance-related issues, our research aimed to analyze, through surveys, the representations that users have of public policies for managing visitor numbers in protected natural sites.

6.3.2. *A principle of regulation accepted, but regulatory measures criticized by users*

Photo-questionnaire surveys carried out in 2015[13] highlight the paradoxical dimension of visitors' perceptions of the public policies used to manage visitor numbers in natural areas: the principle of regulation is accepted (by over 70% of respondents), but its implementation in situ is overwhelmingly rejected (by 58–92% of respondents, depending on the type of measure evaluated) (Figure 6.3).

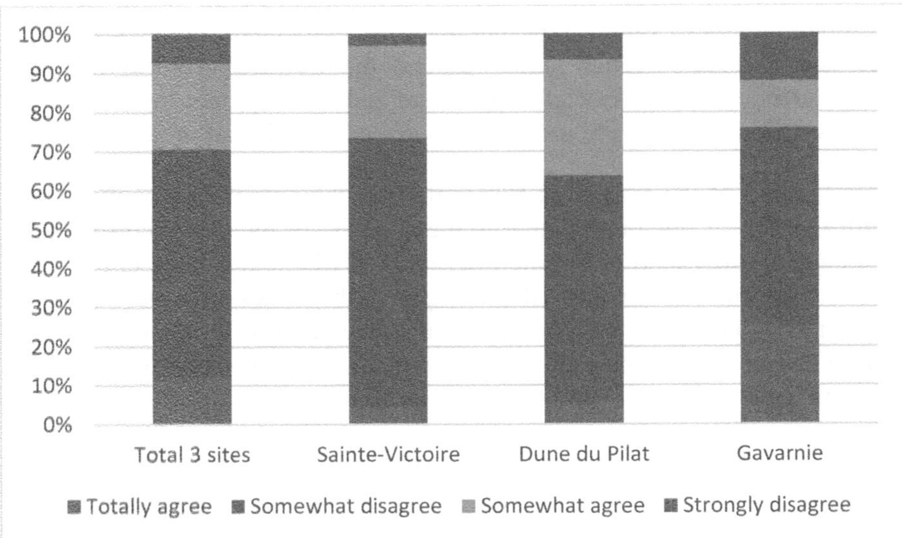

Figure 6.3. *Would you say that measures to regulate visitor flows should be implemented in highly visited natural sites? (source: Clarimont and Vlès (2017))*

Visitors' assessments of the management measures vary from site to site, and from scheme to scheme. Some measures are slightly more popular (such as limiting the hours and days of visits, or banning access to part of the site), while others are strongly criticized (such as allowing guided tours only, or introducing tolls) (Table 6.2). Paid parking is particularly unpopular, likened

13 A total of 256 visitors were surveyed at the three sites, Gavarnie, Dune du Pilat and Massif Sainte-Victoire, in 2015 and 2016.

to a toll: "tolls should not take place in a natural site" (Dune du Pilat 48 interviewee); "Ah yes! Tolls! Natural sites should not be so expensive for families" (Dune du Pilat 49 interviewee); "It pisses me off that the parking lot has to be paid for, it is not a museum!" (Dune du Pilat 54 interviewee).

Would you accept any restrictions?	Yes, but only in high season (%)	Yes, all the time (%)	No (%)	Do not know (%)
Prohibit access to the entire site	12.20	0.80%	86.30%	0.40
Prohibit access to part of the site	30.4	4.70	63.60	1.20
Restrict visiting hours and days	34.10	5.90	58.80	1.20
Limit the number of visitors (quotas)	29.20	2.30	66.50	1.90
Implement tolls	4.70	1.60	92.90	0.80
Move parking areas + shuttles away from the site	17.80	12	68.60	1.60
Authorize guided tours only	1.60	0.80	97.30	0.40
Prohibit certain activities	3.20	15.50	79	2.40

Table 6.2. *Visitor acceptability of visitor management systems (source: Clarimont and Vlès (2017)). For a color version of this table, see www.iste.co.uk/ christofle/tourism2.zip*

However, assessments vary from site to site and from measure to measure. The acceptability of limiting visiting hours and days in high season is higher among visitors to the Grand Site Sainte-Victoire (75%, compared with 20%–30% for the other sites) (Figure 6.4). This observation may be linked to a specific feature of this site, which is already subject to restrictions, with visitor restrictions linked to the risk of fire and forest fires (a risk which was also the reason for the creation of the inter-municipal management board for this area).

For example, 40% of visitors to the Grand Site Sainte-Victoire accept the restricted access to the entire site in the high season, whereas over 98% of users of the Dune du Pilat and Gavarnie reject it. Knowledge of the risk and its management could thus contribute to the acceptability of visitor management measures.

Would you accept these restrictions?

Prohibit access to the entire site

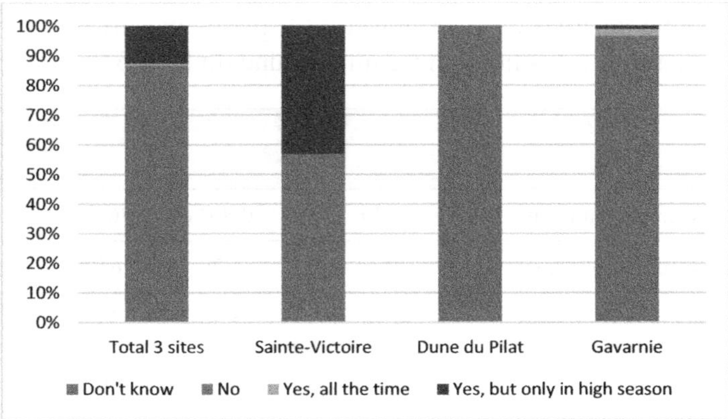

	Total 3 sites	Sainte-Victoire	Dune du Pilat	Gavarnie
Don't know	1	0	0	1
No	220	41	94	85
Yes, all the time	2	0	0	2
Yes, but only in high season	32	31	0	1

Restrict visiting hours and days

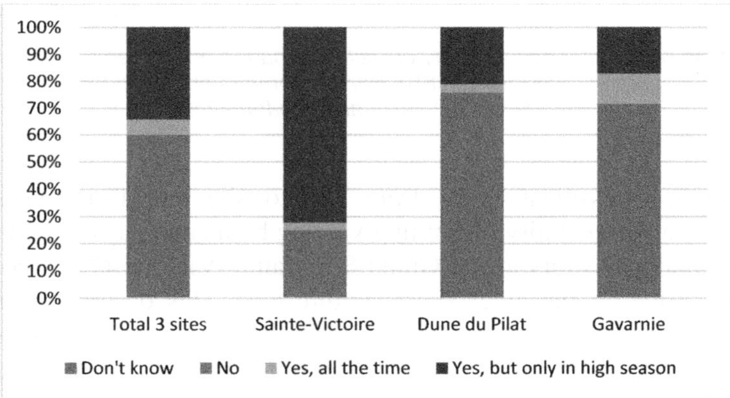

	Total 3 sites	Sainte-Victoire	Dune du Pilat	Gavarnie
Don't know	3	0	3	0
No	150	18	69	63
Yes, all the time	15	2	3	10
Yes, but only in high season	87	52	20	15

Figure 6.4. *Variability in the acceptability of restrictions of use in three natural sites (Dune du Pilat, Gavarnie and Sainte-Victoire) (source: Vlès et al. 2017)*

In another example, in the Port-Cros National Park, an area at risk from wildfire and having introduced a scheme to regulate visitor numbers in 2021 (by limiting the number of passengers on sea shuttles, which now have to be booked in high season), visitors are aware of the challenges of restricted use (Moisson 2023)[14]. A majority of respondents agree with banning access to certain parts of the island in the high season (684 respondents, or 50% of the panel) and even all year round (266 respondents, or 20%), as well as limiting the number of visitors in the high season (778 respondents, or 55%), or even all year round (334 respondents, or 25%) (Figure 6.5). However, limiting the number of tourist activities that can be carried out (traffic and water sports) is more strongly opposed (40% of visitors questioned reject it, whereas only 10%–20% reject the other proposed regulatory measures).

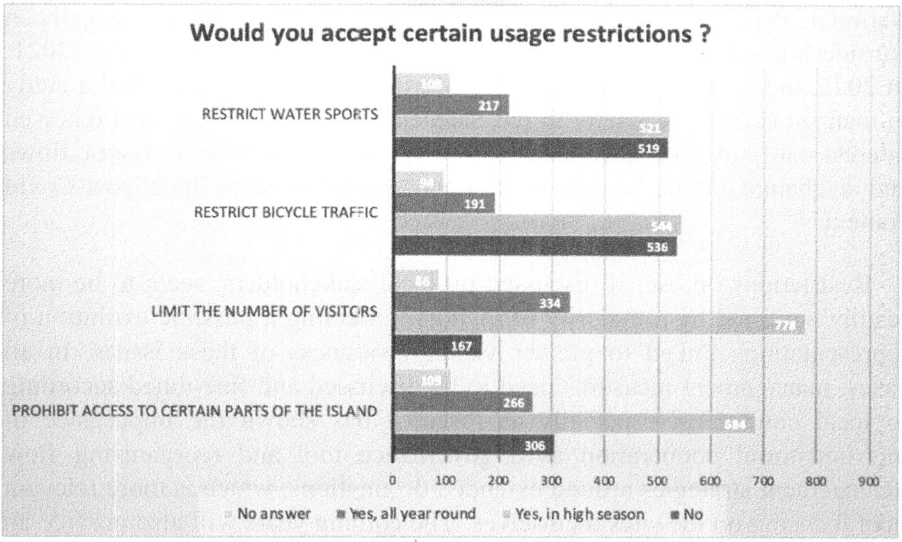

Figure 6.5. *Acceptability of visitor use restrictions on the island of Porquerolles during the summer of 2022 (design: Hatt 2023, based on Moisson (2023))*

6.4. Conclusion

The issue of managing the (over)visiting of natural areas has received a great deal of media coverage in recent years and has, in some cases, been a

14 Results of the Port-Cros National Park visitor satisfaction survey for summer 2022 (questionnaire distributed to 1,365 visitors and processed by C. Moisson).

topical issue for managers for several decades. It invites us to study the measures taken to prohibit or regulate use in natural areas, the methods and difficulties involved in their implementation, and their acceptability to users.

During the surveys conducted in 2015–2016, we observed that the issue of flow management had been integrated into managers' discourse, but that it was difficult to implement due to financial, technical and political challenges (fears of economic losses and/or the discontent of a significant proportion of the electorate being likely to slow down commitment to a voluntary flow management strategy). Though elected representatives and managers were reluctant to integrate the concept of carrying capacity into their discourse and modes of public action in 2015, things have since changed. Inspired in some cases by the approach adopted by the Port-Cros National Park since 2016, many protected area managers have been considering and experimenting with visitor regulation measures since 2021. In 2023, the Cape Corse and Agriate Marine Natural Park launched a study to manage carrying capacity in the Saleccia and Lotu sectors. This renewed interest can partly be attributed to the significant increase in visitor flows and a change in the profile of visitors to natural areas in a post-Covid context.

Restrictions on use, if discussed by local stakeholders, seem to be more readily accepted by a majority of visitors, reflecting a possible evolution of representations linked to greater visitor awareness of these issues. In all cases, management measures need to be discussed and fine-tuned according to local conditions, especially as research has shown the importance of inter-territorial cooperation as a governance tool and reorganizing flow management strategies around extended destinations, which is more relevant than focusing on the sites themselves. The coming years will also provide an opportunity to observe whether or not the new regulatory framework for regulating visitor numbers in natural areas will be used by the elected representatives of the territories concerned, who now have more extensive policing powers.

6.5. References

Alldredge, R.B. (1972). *Some Capacity Theory for Parks and Recreation Areas*. USDA National Park Service, Washington, D.C.

Arnaud, D. (2020). Tourisme de masse à Porquerolles: un été “terriblement parfait”. *Libération*, 25 September [Online]. Available at: https://www.liberation.fr/evenements-libe/2020/09/25/tourisme-de-masse-a-porquerolles-un-ete-terriblement-parfait_1800510/.

Audouit, C. (2008). L’étude de la fréquentation et de ses impacts sur le littoral languedocien. PhD Thesis, Université de Montpellier III, Montpellier.

Bergère, H. and Le Berre, S. (2011). Définition et étalonnage d’un système d’évaluation de la capacité de charge de l’île de Port-Cros (Hyères, France). Report, Scientific Reports of Port-Cros National Park.

Bessière, J., Clarimont, S., Vlès, V. (2016). La ressource patrimoniale, outil de diversification touristique ? Le pôle d’excellence rurale du Néouvielle, entre innovation et recyclage. *Natures Sciences et Sociétés*, 24(3), 217–229. doi: 10.1051/nss/2016034.

Bignon, J. (2019). Rapport du sénat sur la proposition de loi portant diverses mesures tendant à réguler “l’hyper-fréquentation” dans les sites naturels et culturels patrimoniaux. Senate Report, No. 110, Paris.

Boudouresque, C.-F., Perret-Boudouresque, M., Blanfuné, A. (2022). Diversity of marine and brackish macrophytes in the Port-Cros National Park (Provence, France, Mediterranean Sea): Taxa and research effort over space and time. *Diversity*, 14(329), 1–41.

Boue, A. (2022). La capacité de charge et la règlementation des flux de visiteurs au niveau local. Report, Scientific Reports of Port-Cros National Park.

Broadhurst, R. (2001). *Managing Environments for Leisure and Recreation*. Routledge, London/New York.

CGDD – OFB (2021). Les parcs nationaux de France. Chiffres clés édition 2021 [Online]. Available at: https://www.statistiques.developpement-durable.gouv.fr/edition-numerique/parcs-nationaux-2021/pdf/les-parcs-nationaux-de-france-chiffres-cles-edition-2021.pdf.

Chamberlain, K. (1997). *Carrying Capacity*. UNEP, Paris.

Clarimont, S. and Vlès, V. (2017). Impacts des mesures de préservation des sites naturels exceptionnels : Livrable L2. Mesures de préservation des sites et expériences des lieux par les usagers. Research Report, PUCA 2 [Online]. Available at: https://halshs.archives-ouvertes.fr/halshs-01428199v1.

Deldrève, V. and Michel, C. (2019). La démarche de capacité de charge sur Porquerolles (Provence, Parc national de Port-Cros, France) : de la prospective au plan d’actions. Report, Scientific Reports of Port-Cros National Park.

Deprest, F. (1997). *Enquête sur le tourisme de masse*. Belin, Paris.

Duhamel, P. (2023). Le "surtourisme" ou la rupture d'un contrat habitants/touristes : le cas des lieux touristiques en Europe. *L'information géographique*, 87, 100–122.

Duval, M. and Gauchon, C. (2007). Analyse critique d'une politique d'aménagement du territoire, les Opérations Grands Sites. *Annales de géographie*, 654, 147–168.

Gauchon, C. (2002). Les sites naturels classés entre 1906 et 1930 dans les Alpes du Nord : entre tourisme et protection. Bilan et actualité. *Revue de Géographie Alpine*, 90(2), 15–31.

Héritier, S. and Laslaz, L. (2008). *Les parcs nationaux dans le monde.* Ellipses, Paris.

Iorio, E., Geoffroy, D., Pétillon, J. (2020). Distribution and indicator value of intertidal centipedes from Mediterranean beaches within and around Port-Cros National Park (Southern France), with proposal of a simplified monitoring (Chilopoda). *Bulletin de la Société entomologique de France*, 125(1), 41–62.

Jolivet, S. (2021). La police de l'accès aux espaces protégés. Ordre public écologique et politique des "petits pas". Report [Online]. Available at: https://hal.archives-ouvertes.fr/hal-03423101.

Jungmann, L., Lazorthes, B., Barcelo, A., Michel, C. (2021). Étude de satisfaction auprès des visiteurs en vue d'éclairer la capacité de charge de l'île de Porquerolles (Provence, France). Report, Scientific Reports of Port-Cros National Park.

Larrère, R., Lizet, B., Berlan-Barqué, M. (2009). *Histoire des parcs nationaux. Comment prendre soin de la nature ?* Éditions Quæ, Versailles.

Le Berre, S., Brigand, L., Le Corre, N., Peuziat, I. (2013). L'apport du Parc national de Port-Cros à la réflexion sur les usages récréatifs et leurs suivis dans les aires protégées : les observatoires Bountîles Port-Cros et Porquerolles. Report, Scientific Reports of Port-Cros National Park.

MEEM (Ministère de l'Environnement, de l'Energie et de la Mer) (2017). La fonction touristique des territoires : facteur de pression ou de préservation de l'environnement ? [Online]. Available at: https://www.statistiques.developpement-durable.gouv.fr/sites/default/files/2018-10/datalab-17-la-fonction-touristique-des-territoires...mars2017a.pdf.

Moisson, C. (2023). La gestion de la fréquentation touristique des espaces naturels protégés français. Le cas de Porquerolles, Parc National de Port-Cros. Master's Thesis, Aix-Marseille Université, Aix-Marseille.

Navarro Jurado, E., Mihaela Damian, I., Fernández-Morales, A. (2013). Carrying capacity model applied in Coastal destinations. *Annals of Tourism Research*, 43, 1–19.

Pellegrin-Romeggio, F. (2020). Une nouvelle compétence d'assembleur pour une gestion dynamique du tourisme local. *Revue d'économie régionale et urbaine*, 2, 289–310.

Stock, M. (2003). *Le tourisme : acteurs, lieux et enjeux*. Belin, Paris.

Thoenig, J.C. (2014). *Dictionnaire des politiques publiques*, 4th edition. Presses de Sciences Po, Paris.

Van der Yeught, C. (2018). Contribution des entreprises touristique à la maîtrise de la capacité de charge de Porquerolles et au "caractère" du Parc national de Port-Cros (Provence, France). Report, Scientific Reports of Port-Cros National Park.

Violier, P. (2016). La troisième révolution touristique. *Mondes du Tourisme*, special edition [Online]. Available at: http://journals.openedition.org/tourisme/1256.

Vlès, V. (2018). Hésitations et recompositions dans la gestion des flux de fréquentation dans les sites naturels exceptionnels. *Via Tourism Review*, 11/12 [Online]. Available at: http://journals.openedition.org/viatourism/1816.

Vlès, V., Clarimont, S., Hatt, E., Benos, R., Piriou, J., Moulinie, V., Bessiere, J., Torrente, P. (2017). Impacts des mesures de préservation des sites naturels exceptionnels : rapport final de recherche. Report, PUCA [Online]. Available at: https://halshs.archives-ouvertes.fr/hal-01500485v1.

7

Metropolitan Areas and Local Tourism

7.1. Introduction

The Covid crisis has undoubtedly had a severe impact on international tourism, limiting the number of foreign tourists arriving in France, as well as the number of French tourists leaving the country. However, the effects of this health crisis need to be put into perspective. In a context of anxiety and lack of visibility in the short and medium term, which forces us to minimize risks when booking rentals and transport tickets, tourists tend to limit their travels around their home area: "we are not going as far". It is highly likely that we will see a redistribution of tourist flows, around the major metropolises, linked to local tourism.

Under these conditions, which metropolitan leisure areas can be identified? To do this, we use a travel simulation tool. Based on a gravity model that simulates motorized travel on a road graph as a function of accessibilities and services, we will determine the probability of visits to tourist areas bordering metropolitan areas, using the Côte d'Azur metropolitan area as an example. The model presented is also intended to serve as a decision-support tool for policies aimed at developing sustainable tourism.

7.2. Metropolises and local leisure activities

The issue of the influence of major urban centers on the number of tourists visiting neighboring areas is not new. A special issue of the magazine *Norois* – "Approches géographiques des loisirs" (1983) – showed

Chapter written by Fabrice DECOUPIGNY.

that leisure activities linked to the recreational activities of city residents played a part in structuring tourist activities, both inside and outside urban areas, by contributing to the consolidation of a tourist offer. Indeed, the services associated with this offer are also used by the local population, who consume them in their leisure time. In turn, this tourist offer, which is seasonal, also becomes a daily offering for the resident population, thus creating a year-round clientele. This phenomenon also applies to one-off events such as festivals. The latter, which spearhead the summer tourist appeal of certain regions, contribute to the liveliness of the area by creating an identity that the local population makes its own (Brennetot 2004). Bear in mind that local attendance at festivals in France represents, on average, over 50% of the population (Négrier et al. 2010). Local residents are the first to benefit in their daily lives from the attractiveness of tourism, as it reinforces and diversifies the existing range of services.

In recent years, there has been an increase in the number of second homes, which has led to an increase in secondary residency (Bachimon 2018). While the major "traditional" tourist regions (mountains and coastline) retain a high residential rate (number of second homes per 1,000 inhabitants), metropolitan areas gravitating around major urban hubs have seen an increase in residences (Kadri 2014; Léger 2017). The geography of second homes has not changed as a result, but it seems that the option of being closer to home is increasingly favored, as has been observed in Hauts-de-France, where three quarters of second-home owners live less than two hours away (Danielou and Dufeutrelle 2021).

Generally speaking, there is a decline in second homes within the inner peri-urban boundary, corresponding to their transformation into primary residences, unlike the outer zone, where they are growing (Violier et al. 2021). It remains difficult to fully measure the number of second homes in the center of metropolises due to the expanded range offered by reservation platforms.

On a French scale, a quick analysis of INSEE figures (1999–2018) shows a metropolization of the location of second homes. We can observe two phenomena:

– The first: a sharp increase in second homes in large urban centers (towns with over 30,000 inhabitants) (Figure 7.1(A)). Almost all major cities are seeing their residential function strengthen.

– The second: a fall in the average distance of second homes from urban centers (Figure 7.1(B)), suggesting that large urban areas are reinforcing their residential function by concentrating second homes within a radius of 50–60 km.

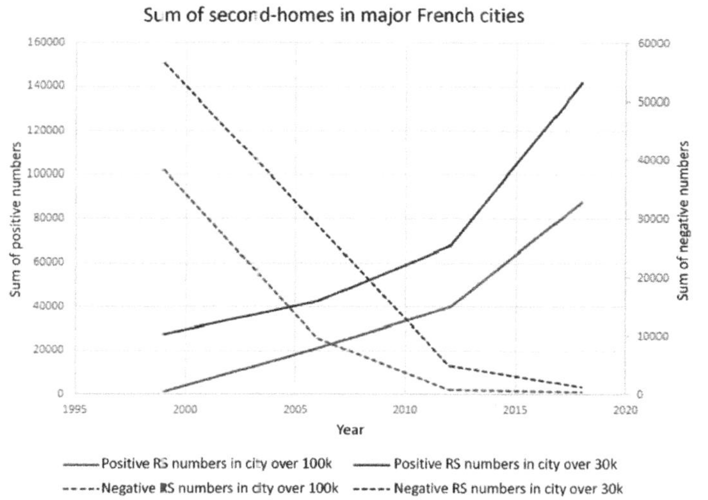

a)

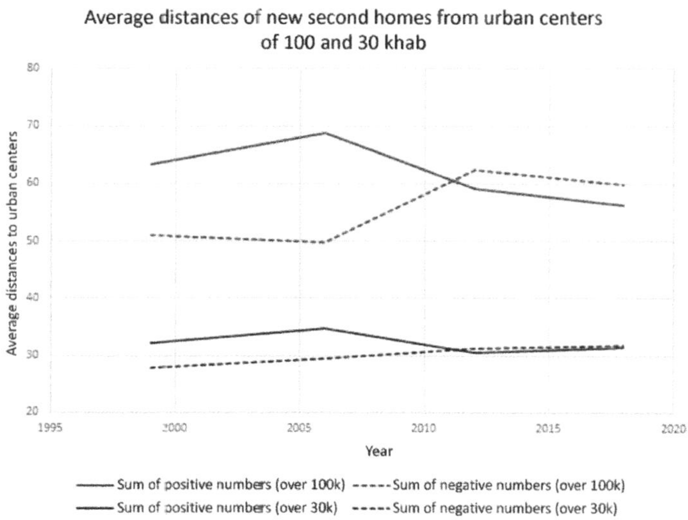

b)

Figure 7.1. *Changes in the location of second homes in France between 1999 and 2018. For a color version of this figure, see www.iste.co.uk/christofle/tourism2.zip*

Undeniably, the location of second homes on the borders of metropolitan areas has an impact on tourism development. Local visitors not only ensures the region's resilience in the face of external shocks caused by crises, but also a certain agility in offering tourism products, which are perpetuated by a local population that consumes them with a certain recurrence. For example, in the Alpes-Maritimes, 75% of second homes in the upper and middle country belong to owners from the PACA region, whereas on the coastal strip, 75% of those with priority status live outside the region. It would appear that the presence of a nearby homeowner population has helped to limit the impact of the Covid crisis inland of major metropolises, by enabling activities to continue. In fact, tourism figures for the Nice metropolitan area in the summers of 2020 and 2021 show an increase in visitor numbers in the upper and middle country (activity reports 2020 and 2021, Nice Côte d'Azur Metropolitan Tourist Office). During the winter of 2020/2021, even though the ski lifts were closed, the Alpes-Maritimes resorts benefitted from good visitor numbers. This phenomenon was repeated the following winter, when snow levels did not allow these resorts to open their lifts to 100% capacity. This confirms the observations made in other regions, where staycation – the phenomenon of taking vacations close to home – is becoming increasingly popular (Lenoble and Romeyer 2020).

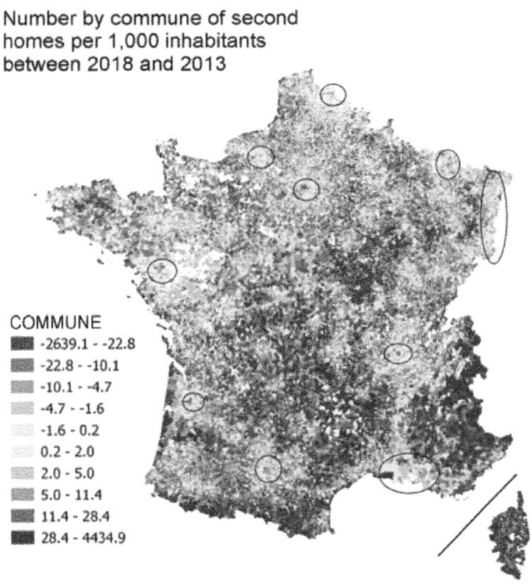

Figure 7.2. *(A) Changes in the residential function between 2013 and 2018 in the main French metropolises (sources: INSEE 2020, Fabrice Decoupigny, UMR ESPACE, UCA 2023). For a color version of this figure, see www.iste.co.uk/christofle/tourism2.zip*

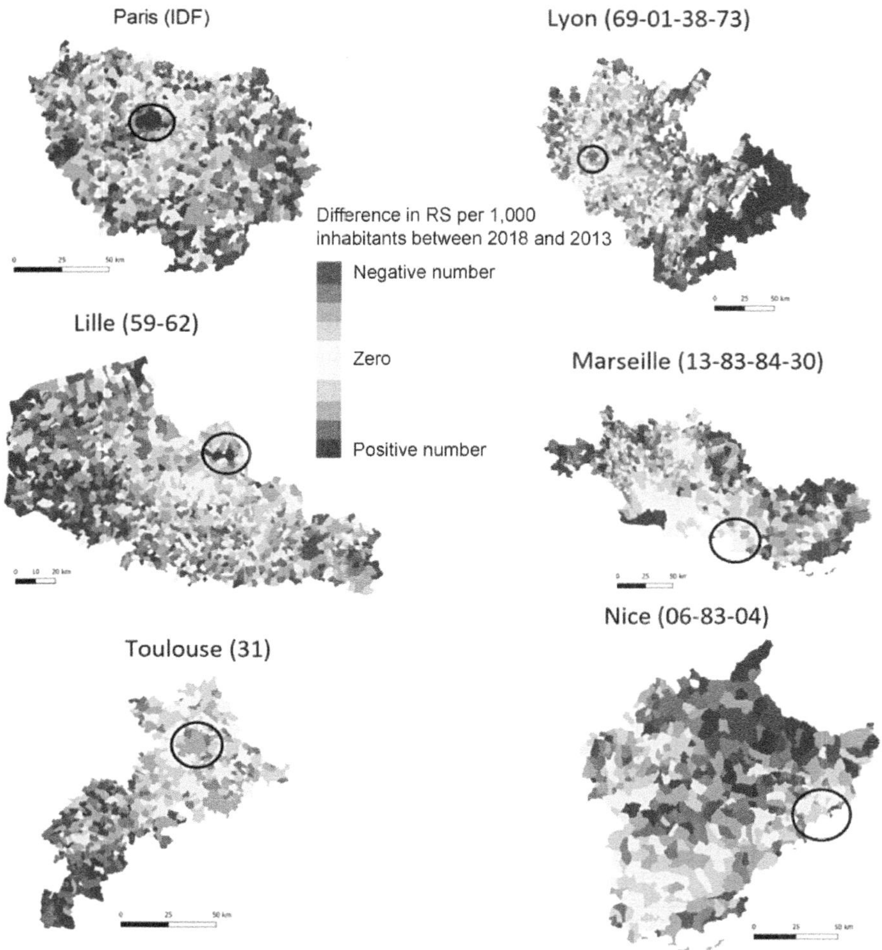

Figure 7.2. *(B) Changes in the residential function between 2013 and 2018 in the main French metropolises (sources: INSEE 2020, Fabrice Decoupigny, UMR ESPACE, UCA 2023). For a color version of this figure, see www.iste.co.uk/christofle/tourism2.zip*

Observations show that tourist numbers have not collapsed in the tourist areas around major metropolises. It seems highly likely that this phenomenon is driven by a city-dwelling population in large metropolises who move around for recreational activities.

7.3. Impact of second homes on attractiveness

However, we have few, if any, figures or surveys on the leisure practices of these populations. Generally speaking, since they know the area well, they do not go to tourist information points that register visitors. Furthermore, since they often travel on a daily basis, they do not use commercial accommodation or transportation services. The same applies to the rate of use of second homes. If they do exist, they are one-off studies on limited territories, such as the one carried out on Auzat, an hour and a half from Toulouse, which shows a commune populated by "infrequent regional visitors" (Bachimon et al. 2017). Remember that INSEE does not conduct vacation surveys, nor weekend travel surveys. It is therefore difficult to have a general idea of the extent of the impact of visitor numbers generated by the occupancy rate of secondary residences, but also of recreational visitor numbers within a 1.5- to 2-hour distance from urban centers.

There is a possible explanation for the continued increase in urban pressure in these areas. This pressure, which remains positive, is not linked to the urbanization of these communes, but rather to the growth in the number of second homes, a value that has risen sharply since 2012, accompanied by a drop in the average distance to major urban centers (Table 7.1).

		Second homes				
			1999	2006	2012	2018
Average distance from a town	more than 100 khab	Sum of positive balances (cities over 100k)	38.6	37.6	26.6	26.9
		Sum of negative balances (cities over 100k)	32.6	35.7	29.6	39.4
	over 30 khab	Sum of positive balances (cities over 30k)	26.7	22.8	15.6	15
		Sum of negative balances (cities over 30k)	20.3	22	20.6	19.5
Sum of positive balances of RS			41832	41595	21720	30401
Sum of negative balances of RS			-8413	-6815	-5517	-6664
Balance RS			33419	34780	16203	23737
Number of second homes in cities	over 100khab	Sum of positive balances	488	8120	1601	2945
		Sum of negative balances	-375	-188	0	-226
	over 30khab	Sum of positive balances	19260	16031	8864	15916
		Sum of negative balances	-1060	-2906	-15916	-400

Table 7.1. *Number of second homes in the Var and Alpes-Maritimes counties and average distances in kilometers to towns. For a color version of this table, see www.iste.co.uk/christofle/tourism2.zip*

As a result, the frequency of use of second homes is increasing. This growth in the number of second homes on the outskirts of major cities is not confined to the Côte d'Azur, but has also been observed throughout France.

These second homes are located between a 30 minute and 1.5 hour drive from major urban centers. There are therefore rural communes within the metropolitan zone's area of influence that have a leisure and relaxation function. Between 40% and 50% of weekly traffic on the RN 202, the main road linking Nice to its inland is concentrated at weekends. Furthermore, 75% of second homes in the upper and middle country are owned by people living in the PACA region, while 75% of second homes on the coast are owned by people living outside the PACA region.

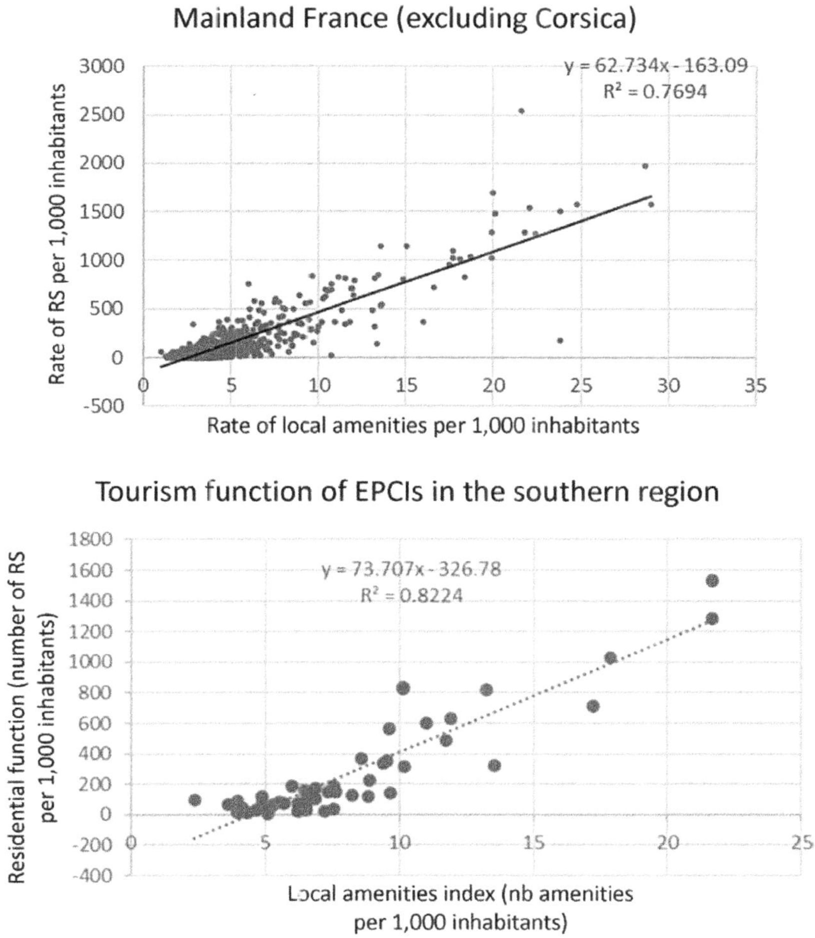

Figure 7.3. *Statistical correlations between the presence of local services and second homes*

The metropolitan territory can therefore appear to be "variable geometry". On weekdays, we have converging and tangential flows confined to an urban area, dominated by commutes to and from work. At weekends, the urban territory expands, exporting visitor flows to areas "outside the city". These divergent flows leave the perimeter of the typical urban area and move toward so-called rural or natural territories.

In order to identify metropolitan leisure areas, we will hypothesize that the rate of second homes is a determining variable in the attractiveness of tourist areas. If an area is regularly visited by an "intermittent" population, we assume that this visit has an impact on local services. Indeed, owners of second homes (between 12% and 15% of the French population) are likely to make greater use of certain types of local shops when they arrive at their holiday destination (town or country). We assume that this population, living in the nearby metropolis (less than two hours away), is likely to visit more often and thus support the year-round maintenance of local shops.

Using INSEE's 2019 permanent equipment database, which gives the number of facilities and services in the commune (from the number of doctors to theaters), we have selected three types of local services: grocery stores, restaurants and bakeries. We exclude tourist facilities (campsites, hotels and information points), as these are used by the nonresident tourist population.

We can thus see that the residential function and the proximity to amenities index are strongly correlated (Figure 7.3). We can therefore assume that local amenities are a marker of tourist and leisure attractiveness.

7.4. Prospective simulations of attractiveness

Using a gravity-based travel model, we simulate the use of areas on the outskirts of major metropolises, in order to understand the probability of travel from these urban centers as a function of attractiveness indicators, which do not exclusively focus on tourist capacity (number of beds).

To do this, we have modeled the Côte d'Azur region and its inland in a road graph that integrates the entire Côte d'Azur metropolis, stretching from Menton to the east of Var.

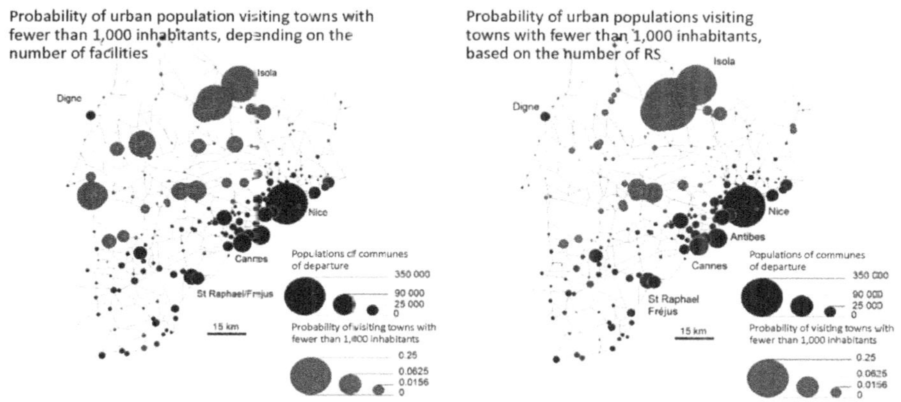

a) b)

Figure 7.4. *Probability of traffic within 120 min of the Côte d'Azur's upper and middle country towns (in red) from all towns (in blue, population size). (a) Probability of traffic as a function of the number of amenities. (b) Probability of traffic as a function of the number of second homes (sources: INSEE 2020, FRED software, Fabrice Decoupigny, UMR ESPACE, UCA 2023). For a color version of this figure, see www.iste.co.uk/christofle/tourism2.zip*

The simulations in Figure 7.4(B) show a potential concentration of visitor trips in a small number of communes corresponding to winter sports resorts (Isola, Auron, La Colmiane, Valberg, etc.), with a large number of second homes. The simulation results in Figure 7.4(A) show a less concentrated distribution of visitors. The results of the two simulations are similar, as the two attractive variables in the model (number of amenities and number of second homes) are more or less correlated with one another. The only thing that changes is the likely number of visitors. Furthermore, we can see that highly attractive towns are not isolated, but form clusters.

It would seem that there are routes that form more or less differentiated visitor sub-areas (Figure 7.5(A)). We obtained these results by simulating the probabilities that urban dwellers will travel to villages in the upper and middle country, in other words, to residential areas of less than 1,000 inhabitants. Concentration sub-areas appear, focusing along routes. Depending on travel times, certain forms of concentration are more intense on the territory. The model thus reveals traffic sub-areas located in very distinct sectors of the territory (Figure 7.5(B)). These concentrations seem to be correlated by the existence of a reception network that allows for the organization of tour routes. As a result, the relative position of the sites will amplify visitor concentrations in certain sectors and enable the creation of tour routes.

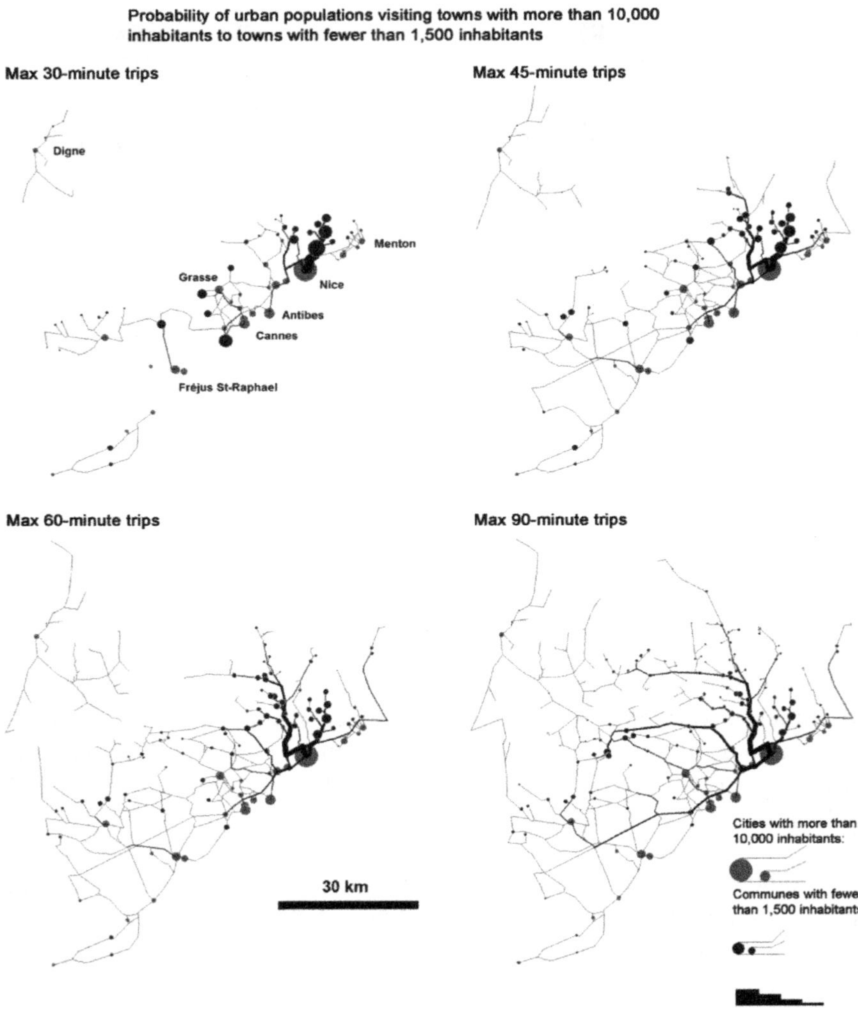

Figure 7.5. *(A) Probability of travel and the emergence of recreational areas. Probability of recreational trip flows from Côte d'Azur metropolitan area. For a color version of this figure, see www.iste.co.uk/christofle/tourism2.zip*

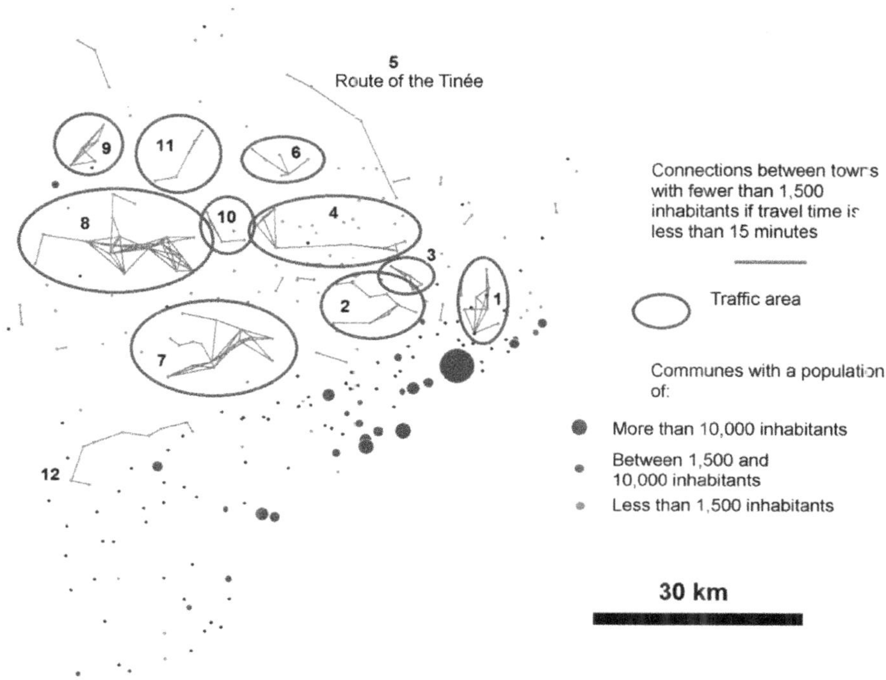

Figure 7.5. *(B) Probability of travel and the emergence of recreational areas. Travel sub-networks in the upper and middle country. For a color version of this figure, see www.iste.co.uk/christofle/tourism2.zip*

7.5. Conclusion

Of course, the model still needs to be improved and calibrated on the basis of counts and surveys carried out in situ, so that prospective simulations can be carried out.

Assessing the impact of the recreational activities of neighboring city-dwellers on the local residential economies inland would enable us to measure the resilience of these areas in the face of external shocks, as well as the latter's ability to sustain leisure activities in the face of constraints on travel and accessibility to urban centers.

7.6. References

Bachimon, P. (2018). De la banalisation de l'extraordinaire. La résidence secondaire du pareil au même. *Bulletin de l'association de géographes français*, 95(4), 568–581.

Bachimon, P., Dérioz, P., Vlès, V. (2017). *Les intermittents du territoire : les différentes facettes de la résidence secondaire*. Les Palabres d'aquí, Palau De Cerdagne.

Brennetot, A. (2004). Des festivals pour animer les territoires. *Annales de géographie*, 113(635), 29–50.

Danielou, F. and Dufeutrelle, J. (2021). Les résidences secondaires : un choix de proximité pour les habitants de la région. *INSEE Flash*, 118, 2.

Kadri, B. (2014). *Dynamiques métropolitaines et développement touristique*. Presses Universitaires du Québec, Montreal.

Léger, J.F. (2017). La géographie des résidences secondaires : une autre lecture des disparités territoriales. *Population et avenir*, 732(2), 4–8.

Lenoble, C. and Romeyer, C. (2020). L'office de tourisme du Grand Lyon pense aussi à ses habitants ! Article du dossier "Staycation et locatourisme". *Revue Espace*, 353, 1–120.

Négrier, E., Djakouane, A., Jourda, M.T. (2010). *Les publics des festivals*. Michel de Maule, Paris.

NOROIS (1983). Les loisirs non touristiques et leur influence sur l'organisation de l'espace. *Norois – Approches géographiques des loisirs*, 120, 479–677.

Violier, P., Duhamel, P., Gay, J.C., Mondou, V. (2021). *Le tourisme en France 1*. ISTE Éditions, London.

8

Hypermobility and Environmental and Societal Challenges

8.1. Introduction

How are individuals adapting their tourist mobilities and demonstrating their agility, in a dual context – the first context being structural, in the face of climatic challenges, and the second being conjunctural, in the face of the crisis caused by the Covid-19 pandemic? The research was carried out on hypermobile tourists, in other words, those with economic capital who make a large number of trips every year, except in 2020.

This chapter is based on a study commissioned and funded by Forum vies mobiles, the SNCF's research and exchange institute, which aimed to understand the behavior of so-called "hypermobile" tourists and identify the drivers of change in relation to the environmental crisis. Commissioned at the start of 2019, the research was disrupted in its progress by the Covid-19 pandemic, and its effects on travel plans has therefore been incorporated into the analysis.

8.2. Methodology

The research was carried out in two stages. A quantitative approach was taken using data from the "Suivi des déplacements touristiques" survey

---

Chapter written by Isabelle FROCHOT, Véronique MONDOU and Philippe VIOLIER.

For a color version of all figures in this chapter, see www.iste.co.uk/christofle/tourism2.zip.

conducted by Kantar on behalf of the Direction générale des entreprises (Enterprises General Directorate) of the French Ministry of Economy and Finance. Note that 20,000 households residing in France were surveyed each quarter. This first phase enabled us to identify those individuals who make the greatest number of trips in the course of a year (at least seven), as well as to define their profiles. Only personal trips motivated by pleasure were considered, not professional mobility.

A qualitative approach was then carried out with a sample of 30 individuals selected by Kantar in order to delve deeper into the practices and motivations of the so-called hypermobile tourists. In a qualitative approach, there is no satisfactory quantitative threshold in itself. It is the attainment of homogeneity and the recurrence of responses that us to consider whether or not the sample size is satisfactory. The 30 interviews carried out made it possible to achieve this semantic saturation. The survey was conducted in 2020, during the period affected by the Covid pandemic. The disruptions caused by the health situation and its possible impact on mobility were integrated into the research. The interviews, lasting between 1 and 1.5 hours, enabled us to record all journeys made in 2018 and 2019, the pre-pandemic period, as well as those made – or planned – in 2020. The descriptive aspect enabled us to trace the practices of these tourists: destination, project, mode of transport, group composition, which we then translated into schematic maps. Beyond the factual aspects, the questions focused on the motivations and values given by people to these trips, as well as on the reasons for their modal choices. Last but not least, the aim was to broaden reflection on environmental awareness to everyday life, and not just to tourist trips.

8.3. Analytical framework

Working on the behavior of hypermobile tourists forces us to question the meaning given to tourism. There is a strong temptation in discourse to consider tourism as a futile activity, which individuals could therefore do without. Yet work on tourism carried out since the late 1990s (MIT Team 2002; Knafou and Stock 2013) has highlighted all the stresses that have been placed on the individual since the advent of industrial society. Its deployment has been accompanied by the introduction of time away from work, the function of which is to allow for the relative release of stress. However, only a fraction of this free time is really effective, according to the spectrum proposed by Norbert Élias and Eric Dunning (1995): traveling outside of everyday life is among the most *recreational* of practices (MIT Team 2002). This change of space means leaving the usual places, which can be alienating and part of the stresses that weigh on daily life, and heading to dedicated places that are designed to encourage the release of stress. Considering tourism as a system that contributes to the recreation of individuals actually rules out the idea that individuals can live without tourism, which is potentially perceived as a futile activity.

Hypermobile tourists are a relevant category to study, as they are identified as the biggest contributors to greenhouse gas emissions (Gössling et al. 2012; Gössling and Humpe 2020; Büchs and Mattioli 2022). The behavior of hypermobile tourists is a broader reflection of the place occupied by mobility in contemporary societies, a point that Sheller and Urry (2006) refer to as the *mobility turn*, a concept considered to be spatially structuring and guiding current lifestyles. In particular, Urry (2005) analyzes the role of the car and its corollary "automobility", which "re-configure[s] modes of sociability". This paves the way for the notion of mobility as "capital" (Lévy 2013; Stock 2019), along the lines of the theory developed by Bourdieu. This implies that mobility capital enables differentiated access to resources. According to the literature (Gössling and Stavrinidi 2015), hypermobility is supported by two stimuli. First, the valorization of network capital is all the more significant when the distance, frequency and dispersion of trips favor specific modes of transport and destinations. Second, the social glorification of mobility is conveyed through various media and telecommunication channels. Until recently, these stimuli echoed an elitist approach to tourism. The latter testifies to financial "power" and a superior social status as prerequisites to the practice of travel without the boundaries of time and space. Now, hypermobility can be mass-produced. However, beyond the environmental impact, the negative externalities of hypermobility are undeniable on a psychological and even societal level, fueling global risks. Cohen and Gössling (2015) speak of the dark side of hypermobility.

This social inequity is, however, accompanied by a massification of tourist mobility, notably linked to the increase in air travel (Gössling et al. 2009). The latter is controversial and paradoxical. Authors, such as Gössling et al. (2019), highlight the affirmation of air travel as a social norm. On the other hand, under the impetus of low-cost airlines, which place lower prices than the competition at the heart of their model, we have seen a general decline in air fares and the spread of very low prices that are lower than those of other modes of transport. As a result, and even if the statistics show an increase in the number of air trips, some researchers (Demoli and Subtil 2019) show that it is, above all, a question of "quantitative democratization – in other words, a uniform increase in the likelihood of air travel – accompanied by a form of polarization, in other words, a multiplication of trips rather than a multiplication of travelers".

Lastly, this research is part of the field analyzing the transfer of sustainable behaviors from everyday life to tourism practices, including the attitude-behavior gap (Gössling and Nilsson 2010; Miller et al. 2015; Ramchurjee and Suresha 2015; Juvan and Dolnicar 2016). This refers to the fact that many consumers claim to be mindful of environmental issues, but in reality, climate change awareness seems to have little impact on tourist travel.

8.4. Main results

8.4.1. *Varied combinations*

Collectively, our results show that hypermobility can be broken down into combinations of practices, locations and modes of transport (Table 8.1). We will see later that these practices also vary according to household composition and the nature of the networks of family and friends.

Practice	Destinations	Preferred means of transport
Socialization	Metropolitan France	Car
	International/DOM	Plane
Discovery	International	Plane
Rest	Metropolitan France	Car
Games/sport	Metropolitan France	Car

Table 8.1. *Combinations of tourism practices, destinations and choice of modes of transport (source: interviews)*

The discovery project (the most frequently cited item) has very little to do with proximity (Table 8.1). It is a practice associated with international and long-distance travel. Stays in France, on the other hand, are more closely associated with rest or games/sports projects, and in part with sociability, such as visits to children and grandchildren at their second home, or visits to friends at short distances. Furthermore, the absence of family stresses, particularly those related to children, translates into greater mobility, as shown in Figure 8.1.

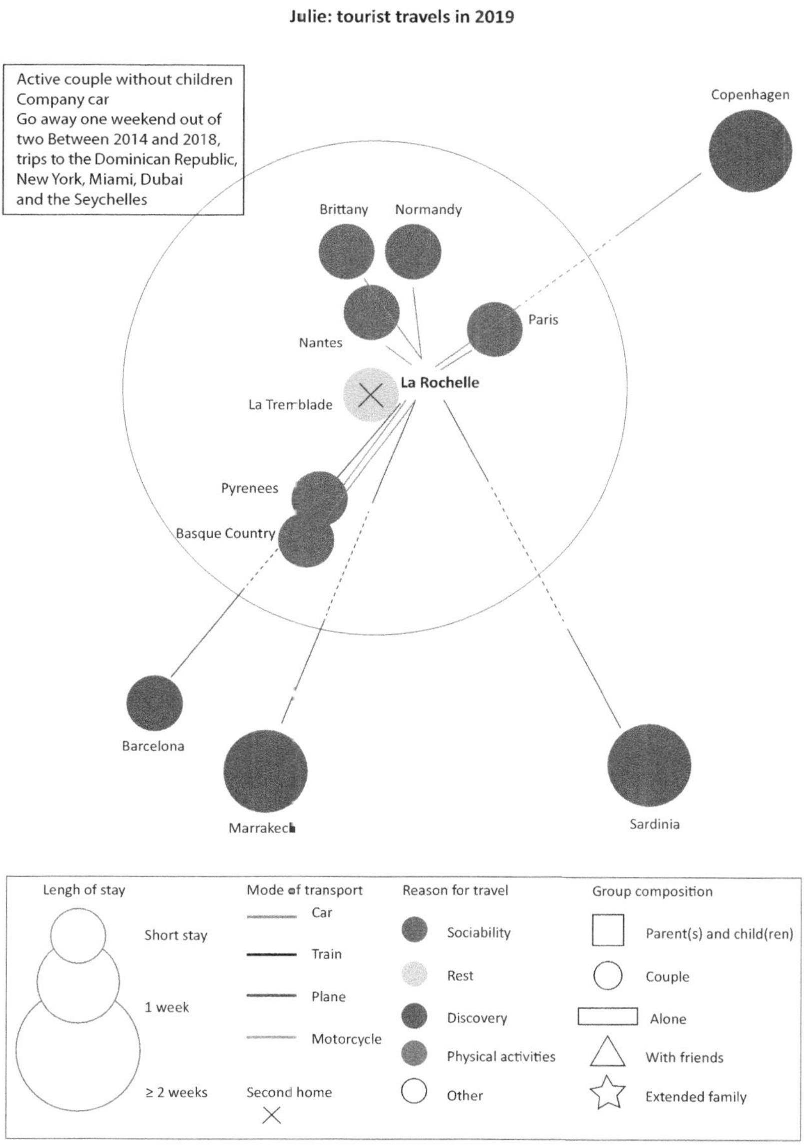

Figure 8.1. *Combinations of tourism project, destination and mode of transport implemented by Julie (source: interview). The legend applies to Figures 8.1–8.6*

The composition of the group can also lead to different practices. Figure 8.2 identifies different combinations: rest is mostly associated with family, whereas discovery and sociability are mostly associated with couples.

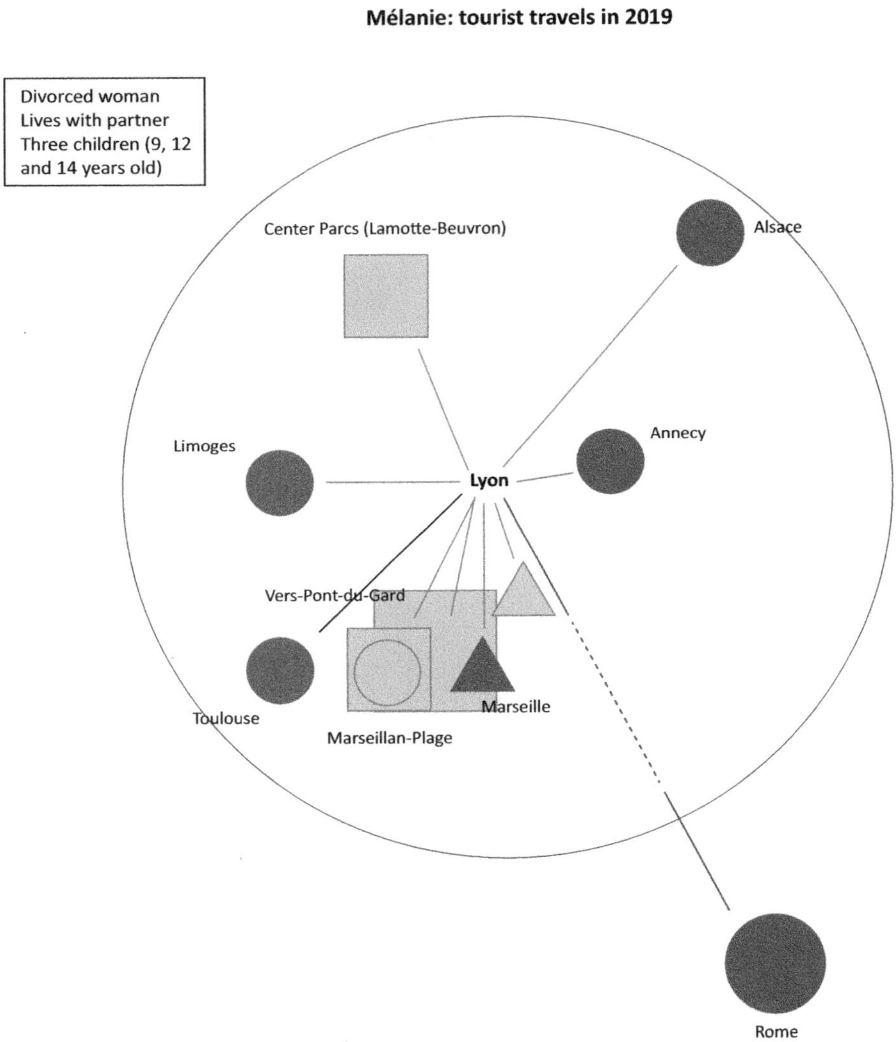

Figure 8.2. *Combinations of tourism project, destination and mode of transport implemented by Mélanie (source: interview). Legend: see Figure 8.1*

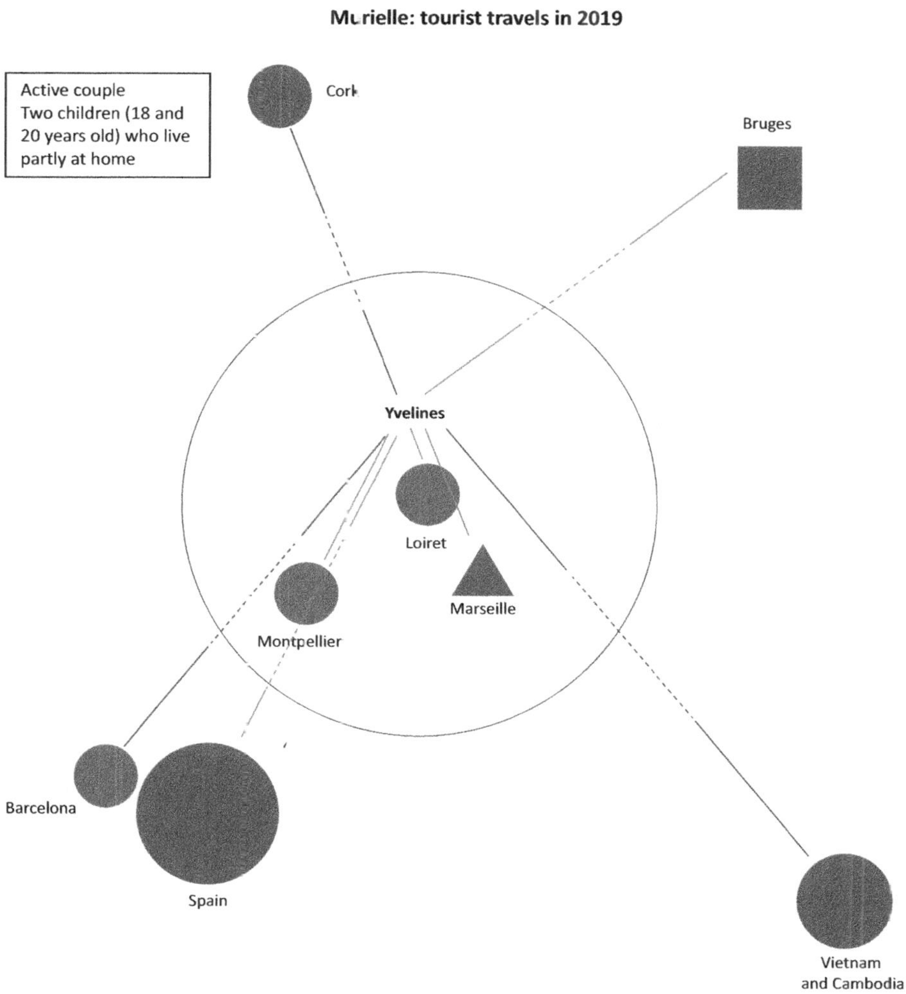

Figure 8.3. *Combinations of tourism project, destination and mode of transport implemented by Murielle (source: interview). Legend: see Figure 8.1*

Mobility is also the result of globalization. Sociability flows (visiting family/friends) are highly represented both in France and abroad, like Murielle, who visited her friends in Barcelona (Figure 8.3), or with overseas departments, between children studying abroad, the expatriation of working people and retirees visiting their expatriate children. Mauricette and her husband, for example, visit their children in Reunion and French Polynesia every year. However, this has not stopped them from taking advantage of their stay in Réunion to discover Russia and Mauritius in 2019.

Proximity does not exclude repeat trips, since the cases we have encountered are part of hypermobility and correspond to a choice, or are the result of economic constraints. In the first case, in a family that is well-off, the parents believe that foreign trips are an important stage in the children's development, and that France should be preferred for the youngest. A long-distance trip was planned, but had to be postponed due to the outbreak of the pandemic. In the second case, a divorced mother with a limited income and three dependent children limits her travels to France, regardless of the intention (discovery, socializing and rest).

In terms of the choice of mode, two means of transport dominate: car and plane. Each of these modes has a special place in the motive/destination combination.

Thus, the car is associated with sociability and rest, as these motives are themselves mostly linked to France. Air travel is primarily associated with discovery, and with trips abroad or to overseas France. This mode of transport is of course favored for intercontinental travel, but it is also used for short stays in neighboring countries. Low-cost offers are clearly identified by respondents as an incentive for tourist travel, or for visiting friends and family. Proximity to airports where low-cost airlines have a strong presence also facilitates the use of this type of service. Cars are popular for their ubiquitous quality and practicality, especially for families with children. From a spatial point of view, the car can be used to cover the "last mile", to get around once you have arrived at your destination, and for roaming.

Lastly, the train is only briefly mentioned for tourist travel. Its use is only mentioned for journeys to major cities (Paris, Marseille), when it combines both speed and a solution to parking problems. It is more often associated with professional mobility, or with people who have few or no modal alternatives, especially young people. The modal choice is therefore divided between road and air, depending on the mobility plans of the people concerned.

8.4.2. *Effects of the pandemic*

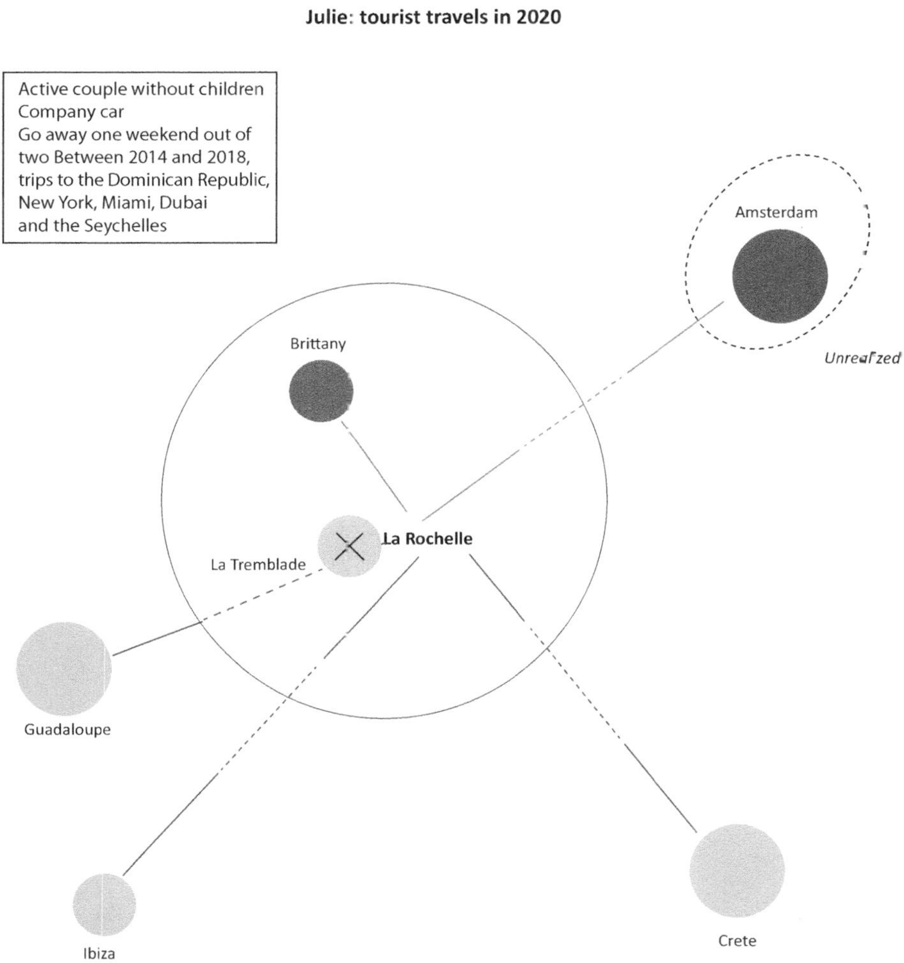

Figure 8.4. *Combinations of tourism project, destination and mode of transport implemented in 2020 by Julie: a combination that was little affected by pandemic-related restrictions (source: interview). Legend: see Figure 8.1*

The pandemic led the public authorities to impose severe restrictions on travel, which was totally banned at the height of the crisis, both abroad and in France. Logically, tourist mobility was drastically reduced and refocused on France as soon as the situation was less tense. However, a few individuals managed to seize the opportunities, notably to destinations that were able to pull through[1] (Figures 8.4 and 8.5).

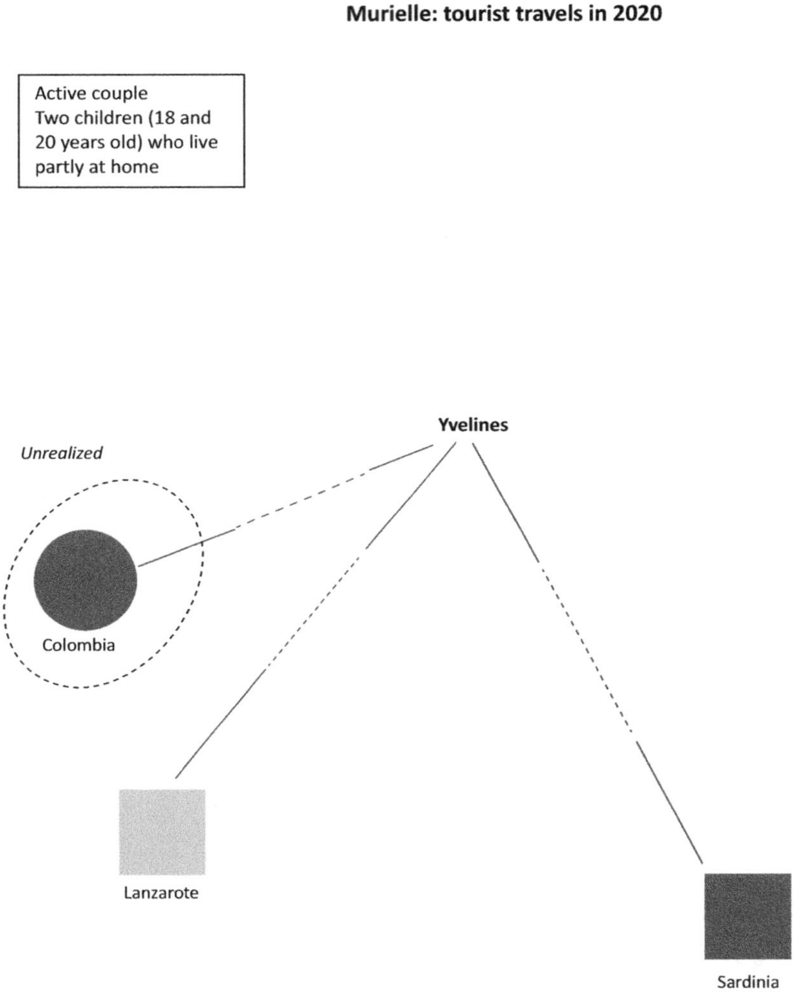

Figure 8.5. *Combinations of tourism project, destination and mode of transport in 2020 by Murielle: a combination partially affected by pandemic-related restrictions (source: interview). Legend: see Figure 8.1*

1 To facilitate comparison between combinations made in 2019 and those made in 2020, in other words, adapted to the Covid pandemic, the individuals are identical in both sets of figures.

In addition to the change in destination, there was also a discrepancy between motives before and during the health crisis. Intentions were dominated by sociability and rest, while discovery was restricted (Figure 8.6).

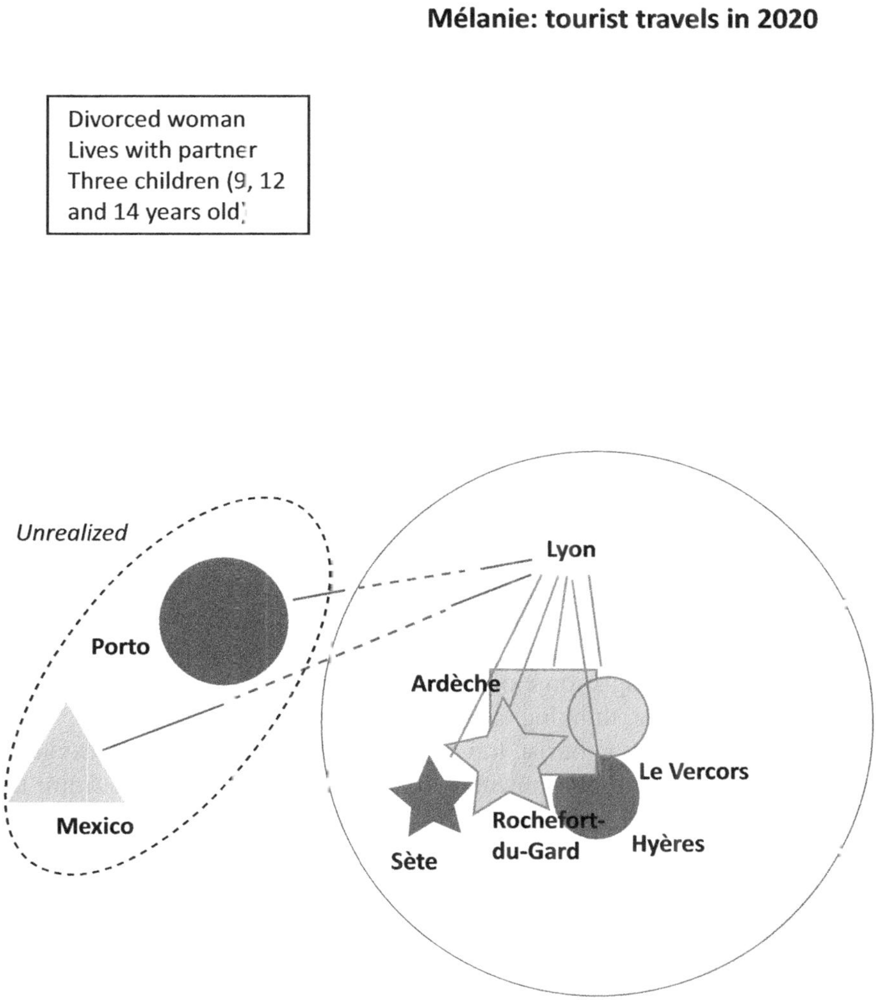

Figure 8.6. *Combinations of tourism project, destination and mode of transport implemented in 2020 by Mélanie: a combination that was refocused on France following the pandemic (source: interview). Legend: see Figure 8.1*

8.4.3. *Effects of lifting restrictions*

The lifting of restrictions and the return to free circulation have resulted in mobility being resumed and the reactivation of projects that had simply been postponed. No questions were raised in the interviews, nor were any asked about the modes of transport used. Refocusing on France is seen as a last resort in the face of the crisis, but not as a sustainable alternative to international travel. Since discovery is associated with remoteness, the latter is not, for this category, rivaled by local tourism. At the same time, even though some researchers are calling for a reconsideration of the air travel system in the light of the health crisis (Gössling and Humpe 2020), air travel is not ruled out in favor of modes that have less impact in terms of pollutant emissions.

8.5. Discussion: a stark observation

The attitude-behavior gap (Juvan and Dolnicar 2016) is confirmed. The majority of interviewees declare that they were aware of sustainable development issues. These concerns are reflected in the implementation of numerous ethical practices in their daily lives. These practices apply to the home, with waste sorting, controlled management of electricity and water consumption, short-distance sourcing, etc. These behaviors also apply to daily travel, where car-sharing is organized and public transport and cycling are favored. Even though some of those that were questioned used cars, the majority claim to be thinking about alternative modes. However, these attitudes do not lead to tourist travel being rethought, which is excluded from this reflection. Environmental considerations are absent from the decision-making process, whether for destinations or modal choices. Discovery is a powerful motivator that, as mentioned above, is associated with remoteness. The use of the plane is thus justified, but even for a short distance (less than two-hour flight), the idea of rejecting plane travel was not brought up. Overall, our results confirm certain findings already established by other researchers. Miller et al. (2015) measured tourist behavior in favor of the environment. The authors confirm that, although these tourists demonstrate a positive attitude toward the environment in their daily lives, they only engage in pro-environmental actions during their travels if this is not binding. Another study by Ramchurjee and Suresha (2015) also identified that depending on tourists' different levels of education, and even if they are aware of the impact of their behavior, they are not ready to act in favor of the environment when visiting a destination.

This resistance to environmental commitment can be explained by elements shared by the tourists questioned in this study: the idea of tourism as an exceptional time–space conducive to recreation, and as such, an escape from the considerations and constraints of everyday life (MIT Team 2002). Moreover, hypermobile tourists have a high level of mobility capital, and discovery, the driving force behind travel, gives mobility a cultural aspect. Households with children claim that mobility plays a role in their upbringing. Tourist travel is therefore totally integrated into the lifestyle of this category of tourists. Ultimately, the lack of information or modal alternatives (Hares et al. 2010) is a limiting factor.

Juvan and Dolnicar (2016) have highlighted the tendency to underestimate the situation, to shift responsibility to the most serious cases or to deny our own responsibilities. These elements did not emerge conclusively from our study and, in fact, a certain impunity was assumed among the majority of respondents.

Moreover, Gössling and Nilsson (2010) have clearly identified that self-image, social position and a form of self-worth can be associated with a "necessity" to travel as a social norm. For the respondents interviewed in this study, it seems clear that their travels are part of a socially embedded and valued way of life. Hibbert et al. (2013) identified that society views highly mobile lifestyles in a positive light: high mobility is associated with a high degree of "encounters", that is to say, an individual's position in society is reflected in mobility plans, ultimately necessitating air travel. The results of this study did not directly identify similar mechanisms. However, it is clear from the interviews that this ability to travel often and far is a sign of status in society that characterizes them, which they value.

Even if they are committed to a sustainable approach, the hypermobile tourists that were interviewed do not systematically seek to offset their journeys with other potentially positive impacts (actions benefiting local communities, for example). Research shows that price could also be hindering a transition toward mobility that consumes less high-carbon energy (Budeanu 2007; Carrus et al. 2008; Pulido-Fernandez and Lopez-Sanchez 2016). However, hypermobile tourists do not refer to this financial aspect and even claim to be willing to pay more for the purchase and use of more sustainable services. Our sample is made up of households with incomes above the French median. The average monthly income is 5,813€, in other words, 3.2 times the median income for "a person living alone" (1,837€ in 2019) and one and a half times the same indicator for a couple with two children under 14 (3,857€) (source: INSEE). However, one individual has a very high income. If we exclude them from our sample, the average income is reduced to 4,979€, which is still significantly higher than the median income. The difficulty here is not financial, and tourist mobility is so deeply rooted in the lifestyles of hypermobile tourists that it seems difficult to transform.

8.6. Conclusion

There is a total paradox between pro-environmental practices that are very much a part of everyday life, and the nonexistence of such practices when it comes to tourist travel, with the environmental aspect "consciously" left out of the decision-making process.

The attitude-behavior gap refers to the fact that many consumers claim to be aware of environmental issues, but that this awareness is not reflected in their behavior. When it comes to traveling even short distances, air travel is preferred, followed by the use of cars. Trains are only used for journeys between major cities. In fact, awareness of climate change seems to have little impact on tourist mobility outside of France.

The hedonic aspect of vacations clearly plays a key role in this equation. The recreational role of tourism (MIT Team 2002) and the meaning it takes on in industrial society also account for this resistance. On the other hand, discovery and travel are seen as essential to the lives of those that were surveyed. This discovery is mainly associated with long-distance travel, for which there are few alternatives to air transport. Yet, it is long-haul air travel that is responsible for the majority of CO_2 emissions (Dobruszkes et al. 2022). Squaring this circle will therefore be a complicated challenge.

8.7. References

Büchs, M. and Mattioli, G. (2022). How socially just are taxes on air travel and 'frequent flyer levies'? *Journal of Sustainable Tourism*, 32(1), 62–84. doi: 10.1080/09669582.2022.2115050.

Budeau, A. (2007). Sustainable tourist behaviour – A discussion of opportunities for change. *International Journal of Consumer Studies*, 31(5), 499–508.

Carrus, G., Passafaro, P., Bonnes, M. (2008). Emotions, habits and rational choices in ecological behaviours: The case of recycling and use of public transportation. *Journal of Environmental Psychology*, 28(1), 51–62.

Cohen, S.A. and Gössling, S. (2015). A darker side of hypermobility. *Environment and Planning A*, 41(8), 1661–1679. doi: 10.1177/0308518X15597124.

Cottrell, S.P. and Graefe, A.R. (1997). Testing a conceptual framework of responsible environmental behavior. *The Journal of Environmental Education*, 29(1), 17–27.

Crutzen, P.J. and Stoermer, E.F. (2000). The "Anthropocene". *Global Change Newsletters*, 41, 17–18.

Cuvelier, P. (1998). *Anciennes et nouvelles formes de tourisme. Une approche socioéconomique*. L'Harmattan, Paris.

Demoli, Y. and Subtil, J. (2019). Boarding classes. Mesurer la démocratisation du transport aérien en France (1974–2008). *Sociologie*, 10(2), 131–151 [Online]. Available at: https://www.cairn.info/revue-sociologie-2019-2-page-131.htm.

Dobruszkes, F., Mattioli, G., Mathieu, L. (2022). Banning super short-haul flights: Environmental evidence or political turbulence? *Journal of Transport Geography*, 104, 103457. doi: 10.1016/j.jtrangeo.2022.103457.

Gössling, S. (2020). Risks, resilience, and pathways to sustainable aviation: A COVID-19 perspective. *Journal of Air Transport Management*, 89, 101933. doi: 10.1016/j.jairtraman.2020.101933.

Gössling, S. and Humpe, A. (2020). The global scale, distribution and growth of aviation: Implications for climate change. *Global Environmental Change*, 65, 102194. doi: 10.1016/j.gloenvcha.2020.102194.

Gössling, S. and Nilsson, H. (2010). Frequent flyer programs and the reproduction of aero-mobility. *Environment and Planning A*, 42(1), 241–252.

Gössling, S. and Stavrinidi, I. (2015). Frequent flyer programs and the reproduction of aero-mobility. *Environment and Planning A*, 42, 241–252.

Gössling, S., Ceron, J-P., Dubois, G., Hall, M.C. (2009). Hypermobile travellers. In *Climate Change and Aviation, Issues, Challenges and Solutions*, Gössling, S. and Upham, P. (eds). Routledge, London.

Gössling, S., Hall, C.M., Weaver, D.B.J. (2012). *Sustainable Tourism Futures*. Routledge, London.

Gössling, S., Hanna, P., Higham, J., Cohen, S., Hopkins, D. (2019). Can we fly less? Evaluating the 'necessity' of air travel. *Journal of Air Transport Management*, 81, 101722. doi: 10.1016/j.jairtraman.2019.101722.

Hares, A., Dickinson, J., Wilkes, K. (2010). Climate change and the air travel decisions of UK tourists. *Journal of Transport Geography*, 18(3), 466–473. doi: 10.1016/j.jtrangeo.2009.06.018.

Hibbert, J.F., Dickinson, J.E., Gössling, S., Curtin, S. (2013). Identity and tourism mobility: An exploration of the attitude-behaviour gap. *Journal of Sustainable Tourism*, 21(7), 999–1016. doi: 10.1080/09669582.2013.826232.

Juvan, E. and Dolnicar S. (2016). Measuring environmentally sustainable tourist behaviour. *Annals of Tourism Research*, 59, 30–44.

Knafou, R. and Stock, M. (2013). Tourisme. In *Dictionnaire de la géographie et de l'espace des sociétés*, Lévy, J. and Lussault, M. (eds). Belin, Paris.

Lévy, J. (2013). Capital spatial. In *Dictionnaire de la géographie et de l'espace des sociétés*, Lévy, J. and Lussault, M. (eds). Belin, Paris.

Miller, D., Merrilees, B., Coghlan, A. (2015). Sustainable urban tourism: Understanding and developing visitor pro-environmental behaviours. *Journal of Sustainable Tourism*, 23(1), 26–46.

MIT Team (2002). *Tourisme 1. Lieux communs*. Belin, Paris.

Pulido-Fernández, J.I. and López-Sánchez, Y. (2016). Are tourists really willing to pay more for sustainable destinations? *Sustainability*, 8(12), 1240–1260.

Ramchurjee, N.A. and Suresha, S. (2015). Are tourists' environmental behavior affected by their environmental perceptions and beliefs? *Journal of Environmental and Tourism Analyses*, 3(1), 26–44.

Sheller, M. and Urry, J. (2006). The new mobilities paradigm. *Environment and Planning A: Economy and Space*, 38(2), 207–226. doi: 10.1068/a37268.

Stock, M. (2019). Mobilités. In *Vocabulaire des histoires de vie et de la recherche biographique*, Delory-Momberger, C. (ed.). Érès, Paris.

Urry, J. (2005). *Sociologie des mobilités. Une nouvelle frontière pour la sociologie ?* Armand Colin, Paris.

9

Feedback on Soft Mobility and Sustainable Tourism in Côte d'Opale: The Bicycle, a Vector of Agility

Since 2020, the crisis linked to the Covid-19 pandemic has had a profound impact on the tourism sector. This unprecedented context leads us to question the sector's capacity for resilience[1] and the sustainability of initiatives taken by all players in the region: from institutional strategies to the composition of new service offerings, and even to user behavior, sustainable tourism now seems to be a marker of ongoing change. The critical phenomenon induced by the Covid-19 epidemic calls into question the strategic models of tourist development, seeking to move beyond a short-term situation.

In addition to this health crisis, there are other stress factors (climate, energy and inflation) that require decisions to be taken for sustainable tourism. This questioning by academics (Marcotte et al. 2020) seems to have been taken up by politicians. The French government has presented its

---

Chapter written by Jean-Denis HUE and Vincent HERBERT.

1 The second concept aims to go beyond adapting to shocks, to "develop new paths to growth. [Here] resilience refers to the ability to renew oneself after the occurrence of risks. Resilience and stability are therefore different, insofar as resilience does not mean returning to the initial situation" (Boschama 2015). More than just a strategic tool for coping with crisis, resilience then becomes a vector for strategic innovation. We will refer to this notion here as "dynamic resilience", understood as "the capacity to invent new resources or values in a context of change" (Hamdouch et al. 2012; Masclanis 2020).

strategy through "Destination France"[2], stating its intention to become the world's leading destination for sustainable tourism, and by 2030, the leading destination for bicycle tourism. These announcements determine the development of a tourism policy, providing a strategic framework whose effects will need to be measured.

9.1. Action research to understand local mobility issues

The context of this reflection is part of a doctoral program co-funded by the Fondation de France and the Université du Littoral-Côte-d'Opale (ULCO) since 2020.

The method consists of "surveying" the area with institutional players, visitors and residents of the Côte d'Opale. Various tools are used to build up a primary database on innovative initiatives and local authority strategies, as well as on new user practices, both pedestrian and sedentary.

The field observation was carried out by the SAP association (Société anonyme et populaire – anonymous and popular society), in collaboration with other structures enabling the organization of events on the territory between summer 2020 and summer 2022. A variety of systems are in place.

We run tutored workshops either with students from ULCO's tourism master's program ("territorial workshops"), or in BTS, or with young people on civic service. During these workshops, we gave them the task of creating bicycle itineraries. The aim was to design routes, meet with professional players, find unifying themes and promote new cycle tourism services. Some of these projects were set up as "challenges" to be presented at an "ecothon" in Dunkirk in January 2023, which, in the form of a hackathon, re-assessed the opportunity to develop these projects with a jury made up of associative, institutional and academic players.

Lastly, in order to address these cross-disciplinary issues, we led a focus group with an expert in mobility and intermodality. These practices enabled us to map out the resources that could be mobilized in the area, as well as the network of players likely to create the bicycle tourism offer.

2 See: https://www.gouvernement.fr/dossier-de-presse/12545-dossier-de-presse-du-premier-ministre-jean-castex-presentation-du-plan-destination-france.

We exchanged views with local users using questionnaires that were co-designed with local players. We chose to intervene either at bike-themed events, or at cultural and social summer events. One of the most widely used methods is probably the "barbe à questions" ("cotton candy questioning") approach, whereby visitors of an event are asked to answer a short questionnaire in exchange for a piece of cotton candy (Figure 9.1).

Figure 9.1. *"Barbe à questions", Sea festival, Boulogne-sur-Mer, July 12, 2023 (Vincent Herbert © 2023). For a color version of this figure, see www.iste.co.uk/christofle/tourism2.zip*

We enriched and complemented our approach with interviews conducted with tourists and local residents during informal meetings, as well as with institutional representatives and various local operators such as the Opale vélo service association, the Vélos de Nico, Belles Échappées, Deux Caps découverte companies, the Guînes tourist office, the Rivages propres association and the Agence de développement et de réservation touristique (ADRT) Pas-de-Calais tourisme.

Lastly, we collected over 800 questionnaires on cycling in the Côte d'Opale region, and conducted 11 interviews with stakeholders and users. These original data enable us to make an initial assessment of the orientation of territorial policies in terms of soft mobility through the prism of the bicycle.

9.2. Institutional agility as a marker of "direction" for an ecotourism policy

The agility of institutional players in terms of reaction and sustainable adaptation to critical situations is based on their willingness to coordinate territorial planning and development policies. The Loi d'Orientation des Mobilités (LOM, 2019) enables local authorities to implement mobility plans and become operators of soft and active mobility. The LOM thus enables investment in public transport capacity, intermodal mobility and, in particular, the "bicycle plan"[3]. These investments represent an opportunity to rethink the way users travel, whether they are residents or tourists. It should be remembered that tourism is a sector with a particularly high impact in terms of CO_2 emissions[4], due to tourism practices based on polluting mobility. Our summer survey (2022) of the Côte d'Opale tourists revealed that over 80% came to the site by car[5]. If the aim is to reduce the negative impact of tourism on climate change, we need to offer facilities that facilitate other forms of mobility, such as cycling.

The Pas-de-Calais department, through the prism of ADRT Pas-de-Calais tourism, whose board of directors is made up of department elected representatives, has made the decision to put cycling at the heart of its tourism appeal policy[6]. As part of the Interreg "Eurocyclo" project launched in 2017, it has been able to assess, experiment with and promote bike tourism on its territory. This European funding, which aims to facilitate exchanges of experience between territories with diverse practices, has enabled the department to lay the foundations of a development strategy and support operators sharing its opportunity diagnosis. According to one project manager: "We are still in the early stages, so we need to look at this development over a longer timeframe, and with much greater resources"[7].

3 See: https://www.ecologie.gouv.fr/sites/default/files/22165_DP-Plan-velo-VF.pdf.

4 See: https://presse.ademe.fr/2021/06/le-tourisme-durable-en-france-un-levier-de-relance-ecologique.html.

5 Results from our summer questionnaire on cycling (232 respondents).

6 See: https://velo-rando-pasdecalais.com/pas-de-calais-a-velo/.

7 Interview with a representative of Pas-de-Calais tourisme, September 2022.

In conjunction with the France vélo tourisme association[8], this operator is promoting the "Accueil vélo" brand to organize roaming on its territory. The aim is to identify places offering rental, accommodation and catering for tourists on bicycles.

The operator seeks to reinforce a national strategy by supporting local initiatives, but this policy does not yet constitute a sufficient network to "brand" the region and its players. As this label has a cost, some private operators point out that "they would not have wanted it if the department had not taken it on", while expressing a certain pride in having been identified and chosen[9].

For this network to be able to offer tourists the opportunity of a quality itinerary, we need to multiply its membership to create appealing conditions. Pas-de-Calais tourism works with the tourist offices in its area to promote the Accueil vélo brand and, more broadly, bicycle tourism. The aim is to not just label the area, but rather to create synergies, to show what is visible, and give space to cycling. With this in mind, more and more routes are being developed and signposted, and are being promoted to tourists (Figure 9.2).

For this dynamic to be coherent and attractive, it is important that the inter-communal bodies position themselves and invest in the facilities needed to create these flows. The Communauté de communes de la Région d'Audruicq (CCRA) has, under the LOM law, chosen to take responsibility for soft and active mobility, and recruited a "mobility" project manager back in March 2022.

While the first task is to rethink mobility plans, particularly intermodal ones, cycling practices are increasingly considered, even if "elected representatives do not yet have a fully-fledged cycling culture"[10]. However, their aim is to acquire local expertise so as to be able to "orient" development projects, to be able to mobilize other funding[11], or to support territorial dynamics.

---

8 See: https://www.francevelotourisme.com/sites/default/files/inline-files/FVT_dossier_de_presse_2022.pdf.

9 Interview with a bicycle operator in July 2022.

10 Interview with a project manager in September 2022.

11 See: https://developper-velotourisme.ademe.fr/.

Figure 9.2. *Tourist map from ADRT Pas-de-Calais tourisme (source: ADRT, Pas-de-Calais tourisme). For a color version of this figure, see www.iste.co.uk/christofle/tourism2.zip*

In this respect, the deployment of the Vélomaritime (cycle route No. 4) is a sure way to develop tourism (Figure 9.3).

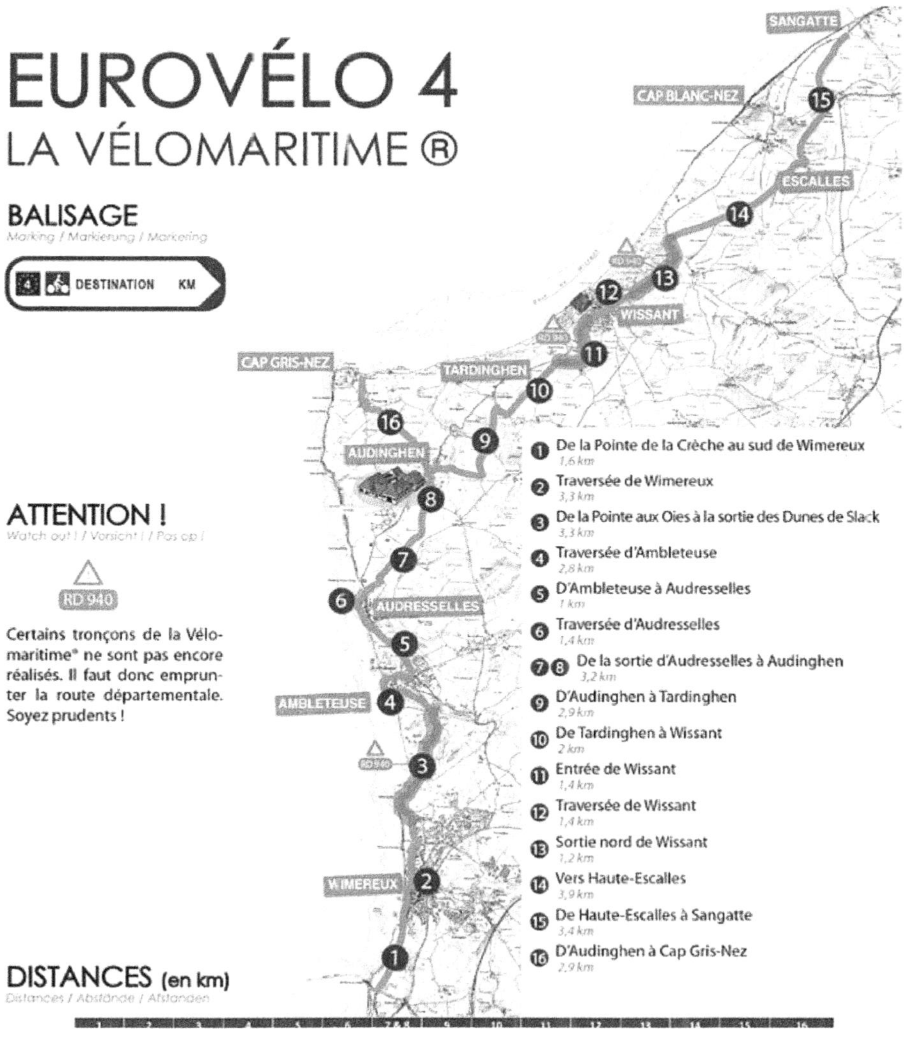

Figure 9.3. *Layout of cycle route No. 4*[12]*. For a color version of this figure, see www.iste.co.uk/christofle/tourism2.zip*

12 See: https://www.lavelomaritime.fr/itineraire/boulogne-sur-mer-calais.

The arguments put forward by the France vélo tourisme association, in particular, highlight visitor numbers and economic benefits, comparing them with those of the Loire à vélo[13]. These quantitative data seem to be gradually arousing the interest of local authorities. This coastal cycle route links Bruges (Belgium) to Roscoff (France). It is a strategic route, linking France to European countries where cycling is highly developed and an integral part of everyday life.

Tourists visiting the Côte d'Opale from Belgium, the Netherlands and Germany account for almost a third of all visits, and their numbers are increasing[14]. Communication about the Vélomaritime began after the health crisis, and the route is now over 80% complete. However, it is worth noting that this route is not made up of new trails, but more than 60% of upgrades to existing routes. This communicative agility enables institutions to build momentum at little cost. Nonetheless, the Vélomaritime is a strategic tool for linking tourist operators and local authorities around a bicycle tourism project (see Destination France). In view of current trends in tourism practices, this development can only serve to increase visitor numbers in the long term.

While we have noted that strategic policies in favor of bicycle tourism are being implemented, they do not seem to be up to the challenges of regional development. It is undeniable that strategies are being announced, that national and European experiences are proving the value of bicycle tourism for the development of tourism in a given region, and that expertise is being developed by associations. For this dynamic to be implemented, cohesion between the various institutions is necessary and remains to be developed, as we have emphasized. Above all, it deserves to be taken up by local residents and private operators alike.

9.3. The bicycle, a translation of "agile" practices for users

Although locals are considered to be part of tourist hospitality, and a much sought-after, high-quality source of information, the Vélomaritime is

13 See: https://pro-tourismeloiret.com/actualite/bilan-de-frequentation-des-veloroutes-juillet-2022/.

14 "+44% of overnight stays by Dutch tourists compared with 2019, +11.7% of overnight stays by German tourists compared with 2019", (Mr. Fasquel, press conference on October 4, 2022).

still not a major tourist attraction. Only 20% of those questioned were aware of Vélomaritime[15]. Communication in its favor does not yet seem to have reached its primary target: local residents.

For any sustainable tourism development plan, it is important to involve local residents or "natives" in development strategies. They bring their local expertise to the table, and support developments through recreational, day-trip, leisure and everyday use. One of the first results of local expertise is that, while they perceive "the beginnings of improvements", they consider the current facilities to be insufficient[16]. During discussions prompted by the questionnaire, a feeling of insecurity was expressed concerning the use of bicycles for family outings.

Most of those questioned (70%) believe that cycling will develop strongly over the next few years. They put forward the idea of ecological awareness, but also put forward economic reasons encouraging people to use bicycles for their mobility. Note that 80% of them express a desire to cycle on holiday, especially for excursions (less than 50 km), and 18% for extra-regional tourism

According to our summer observations, bicycle tourism is mainly practiced on an occasional basis during tourist stays. It is an opportunity to immerse yourself in the area, discovering the landscape. Tourist offices confirm this trend, pointing out that visitors are increasingly asking for brochures on bicycle touring.

The proportion of visitors who actually cycle on the Côte d'Opale is still very small. However, the people we interviewed had already visited the area and were following the Vélomaritime itinerary. We met a couple with a small child that was being towed in a bicycle trailer, who had arrived from the Lille region by train.

This time, they wanted to repeat the journey with their child, having developed an intrigue for this kind of mobility, "considered to be ecologically sound", but above all to "share the beauty of the landscapes" offered by the route with their family. However, they did point out some faults in the signposting, both in terms of directions and the choice of unsafe

15 Results from our summer questionnaire on cycling (232 respondents).

16 Results from our summer questionnaire on cycling (232 respondents).

passages[17]. They had not booked all of the accommodation, and were mainly looking for campsites to stop over at.

We also spoke to a Belgian couple in their seventies who were returning from the Baie de Somme by TER (regional express train) with their bikes. They use their bikes on a daily basis, and especially during their vacations. They estimate that they have cycled over 300,000 km. They know the region, and “love its landscapes”. They think that “the facilities are well done in France, and that while the French are polite and welcoming, they do not know their area”. For them, cycling is essential for maintaining good health, which is why they started and continue to ride, “especially when you look at the state” of their fellow cyclists. However, they also emphasize the psychological, mental need “to go the distance, to make an effort, to get to the top of a hill”.

These tourists are representative of the segments targeted by the region’s attractiveness policies (passionate explorer couple), attracted by the discovery of landscapes. They show a certain agility, relying on their expertise and knowledge that they have already acquired. However, the choice of intermodal mobility between train and bike seems anecdotal for the time being, as we have yet to see rail trains fully dedicated to the transport of touring cyclists, as is the case for the Loire à vélo.

While cycle paths need to be developed and signposted to facilitate cycling, it is also important that a rental service be made available to users. As we have already pointed out, many tourists access the region by car. While they prefer to explore the countryside on foot, there is a growing demand for bicycle touring. To meet this need, rental services have been set up.

The institutions have launched this service offering. As soon as it was created in 2014, the Maison du site des Deux Caps offered traditional and electric bike rental services. This first operator was followed by private operators on other sites. A network of operators wishing to make bike rentals available to visitors is forming. Since 2019, we have noticed that the rental offer has doubled. These are charged by the day or half-day, mainly on electrically assisted bikes, making it easier to experience the landscape in a demanding topographical context. Customers can be accompanied by a

17 Boulogne-sur-Mer, interview in June 2022, insecurity linked to the passage at the Wissant exit in particular.

guide, or ride independently. They use the operators' applications to discover the different routes on offer[18]. The strengthening of private initiatives (for example, the Opale vélo services association[19], or the les Vélos de Nico company[20]) is encouraging the emergence of spatial agility for tourists.

This rental service is complemented by the development of cycling events in the area. This year, we noted over thirty local races organized in the area under observation, including a stage of the Tour de France. In addition to these sporting events, other, more "experiential" events seem to be emerging, such as the one proposed by the Maison mer collective, and its "Vélo disco"[21]. These events are accompanied by the development of a range of accommodation, aimed specifically at welcoming bicycle tourists[22].

Although we are seeing an evolution in bicycle tourism practices, it is based on a referential change from users seeking to experiment, maintain or develop their ability to get around by bike. This gentle, active mobility, conducive to a landscape experience, is supported by a growing range of services. Our qualitative observations suggest a spatial and temporal development, which would benefit from being confirmed by the installation of eco-meters, giving us the possibility of a quantitative study[23].

9.4. Conclusion

Our observations and field surveys have led us to propose an initial typology of the different profiles of bicycle tourists. We can thus identify:

– tourists/second-home residents;

– regional residents with family or friends;

– traveling seniors;

– sport enthusiasts.

18 See: https://www.outdooractive.com/fr/route/vtt/nord-pas-de-calais/sur-les-traces-de-la-seconde-guerre-mondiale-au-cap-gris-nez/238666621/ (course created with ULCO students).

19 See: https://opaleveloservices.fr/.

20 See: https://www.velo-wissant.com/.

21 See: https://www.youtube.com/watch?v=rMH0r5Gmkow.

22 See: https://www.facebook.com/auxportesdeslacs/.

23 See: https://www.velo-territoires.org/observatoires/plateforme-nationale-de-frequentation/.

Table 9.1 shows the categories of bicycle tourists encountered during our surveys and their main traits.

	Belgians in residence	Regional families	Traveling seniors
Motivations	Quality of life Landscape appeal	Proximity Landscape appeal	Landscape appeal French hospitality
Modalities	Several bicycles available	Additional equipment (panniers, children's trailer, electric assistance) Train	Intermodality ("300 km on the odometer!") Train
Meaning	"Way of life" Everyday habits	Getting out of the city Ecological mobility Sharing, transmitting	Physical health Mental health
Limits	"Much to do"	Unsafe passages	Need for local ownership
Accommodation	Second home	Campsite	Bed and breakfast

Table 9.1. *Main profiles of cycle tourists encountered on the Côte d'Opale (Hue and Herbert 2023)*

From our field survey, we have determined the characteristic profiles of users engaged in cycling itineraries. They illustrate the eco-modern transition (Corneloup 2021) in tourism practices that territories are adapting to.

The agile discovery of the Côte d'Opale region is facilitated by developments, signposting and digital applications[24], which provide "directions" for their itineraries. The "translation" of users is made possible by the electrical evolution of equipment, the increase in rental services and intermodal possibilities. Bicycle tourism gives "meaning" to a tourist attraction policy that seeks to integrate sustainable tourism principles into its development. In order to consolidate this dynamic, and to make it ever more coherent and visible, it now seems necessary to link public and private players through contractual arrangements that reinforce local initiatives. The regional council's proposal for a tourism outreach contract[25] would, in this respect, be interesting to observe.

24 See: https://www.outdooractive.com/fr/route/vtt/nord-pas-de-calais/sur-les-traces-de-la-seconde-guerre-mondiale-au-cap-gris-nez/238666621/.

25 See: https://guide-aides.hautsdefrance.fr/dispositif855.

9.5. References

Berque, A. (2009). *Écoumène. Introduction à l'étude des milieux humains*. Belin, Paris.

Boschma, R. (2015). Towards an evolutionary perspective on regional resilience *Regional Studies*, 49(5), 733–751. doi: 10.1080/00343404.2014.959481.

Coriat, B. (2021). *La pandémie, l'anthropocène et le bien commun*. Les Liens qui Libèrent, Paris.

Corneloup, J. (2021). *La transition récréative, une utopie transmoderne*. Presses Universitaires de Rouen et du Havre, Rouen.

Hamdouch, A., Depret, M.H., Tanguy, C. (2012). *Mondialisation et résilience des territoires : trajectoires, dynamiques d'acteurs et expériences*. Presses de l'Université du Québec, Quebec.

Hue, J.D. and Herbert, V. (2023). Retour d'expériences de mobilité douce et de tourisme durable en côte d'Opale : la bicyclette, vecteur d'agilité. Report [Online]. Available at: https://hal.science/hal-04146815v1/document.

Knafou, R. (2021). *Réinventer le tourisme, sauver nos vacances sans détruire le monde*. Éditions du Faubourg, Paris.

Marcotte, P., Reda Khomsi, M., Falardeau, I., Roult, R., Lapointe, D. (2020). Tourisme et Covid-19. *Téoros* [Online]. Available at: http://journals.openedition.org/teoros/7976 [Accessed 1 February 2021].

Masclanis, F. (2020). Résilience et tourisme : d'une crise conjoncturelle à une mutation structurelle ? *Téoros* [Online]. Available at: http://journals.openedition.org/teoros/7891 [Accessed 2 February 2021].

Conclusion

C.1. Tourism, territories and actors: from adaptation to agility

The initial findings demonstrate that tourism is a reactive and adaptive sector. In a short time, this activity has largely recovered the “deficit” caused by the major crisis of the Covid-19 pandemic and has returned to significant levels of activity. Indeed, after the dramatic decline of 2020 and 2021, the UNWTO[1] reported more than 900 million international arrivals in 2022, already twice the figures recorded in 2021, although still at 63% of pre-pandemic levels (UNWTO 2023). In 2023, 1.3 billion international arrivals were noted, representing a 44% increase compared to 2022, with a full return to pre-pandemic figures expected in 2024 (UNWTO 2024). This recovery, as swift as it is remarkable, indeed reflects the influence of tourism on citizens’ lives. Whether it concerns flows for leisure, business, events, meetings or conferences at local, national and international scales, tourism remains a “global” phenomenon (Arionesei et al. 2014), increasingly *permeating* places and societies. We could say that tourism is reclaiming its place, continuing to expand geographically while, in a post-Covid shift, giving a renewed opportunity to the locals (Yu et al. 2023). It continues to shape territories and organizations, influence ways of living and even thinking, and maintain close ties with the economic, political, geopolitical, societal and social realms. However, the crisis has left its mark in a context of heightened uncertainties and transitions (ecological, digital, demographic

---

Conclusion written by Sylvie CHRISTOFLE.

1 Now UN Tourism.

and more), accelerating certain changes and encouraging destinations and organizations to demonstrate agility.

Dynamism and forward-looking visions thus emerge as key points in the evolution of destinations and the creation of trajectories within an "agile" model, taking into account both global changes and more localized phenomena. The role of public and private actors, at all scales, is crucial, and depending on the contexts, each destination has its own trajectory, which can remain linear, bend or change direction. Territorial and organizational agility can then be expressed through active replications of proven effective models, accelerations of changes, even transformations or reinventions. This book has developed discourse analyses, conveyed both in the press and in scientific literature, theoretical benchmarks and responses to the upheavals induced by major ongoing transitions. These gauge tourism agility through policies for planning and redesigning spaces, marketing and communication strategies, technological, digital, and societal innovations, the development of activities complementary to traditional tourism, increasingly mixed experiences and offers targeting both tourist populations and local inhabitants simultaneously. Tourism agility lies at the heart of a certain functional and spatial redeployment of the activity, of adjustments between stakeholders, which are the seeds of current and future territorial and organizational strategies.

Theories regarding complex adaptive systems have been developing since the 2000s (Baggio 2008; Baggio et al. 2010; Brouder and Eriksson 2013; Ma and Hassink 2013; Hartman 2018). In the face of uncertainty, strategies and policies of action through adaptability processes, even agility, have been implemented by destinations at different scales and are presented in this book. These ways of viewing the world and tourism indeed seem to be responses to a contemporary context of instability (Hartman 2021). However, destinations need time to implement and appropriate agile processes. Indeed, the recombination and reorganization of both material and immaterial structures to make them more agile and resilient to shocks and crises are processes of systemic optimization, hence complex (Christofle 2023). Not all destinations can easily implement agile processes on a large scale, impacting both public and private stakeholders, groups and individuals, political and tourism governance, and the inclusion of inhabitants, tourists and so on. Due to their size, geographic, political or even geopolitical environments, cultural context, level of tourism development, structural flexibility and other factors, destinations differ, as do the actions taken to foster tourism agility. Some stable, wealthy and robust territories can draw on multiple pillars of this agility. Others may choose to base their evolution on greater technological agility, destination management, marketing and so on. Still, others focus on incremental strategies to develop and consolidate societal tourism agility, dynamic integration into ecological transition and sustainability. As the authors have shown, agility can thus help destinations more easily cope with current and future shocks and crises, whether by consolidating, increasing, diversifying, refocusing or mixing the tourism function of the studied location and allowing a contemporary understanding of the connections and correlations among stakeholders.

Viewed as complex adaptive systems, destinations can use tourism agility as a governance tool. Indeed, in a systemic framework composed of diverse relationships and interactions, agile processes can develop or consolidate the resilience of places and tourism organizations (Zeghni and Fabry 2020). Resilience can be understood as a response to contemporary challenges, both structural (ecological transition, digital and technological changes, etc.) and situational (health crises, geopolitical crises, etc.) that tourism faces. Essentially, for the destinations and organizations analyzed here, the challenge is to learn how to or know how to adjust policies, both public and private, with agility. A resilient destination is, in fact, intrinsically capable of designing and agilely implementing two main types of responses. First, it must flexibly manage disruptions, exogenous and endogenous shocks, with the ability to adapt as quickly and effectively as possible through stakeholder dynamics to better withstand risks and shape change; at the same time, it must embed the territory and its stakeholders into sustainability for balanced environmental, social and economic development, reducing vulnerability (Adger 2003; Hudson 2010; Fabry and Zeghni 2020).

In conclusion, the 18 texts presented have offered a framework for reflecting on the increasingly critical issue of the agility of tourism organizations and territories in the face of contemporary mutations, crises and uncertainties, whether through active replications, accelerated transitions or even model reinventions. This book is the result of contributions from 38 researchers, who are sincerely thanked here for their input.

C.2. References

Adger, W.N. (2003). Building resilience to promote sustainability. *IHDP Update*, 2, 1–3.

Arionesei, G., Stanciu, P., Moroşan, S.A.A., Cosma, P.D.S.M.R. (2014). Tourism today: Why is it a global phenomenon. In *International Conference on Sustainable Development in Conditions of Economic Instability*, Satu-Mare.

Baggio, R. (2008). Symptoms of complexity in a tourism system. *Tourism Analysis*, 13(1), 1–20.

Baggio, R., Scott, N., Cooper, C. (2010). Improving tourism destination governance: A complexity science approach. *Tourism Review*, 65(4), 51–60.

Brouder, P. and Eriksson, R.H. (2013). Tourism evolution: On the synergies of tourism studies and evolutionary economic geography. *Annals of Tourism Research*, 43, 370–389.

Christofle, S. (2023). Tourism and meeting incentive convention event (MICE) tourism in Europe, systemic shock, structural transformations and resilience. In *Resilience and Regional Development: New Roadmaps*, Pascariu, G.C., Ţigănaşu, R., Kourtit, K., Nijkamp, P. (eds). Edward Elgar Publishing, London.

Hartman, S. (2018). Towards adaptive tourism areas: Using fitness landscapes for managing and futureproofing tourism area development. *Journal of Tourism Futures*, 4(2), 152–162.

Hartman, S. (2021). Adaptive tourism areas in times of change. *Annals of Tourism Research*, 87, 102987.

Hatt, E. (2022). Quelles transitions des territoires touristiques dans un contexte de changement climatique ? *Journée d'étude ADEME, OFB, CEREMA et Région Sud "Tourisme et changement climatique en PACA"* [Online]. Available at: https://shs.hal.science/halshs-03849901v1

Hudson, R. (2010). Resilient regions in an uncertain world: Wishful thinking or a practical reality? *Cambridge Journal of Regions, Economy and Society*, 3(1), 11–25.

Ma, M. and Hassink, R. (2013). An evolutionary perspective on tourism area development. *Annals of Tourism Research*, 41, 89–109.

Morice, J.R. (2023). Le concept d'infusion en géographie : une approche par le tourisme. *L'Information géographique*, 87(2), 46–63.

UNWTO (2023). Le tourisme en bonne voie pour retrouver ses niveaux d'avant la pandémie dans certaines régions [Online]. Available at: https://www.unwto.org/fr/news/le-tourisme-en-bonne-voie-pour-retrouver-en-2023-ses-niveaux-d-avant-la-pandemie-dans-certaines-regions.

UNWTO (2024). Le tourisme international atteindra en 2024 les niveaux d'avant la pandémie [Online]. Available at: https://www.unwto.org/fr/news/le-touris-me-international-atteindra-en-2024-les-niveaux-davant-la-pandemie.

Yu, L., Zhao, P., Tang, J., Pang, L. (2023). Changes in tourist mobility after COVID-19 outbreaks. *Annals of Tourism Research*, 98, 103522.

Zeghni, S. and Fabry, N. (2020). Résiliences, destinations, gouvernance : un cadre d'analyse. In *4ème Journée d'Etude du Tourisme de Nice-JET*. MSHS Sud-Est, Université Côte d'Azur, Nice.

List of Authors for the Two Volumes

Henri ALEXIS
SIC.Lab Méditerranée
Université Côte d'Azur
Nice
France

Alexis ANNES
LISST
École d'Ingénieurs de PURPAN
Toulouse
France

Claudine BATAZZI
SIC.Lab Méditerranée
Université Côte d'Azur
Nice
France

Jacinthe BESSIÈRE
CERTOP-ISTHIA
Université de Toulouse
Jean-Jaurès
France

Denis BORIES
ISTHIA
Université de Toulouse
Jean-Jaurès
France

Sylvie CHRISTOFLE
ESPACE
Université Côte d'Azur
Nice
France

Sylvie CLARIMONT
TREE
Université de Pau et des Pays
de l'Adour
France

Salvador Anton CLAVÉ
GRATET
University of Rovira i Virgili
Vila-seca
Spain

Fabrice DECOUPIGNY
ESPACE
Université Côte d'Azur
Nice
France

Sascha DIWERSY
Praxiling
Université Montpellier 3
France

Nathalie FABRY
Dicen-IdF
Université Gustave-Eiffel
Serris
France

Marie-Ève FÉRÉROL
Mairie de Saint-Jean-Pied-de-Port
France

Carine FOURNIER
ESPACE
Aix-Marseille Université
France

Sandrine FOURNIER
CRIISEA
Université de Picardie Jules Verne
Amiens
France

Isabelle FROCHOT
CREGO
Université de Bourgogne
Dijon
France

Jean-Christophe GAY
URMIS
Université Côte d'Azur
Nice
France

Émeline HATT
LIEU
Aix-Marseille Université
France

Vincent HERBERT
TVES
Université du Littoral Côte d'Opale
Dunkirk
France

Jean-Denis HUE
TVES
Université du Littoral Côte d'Opale
Dunkirk
France

David HURON
GRM
Université Côte d'Azur
Nice
France

Boualem KADRI
GRITTS
Université du Québec à Montréal
Canada

Patrizia LAUDATI
SIC.Lab Méditerranée
Université Côte d'Azur
Nice
France

Véronique MAGRI
BCL
Université Côte d'Azur
Nice
France

Jean-Bernard MARSAT
Territoires
INRAE
Clermont-Ferrand
France

Cyril MARTIN-COLONNA
GRITTS
Université du Québec à Montréal
and
Université du Québec
Trois-Rivières
Canada

Véronique MONDOU
ESO-Angers
Université d'Angers
France

Paul-Emmanuel PICHON
CERTOP
Université de Toulouse
Jean-Jaurès
France

Étienne POLGE
Territoires
INRAE
Clermont-Ferrand
France

Noémie RAVAS
CERTOP
Université de Toulouse
Jean-Jaurès
France

Otto REGALADO-PEZÚA
ESAN Graduate School of
Business
Lima
Peru

Shiwei SHEN
DSCICT Ningbo
Ningbo University
China

Juan Carlos SOSA VARELA
Université Ana G. Méndez
San Juan
Porto Rico

Marios SOTIRIADIS
DSCICT Ningbo
Ningbo University
China

Jacques SPINDLER
GRM
Université Côte d'Azur
Nice
France

Leonardo TORO
ESAN Graduate School of Business
Lima
Peru

Laurent VANNI
BCL
Université Côte d'Azur
Nice
France

Philippe VIOLIER
ESO-Angers
Université d'Angers
France

Sylvain ZEGHNI
LVMT
Université Gustave-Eiffel
Serris
France

Index

A, C

D, E

F, G

H, I

L, M

N, O, P

R, S

T, U, V

Summary of Volume 1

Chapter 4. Resilience of a Tourist Destination in the Post-Covid-19 Era: The Case of Val d'Europe Agglomération

Nathalie FABRY and Sylvain ZEGHNI

Part 2. Tourism Agility: Between Technology and Society

Chapter 5. Identification of Digital Skills: A Study of Peruvian Tourist Businesses

Otto REGALADO-PEZÚA, Leonardo TORO and Juan Carlos SOSA VARELA

Chapter 6. Artificial Intelligence and the Search for Meaning in Support of Marketing Agility in Tourism

Denis BORIES and Paul-Emmanuel PICHON

Other titles from

iSTE

in

Science, Society and New Technologies

2025

LEVEAU Pierre-Henry
Tourism, Technologies and Consumption in the 5.0 Era: Discovery and Reflection in the Face of Organizational and Societal Issues
(Tourism and Mobility Systems Set – Volume 10)

2024

BARTHES Angela, CIBIEN Catherine, ROMAGNY Bruno
Biosphere Reserves and Sustainable Development Goals 1: Scientific and Practical Educational Issues in the Mediterranean
(Territory Development Set – Volume 3)
Biosphere Reserves and Sustainable Development Goals 2: Issues, Tensions, Processes and Governance in the Mediterranean
(Territory Development Set – Volume 4)

BOTERO Nataly, LEDOUBLE Hélène, ALLARD-HUVER François
Pesticides: Pluridisciplinary Dialogues in Social and Human Sciences
(Communication, Environment, Science and Society Set – Volume 4)

CATELLANI Andrea, LITS Grégoire
Transitions in Tension: Controversies and Tensions Around Ecological Transitions
(Communication, Environment, Science and Society Set – Volume 3)

DAVALLON Jean
Heritage Traces in the Making: A Communicational Analysis of Modes of Heritagization
(Traces Set – Volume 6)

DEJEAN Maxime, L'HOSTIS Marine, LI Meng
Chinese Outbound Tourism: From Source Markets to Destinations
(Tourism and Mobility Systems Set – Volume 8)

GAY Jean-Christophe
Tourismophobia: From "Mass Tourism" to "Overtourism"
(Tourism and Mobility Systems Set – Volume 9)

JULIA Guilhem, FAUCHON Anne, KANAWATI Rushed
AI, Healthcare and Law

KOHLMANN Émilie
Linking with Nature in the Digital Age
(Communication, Environment, Science and Society Set – Volume 1)

LEDOUBLE Hélène
Popularizing Science: The Complex Terminological Interactions between Scientific and Press Discourses within the Field of Agroecology
(Communication, Environment, Science and Society Set – Volume 2)

LOUART Pierre, PIRIOU Jérôme, VIOLIER Philippe
Tourist Destinations According to Stakeholder Strategies: From Clusters to Local Tourist Systems
(Tourism and Mobility Systems Set – Volume 7)

2023

APCHAIN Thomas
Favela Tours: Building Otherness in the Favelas of Rio de Janeiro
(Tourism and Mobility Systems Set – Volume 6)

CARDON Alain, EL HAMI Abdelkhalak
Fundamental Generation Systems: Computer Science and Artificial Consciousness, the Informational Field of Generation of the Universe, the Sixth Sense of Living Beings
(Digital Sciences Set – Volume 4)

CURULLI Irene G., IKIZ KAYA Deniz, KHAEFI Arghavan
Heritage Education for Climate Action
(Research in Architectural Education Set – Volume 2)

ELAMÉ Esoh
The Sustainable City in Africa Facing the Challenge of Liquid Sanitation
(Territory Development Set – Volume 2)

JURCZENKO Emmanuel
Climate Investing: New Strategies and Implementation Challenges

LYUBAREVA Inna, WALDECK Roger
Diversity of Methodological Approaches in Social Sciences: Example of the Analysis of Media and Online Information
(Modeling Methodologies in Social Sciences Set – Volume 3)

PARET Dominique, CRÉGO Pierre, SOLÈRE Pauline
Smart Patches: Biosensors, Graphene and Intra-Body Communications

VENTRE Daniel, GUILLOT Philippe
Electronic Communication Interception Technologies and Issues of Power

VENTRE Daniel, LOISEAU Hugo
Cybercrime during the SARS-CoV-2 Pandemic (2019-2022): Evolutions, Adaptations, Consequences
(Cybersecurity Set – Volume 3)

2022

AIT HADDOU Hassan, TOUBANOS Dimitri, VILLIEN Philippe
Ecological Transition in Education and Research

CARDON Alain
Information Organization of The Universe and Living Things: Generation of Space, Quantum and Molecular Elements, Coactive Generation of Living Organisms and Multiagent Model
(Digital Sciences Set – Volume 3)

CAULI Marie, FAVIER Laurence, JEANNAS Jean-Yves
Digital Dictionary

DAVERNE-BAILLY Carole, WITTORSKI Richard
Research Methodology in Education and Training: Postures, Practices and Forms
(Education Set – Volume 12)

ELAMÉ Esoh
Sustainable Intercultural Urbanism at the Service of the African City of Tomorrow
(Territory Development Set – Volume 1)

FLEURET Sébastien
A Back and Forth Between Tourism and Health: From Medical Tourism to Global Health
(Tourism and Mobility Systems Set – Volume 5)

KAMPELIS Nikos, KOLOKOTSA Denia
Smart Zero-energy Buildings and Communities for Smart Grids
(Engineering, Energy and Architecture Set – Volume 9)

2021

BARDIOT Clarisse
Performing Arts and Digital Humanities: From Traces to Data
(Traces Set – Volume 5)

BENSRHAIR Abdelaziz, BAPIN Thierry
From AI to Autonomous and Connected Vehicles: Advanced Driver-Assistance Systems (ADAS)
(Digital Sciences Set – Volume 2)

BÉRANGER Jérôme
Societal Responsibility of Artificial Intelligence: Towards an Ethical and Eco-responsible AI
(Technological Prospects and Social Applications Set – Volume 4)

CORDELIER Benoit, GALIBERT Oliver
Digital Health Communications
(Technological Prospective and Social Applications Set – Volume 5)

DOUAY Nicolas, MINJA Michael
Urban Planning for Transitions

GALINON-MÉLÉNEC Béatrice
The Trace Odyssey 1: A Journey Beyond Appearances
(Traces Set – Volume 4)

HENRY Antoine
Platform and Collective Intelligence: Digital Ecosystem of Organizations

KOLOKOTSA Denia, KAMPELIS Nikos
Smart Buildings, Smart Communities and Demand Response
(Engineering, Energy and Architecture Set – Volume 8)

LE LAY Stéphane, SAVIGNAC Emmanuelle, LÉNEL Pierre, FRANCES Jean
The Gamification of Society
(Research, Innovative Theories and Methods in SSH Set – Volume 2)

RADI Bouchaïb, EL HAMI Abdelkhalak
Optimizations and Programming: Linear, Non-linear, Dynamic, Stochastic and Applications with Matlab
(Digital Sciences Set – Volume 1)

2020

ALAKTIF Jamila, CALLENS Stéphane
Migration and Climate Change: From the Emergence of Human Cultures to Contemporary Management in Organizations

BARNOUIN Jacques
The World's Construction Mechanism: Trajectories, Imbalances and the Future of Societies
(Interdisciplinarity Between Biological Sciences and Social Sciences Set – Volume 4)

ÇAĞLAR Nur, CURULLI Irene G., SIPAHIOĞLU Işıl Ruhi, MAVROMATIDIS Lazaros E.
Thresholds in Architectural Education
(Engineering, Energy and Architecture Set – Volume 7)

DUBOIS Michel J.F.
Humans in the Making: In the Beginning was Technique
(Social Interdisciplinarity Set – Volume 4)

ETCHEVERRIA Olivier
The Restaurant, A Geographical Approach: From Invention to Gourmet Tourist Destinations
(Tourism and Mobility Systems Set – Volume 3)

GREFE Gwenaëlle, PEYRAT-GUILLARD Dominique
Shapes of Tourism Employment: HRM in the Worlds of Hotels and Air Transport
(Tourism and Mobility Systems Set – Volume 4)

JEANNERET Yves
The Trace Factory
(Traces Set – Volume 3)

KATSAFADOS Petros, MAVROMATIDIS Elias, SPYROU Christos
Numerical Weather Prediction and Data Assimilation
(Engineering, Energy and Architecture Set – Volume 6)

MARTI Caroline
Cultural Mediations of Brands: Unadvertization and Quest for Authority
(Communication Approaches to Commercial Mediation Set – Volume 1)

MAVROMATIDIS Lazaros
Climatic Heterotopias as Spaces of Inclusion: Sew Up the Urban Fabric
(Research in Architectural Education Set – Volume 1)

MOURATIDOU Eleni
Re-presentation Policies of the Fashion Industry: Discourse, Apparatus and Power
(Communication Approaches to Commercial Mediation Set – Volume 2)

SCHMITT Daniel, THÉBAULT Marine, BURCZYKOWSKI Ludovic
Image Beyond the Screen: Projection Mapping

VIOLIER Philippe, with the collaboration of TAUNAY Benjamin
The Tourist Places of the World
(Tourism and Mobility Systems Set – Volume 2)

2019

BRIANÇON Muriel
The Meaning of Otherness in Education: Stakes, Forms, Process, Thoughts and Transfers
(Education Set – Volume 3)

DESCHAMPS Jacqueline
Mediation: A Concept for Information and Communication Sciences
(Concepts to Conceive 21st Century Society Set – Volume 1)

DOUSSET Laurent, PARK Sejin, GUILLE-ESCURET Georges
Kinship, Ecology and History: Renewal of Conjectures
(Interdisciplinarity Between Biological Sciences and Social Sciences Set – Volume 3)

DUPONT Olivier
Power: A Concept for Information and Communication Sciences
(Concepts to Conceive 21st Century Society Set – Volume 2)

FERRARATO Coline
Prospective Philosophy of Software: A Simondonian Study
(Technological Prospects and Social Applications Set – Volume 3)

GUAAYBESS Tourya
The Media in Arab Countries: From Development Theories to Cooperation Policies

HAGÈGE Hélène
Education for Responsibility
(Education Set – Volume 4)

LARDELLIER Pascal
The Ritual Institution of Society
(Traces Set – Volume 2)

LARROCHE Valérie
The Dispositif: A Concept for Information and Communication Sciences
(Concepts to Conceive 21st Century Society Set – Volume 3)

LATERRASSE Jean
Transport and Town Planning: The City in Search of Sustainable Development

LELEU-MERVIEL Sylvie, SCHMITT Daniel, USEILLE Philippe
From UXD to LivXD: Living eXperience Design

LENOIR Virgil Cristian
Ethically Structured Processes
(Innovation and Responsibility Set – Volume 4)

LOPEZ Fanny, PELLEGRINO Margot, COUTARD Olivier
Local Energy Autonomy: Spaces, Scales, Politics
(Urban Engineering Set – Volume 1)

METZGER Jean-Paul
Discourse: A Concept for Information and Communication Sciences
(Concepts to Conceive 21st Century Society Set – Volume 4)

MICHA Irini, VAIOU Dina
Alternative Takes to the City
(Engineering, Energy and Architecture Set – Volume 5)

PÉLISSIER Chrysta
Learner Support in Online Learning Environments

PIETTE Albert
Theoretical Anthropology or How to Observe a Human Being
(Research, Innovative Theories and Methods in SSH Set – Volume 1)

PIRIOU Jérôme
The Tourist Region: A Co-Construction of Tourism Stakeholders
(Tourism and Mobility Systems Set – Volume 1)

PUMAIN Denise
Geographical Modeling: Cities and Territories
(Modeling Methodologies in Social Sciences Set – Volume 2)

WALDECK Roger
Methods and Interdisciplinarity
(Modeling Methodologies in Social Sciences Set – Volume 1)

2018

BARTHES Angela, CHAMPOLLION Pierre, ALPE Yves
Evolutions of the Complex Relationship Between Education and Territories
(Education Set – Volume 1)

BÉRANGER Jérôme
The Algorithmic Code of Ethics: Ethics at the Bedside of the Digital Revolution
(Technological Prospects and Social Applications Set – Volume 2)

DUGUÉ Bernard
Time, Emergences and Communications
(Engineering, Energy and Architecture Set – Volume 4)

GEORGANTOPOULOU Christina G., GEORGANTOPOULOS George A.
Fluid Mechanics in Channel, Pipe and Aerodynamic Design Geometries 1
(Engineering, Energy and Architecture Set – Volume 2)
Fluid Mechanics in Channel, Pipe and Aerodynamic Design Geometries 2
(Engineering, Energy and Architecture Set – Volume 3)

GUILLE-ESCURET Georges
Social Structures and Natural Systems: Is a Scientific Assemblage Workable?
(Social Interdisciplinarity Set – Volume 2)

LARINI Michel, BARTHES Angela
Quantitative and Statistical Data in Education: From Data Collection to Data Processing
(Education Set – Volume 2)

LELEU-MERVIEL Sylvie
Informational Tracking
(Traces Set – Volume 1)

SALGUES Bruno
Society 5.0: Industry of the Future, Technologies, Methods and Tools
(Technological Prospects and Social Applications Set – Volume 1)

TRESTINI Marc
Modeling of Next Generation Digital Learning Environments: Complex Systems Theory

2017

ANICHINI Giulia, CARRARO Flavia, GESLIN Philippe, GUILLE-ESCURET Georges
Technicity vs Scientificity: Complementarities and Rivalries
(Interdisciplinarity Between Biological Sciences and Social Sciences Set – Volume 2)

DUGUÉ Bernard
Information and the World Stage: From Philosophy to Science, the World of Forms and Communications
(Engineering, Energy and Architecture Set – Volume 1)

GESLIN Philippe
Inside Anthropotechnology: User and Culture Centered Experience
(Social Interdisciplinarity Set – Volume 1)

GORIA Stéphane
Methods and Tools for Creative Competitive Intelligence

KEMBELLEC Gérald, BROUDOUX Evelyne
Reading and Writing Knowledge in Scientific Communities: Digital Humanities and Knowledge Construction

MAESSCHALCK Marc
Reflexive Governance for Research and Innovative Knowledge
(Responsible Research and Innovation Set - Volume 6)

PARK Sejin, GUILLE-ESCURET Georges
Sociobiology vs Socioecology: Consequences of an Unraveling Debate
(Interdisciplinarity Between Biological Sciences and Social Sciences Set – Volume 1)

PELLÉ Sophie
Business, Innovation and Responsibility
(Responsible Research and Innovation Set – Volume 7)

2016

ANDRÉ Michel, SAMARAS Zissis
Energy and Environment
(Research for Innovative Transports Set – Volume 1)

BLANQUART Corinne, CLAUSEN Uwe, JACOB Bernard
Towards Innovative Freight and Logistics
(Research for Innovative Transports Set – Volume 2)

COHEN Simon, YANNIS George
Traffic Management
(Research for Innovative Transports Set – Volume 3)

EL FALLAH SEGHROUCHNI Amal, ISHIKAWA Fuyuki, HÉRAULT Laurent, TOKUDA Hideyuki
Enablers for Smart Cities

GIANNI Robert
Responsibility and Freedom: The Ethical Realm of RRI
(Responsible Research and Innovation Set – Volume 2)

GRUNWALD Armin
The Hermeneutic Side of Responsible Research and Innovation
(Responsible Research and Innovation Set – Volume 5)

LENOIR Virgil Cristian
Ethical Efficiency: Responsibility and Contingency
(Responsible Research and Innovation Set – Volume 1)

PELLÉ Sophie, REBER Bernard
From Ethical Review to Responsible Research and Innovation
(Responsible Research and Innovation Set – Volume 3)

REBER Bernard
Precautionary Principle, Pluralism and Deliberation: Science and Ethics
(Responsible Research and Innovation Set – Volume 4)

TORRENTI Jean-Michel, LA TORRE Francesca
Materials and Infrastructures 1
(Research for Innovative Transports Set – Volume 5A
Materials and Infrastructures 2
(Research for Innovative Transports Set – Volume 5B)

VENTRE Daniel
Information Warfare – 2nd edition

YANNIS George, COHEN Simon
Traffic Safety
(Research for Innovative Transports Set – Volume 4)

2015

BRONNER Gérald
Belief and Misbelief Asymmetry on the Internet

2009

VENTRE Daniel
Information Warfare

Printed and bound by CPI Group (UK) Ltd, Croydon, CR0 4YY
28/07/2026
14931342-0003